money_talks_

To Pat
Best wishes

Owen Mon

money *talks*
my autobiography

owen
money

with Alan Wightman

y Lolfa

To my son Matthew, my daughter Katie and my grandchildren Alex and Gabriel.

First impression: 2010

© Copyright Owen Money and Y Lolfa Cyf., 20010

The publishers wish to acknowledge the support of Cyngor Llyfrau Cymru

Cover design: Alan Thomas
Cover photograph: Darryl Corner

ISBN: 978 1847712356

Published, printed and bound in Wales
by Y Lolfa Cyf., Talybont, Ceredigion SY24 5HE
website www.ylolfa.com
e-mail ylolfa@ylolfa.com
tel 01970 832 304
fax 832 782

FOREWORD

I HAD KNOWN OWEN Money for many years when one day he surprised me. He looked me straight in the eye and said, "Rob, I'm a comedian".

I had no idea.

I'd seen his act, of course I had, but in a way that just made it harder to believe. I'd always assumed he was just a very confident man with a moustache and learning difficulties.

Nonetheless, I went on to cast him in the role of my father in the BAFTA eligible series, *Rob Brydon's Annually Retentive*. His performance in the show will be familiar to anyone who has seen it. Time and again he arrived on set punctually, effortlessly wearing the correct costume and happily entertaining the cast and crew all day with his joke.

This book tells the story of Owen's remarkable rise from rags to slightly bigger rags. I applaud him for writing it and wish him luck in his ongoing battle with personal hygiene.

Rob Brydon

CHAPTER ONE

WHEN SOMEONE SUGGESTED THAT now might be a good time to write my autobiography (while I'm still alive!), I thought, "Great! At last I've got the chance to look back at my life. I'll be able to publicly thank the many people who guided me and taught me and helped me along the way, as well as settling old scores against the handful who tried to 'head me off at the pass' over the years." But then I realised that I've been around for over sixty years. That's more than half a century. Plus another ten years. As you can see, I'm very good at mental arithmetic. In fact the number of times I've got mental arithmetic questions wrong, I can count on the fingers of both hands.

So where do I begin to relate sixty years-worth of stories and anecdotes? "To begin at the beginning..." wrote Dylan Thomas. You must have heard of Dylan Thomas. Even if you haven't read his books you're bound to know that he was the Welsh writer and world-class drinker, who a famous singer re-named himself after, back in the 1960s. You know who I'm talking about. *B. J.* Thomas – the man who sang 'Raindrops Keep Falling On My Head'. Remember his follow-up hit? 'Hey, Won't You Play, Another Somebody Done Somebody Wrong Song?' which, famously, was less than a minute long, because the record label had to be twice the normal size to accommodate the song's title.

I'm definitely the man you need to ask when it comes to pop trivia. For example, when those silly rumours were going around that it was Bob Holness who played the saxophone on Gerry Rafferty's 1978 hit 'Baker Street', I was the *only* BBC broadcaster who said it was nonsense. Because I knew that the sax player on the record wasn't the long-time host of *Blockbusters*. No, it was the late great actress and groovy tenor sax player... Dame Thora Hird. So whenever you hear the song on the radio, think of Thora blowing away at her instrument and remember what I told you the next time the 'Bob Holness' question comes up in a pub quiz. You'll get quite a reaction, I promise you.

To 'begin at the beginning' would appear to be the logical, sensible thing to do when writing an autobiography. We've all read enough autobiographies to know that they usually follow a pattern and are generally split into four main sections:

I was born (without this section there'd be very little to fill the other three).

My tough childhood that helped to shape me into the person I am now.

My years of struggle for fame against the odds.

And my eventual big break and subsequent success.

But this book is a little different. For instance, Chapter Three is entirely in colloquial German dialect and if you read Chapter Eleven backwards you'll see that it doubles-up as a recipe for Thai green curry and black pudding. Also, this little book of mine doesn't make any reference to my big break and subsequent success, because, between you and me and the gate post, I'm still waiting for it all to happen.

Okay, I'm just kidding! It was *a joke*. Keep your wits about you because within these pages I can promise you that you'll encounter at least *three* more. I can also guarantee that it contains all the necessary ingredients to make an interesting autobiography, including lots of pages with words on them. It's got humour, tragedy, career triumphs and disappointments, long-held secrets revealed, pathos, jealousy, love, lust and cross-dressing. I'm kidding again. There's absolutely *no* pathos.

So, although it would make sense to 'begin at the beginning' as Dylan Thomas so eloquently put it, as far as I'm aware, in the course of his short but interesting life, Dylan Thomas was never chased around a stage by an amorous pantomime gorilla every night for 12 weeks before eventually being caught and held captive in a cage. He didn't play Rob Brydon's joke-a-minute Dad in a BBC sitcom or host one of the most popular shows on BBC Radio Wales. Or survive an edgy interview with the unpredictable Freddie Starr just after he'd threatened to walk off my BBC One Wales television show *Money in the Bank* purely because *he didn't like the look of the studio* – even though one television studio is very much like another.

Dylan (or 'DT' as the notorious drinker is sometimes appropriately referred to), didn't work with some of the biggest names in popular music like Tom Jones, Shirley Bassey, Glastonbury 2009's 'wrinkly rockers' Status Quo, Julio Iglesias, Willie Nelson, David Essex, Paul Carrack, Dave Edmunds, The Crickets, Joe Brown and long-time Eric Clapton collaborator Andy Fairweather-Low, as well as many of Britain's top comedy greats like Cannon & Ball, Bobby Davro, Joe Pasquale, Jimmy Cricket, Johnny Casson and Tim '20 gags a minute' Vine.

And Dylan definitely didn't have to stand up in a Valleys social club and tell jokes to a restless audience who were not only anxious to get on with the bingo but, thanks to a talkative committee member, also knew exactly how much I was being paid for 45 minutes' work. Although it wasn't a fortune it was as much as, if not more than, most members of the audience earned for a week's hard labour. So was it any wonder they sat through my performance, grim-faced, their arms folded in a 'Go on, make me laugh' gesture?

Although I gave what I thought was a good performance and the committee their money's worth – always important for a performer if he or she wants to be re-booked – the audience were, at best, luke-warm. That's what makes comedy so difficult to analyse. You can tell a load of gags one night and every one of them will get a laugh. The next night, in a different venue, with a different audience, a proportion of those jokes will fail to tickle the audience's funny bones.

Why? Well If I knew the answer to *that* I'd be writing this book while sailing my two million pound yacht around my private island in the Caribbean, with Gordon Ramsay cooking in the galley, Rolf Harris touching-up the paint on the hull, and Angelina Jolie swabbing the decks in a skimpy bikini. Sorry. That was an unforgivably sexist comment which I wish to take back. My apologies to Gordon. The truth is, given the circumstances, that particular club audience weren't in the mood to be entertained and would probably have hated Des O'Connor, Dorothy Squires and Princess Diana if they'd formed a trio and been that night's 'star turn'. Hang on a minute. Des. Dot. Di. Sounds like Welsh Morse Code!

I just had to interrupt my writing for a minute, because after I wrote that last sentence, the doorbell went. They'll steal *anything* around here.

What was I talking about? Oh yes, the differences between me and Dylan Thomas and why I don't intend to begin at the beginning. Old DT didn't fly to America to... oh, alright if you're going to be picky, he *did* fly to America... but *he* didn't go there to make a fascinating documentary series about his musical heroes, get to sing a song in Sam Phillips' legendary Sun Studios and nearly break his neck riding a Harley Davidson through the desert. *He* didn't take a big gamble on starting up his own theatre company. *He* didn't travel the length and breadth of Wales discovering talented performers and giving them the chance to appear on television. *He* didn't spend a four-month long summer season in Blackpool. And to the best of my knowledge *he* was never awarded two... that's right... *two* Sony Awards *and* the MBE. Did you know I was awarded the MBE? One thing's for certain. By the end of this book you will!

So I feel more than entitled not to begin my memoirs in

the beginning and intend to start them any way I like. That's a posh word, 'Memoirs'. I should remember that if I was you, because you won't find many posh words in this book. If it's posh words you want, go and buy a dictionary. Which reminds me, I once looked-up the word 'camouflage' in the dictionary, but couldn't find it anywhere! So it must *really* work.

Okay, so what could be my own individual, Owen Money way of starting my autobiography, avoiding all those well-worn "I was born in…" opening sentences? Well, I can't think of a more appropriate point to begin than the time when I really thought my life was in jeopardy:

The time – March 2006.

The place – Thailand.

The reason – my stroke.

I'd been ill before. I'd been in hospital before. But I'd never been so convinced that there was a real danger that I was on my way out. In many ways I suppose it was inevitable something would go wrong with my health, because not only was I overweight, my workload would have challenged a performer half my age. During 2005 I had taken on every job that was offered to me. This wasn't simply down to greed on my part. You have to bear in mind that the expression 'make hay while the sun shines' applies as much to performers as it does to farmers. And other professions that involve making hay.

While we're popular and in demand, we have to take on any and all work that we're fortunate to be offered, because we're well aware that there will come a time when we won't be offered so many opportunities to entertain an audience. It's a hard fact of life for performers and, like cactus in a desert, it comes with the territory.

While it's true that there's no business like show business, it's also true that sometimes there's just 'no business' even if you were once a big star with a prime time television show and a bill-topping appearance on the Royal Variety Show.

Just ask Michael Barrymore. Any performer will tell you that there are times when the phone doesn't ring. Especially if it's been cut off because the bill hasn't been paid. In fact there have been times in my career when the phone didn't ring for so many weeks I was convinced I'd gone deaf!

I remember reading somewhere that the famous British actor Charles Dance once went through a period of unemployment that lasted almost a *year*! And that was *after* his huge success in *White Mischief* and *The Jewel in the Crown*. Which just goes to show how unpredictable – and scary – a career in show business can be. In fact there is a tongue-in-cheek theory that there are only *four* stages in a performer's career, whether an actor, singer, musician or comedian. I'll explain these four stages for you, using my own name, but it could apply to anyone from Tom Hanks to Jennifer Lopez:

When you're unknown, the big guns running show business ask, "Who's Owen Money?"

As you start to make a name for yourself they ask, "Get me Owen Money!"

Once you've been established for a while, the request goes out, "Get me a young Owen Money".

And when you've fallen out of favour, they again ask, "Who's Owen Money?"

While this theory might raise a smile, it contains more than a grain of truth.

The next time you see an actor or comedian or presenter on TV and you think, "Oh, not him again! He's never off the telly!" do bear in mind that they may only have had two jobs in a year, which might have been filmed six months apart and fate ordained that both programmes just happened to be shown within a couple of weeks of each other.

So towards the end of 2005 I was working all hours. Apart from producing, directing and starring in my usual Owen Money Theatre Company pantomime which toured around Wales between November and February, usually spending two weeks in each venue, I had also agreed with my old friend George Savva to appear in a pre-Christmas cabaret season at his wonderful Cwrt Bleddyn Hotel & Spa, which is set in beautiful grounds just outside Usk, south Wales.

George, who has since sold the hotel and returned to his home country of Cyprus, had many years' experience in the cabaret scene, during its heyday in the 70s and 80s, and had cornered the market in pre-Christmas party nights at the Cwrt Bleddyn throughout December. For the price of their ticket, customers were treated to a sumptuous turkey dinner followed by a trouser-bursting dessert, which in turn was followed by an hour or so of great live entertainment. And me.

In previous years he had booked acts like Dave Berry & the Cruisers and the Rockin' Berries and during the 2005 season he wanted me to share the bill with some other old friends of mine, one of the bands who created the Liverpool sound in the early 60s, The Searchers, who, with a few changes in personnel, were still going strong – and still are today. The band, who had scored hits with 'Sugar and Spice' and 'Sweets for my Sweet', were due on stage at eleven and I was asked to appear around ten-thirty, which was thankfully well after the dinner plates and cutlery had been taken away. Well, no comedian wants his audience to have access to sharp weapons. This meant that as soon as the curtain came down on the pantomime, I had to shower, change and drive down to Usk in record time – while of course always observing the speed limits, your honour!

George had booked me to appear for 24 nights and the place was packed for every one of them, usually with office parties who were well into the booze by the time I got there. A comedian's job is to cheer people up. To put a smile on their faces and put them in a good mood. So it's always a challenge when you face an audience who are *already* in a good mood, because they're out celebrating with their friends and colleagues. They're laughing and joking, they're stuffed full of turkey and Christmas pudding and naturally they've supped more than a few ales during the evening.

In fact the appearance of a comedian at that point, trying to attract their attention, could actually *spoil* their good mood!

However, I am glad to report that the audiences at the Cwrt Bleddyn were very receptive and laughed in all the right places. I say that because sometimes an audience member will only 'get' a joke I've told just as I'm midway through telling the next one. This could be because the joke was a little bit subtle for them or they didn't quite hear the punch line and had to think about it. But nine times out of ten it's because they're smashed out of their brains.

My short, but brilliantly funny spot was immediately followed, with almost military precision, thanks to George Savva's slick organisation, by the Searchers' opening number. In fact I would have stayed on longer than half-an-hour, but for the fact I didn't know all the words to 'Don't Throw Your Love Away... Oh, no, no, no...'

As if I didn't need any added pressure on my health and well-being, apart from my crazy work schedule, I was also heavily involved in a huge business venture called the Merthyr Village Project, a proposed multi-million pound investment in my home town of Merthyr Tydfil. Merthyr was in desperate need of inward investment in new homes and retail premises, which in turn would provide hundreds of jobs for what was, and still is, one of the most deprived areas in the Valleys – and this was some years before the Hoover factory closed, which was another huge blow to the community.

Christmas and New Year's Eve 2005 came and went in a blur and as 2006 began the pantomime continued its all-conquering invasion of Wales, right through until the school half-term holidays in February, creating fun and frolics from Port Talbot to Treorchy and from Aberdare to Cwmbrân. I love performing in pantomimes – there really isn't anything else to touch it in terms of getting a reaction from an audience – but by the time I put on my costume and make-up for that last performance, I was more than ready for a break.

I flew out to Thailand with a crowd of friends to stay at my villa, ready to relax and enjoy the sea and sunshine and other things I like that begin with 's'. I was thinking of salsa music. What were *you* thinking?

For the first week we were out there, I felt fine. Tired, but generally okay. Then one evening – it was St Patrick's Day as it happens, although he didn't personally turn up – after we'd enjoyed a great game of golf, we all went to a bar for a few drinks and although it usually didn't worry me, I found myself finding the music playing in the background very loud. I also felt much hotter than usual. It gets very hot out there but I'm used to it, having holidayed in Thailand many times. That night, however, I really felt the heat draining my strength.

I had a drink or two, but then decided not to have any more alcohol, even though everyone else around me was knocking it back and having a great time. I explained to everyone that I didn't feel too good and I was going back to my villa. I left the bar, made my way home alone and as soon as I arrived at the villa I went straight to bed, feeling really weird.

I woke up in the morning around nine o'clock but because all the others hadn't come back to the villa until four or five in the morning, they were fast asleep, so I had no-one to talk to, to explain how ill I felt. In fact I didn't speak to anyone until just after lunch and when I did, it was noticeable that my speech was slurred. I went down to Pattaya Hospital with Graham Hayward, the man who built my villa for me and when the doctors examined me they thought I had an ear infection. Neither Graham nor me thought that was right, so when we came back to the villa I phoned Kath, my wife, who is a nurse at Morriston Hospital. And even though we haven't been together for several years, we still love each

other and when there's a problem, we're there for each other.
After she'd spoken to me she had a consultation with one of
the hospital doctors. One of them said that I should go back
to the hospital and the other one's advice was for me to take
some aspirins and get on a plane home as fast as possible.
Guess what advice I took?

I got a flight back to the UK the following morning and,
dosed-up with painkillers, I flew back home. I've flown many
times to many destinations, but this was one of the worst
plane journeys I have ever been on. Not because I was scared
of flying – because I'm not. I was feeling very ill and very
frightened because I had no idea what the doctor's prognosis
would be when (if!) I got back home to Wales and I was on
my own, with none of my usual travelling companions.

Something really embarrassing happened on the flight
which just added to the misery I was going through. I ordered
a tomato juice from one of the trolley dollies (I think his
name was Colin) and in my frail state, as I went to pick it up,
I knocked it over the woman sat next to me. And it wasn't a
small spill. I dropped the lot all over the woman, who wiped
the floor with me. She was absolutely furious. Of course I
apologised several times, but whether she heard me while she
shouted and screamed at me, I don't know. Naturally, from
my slurred speech, she thought that I was drunk. There was
no way I was going to tell her "I've had a stroke" because I
don't think I could have got the words out coherently and
besides I didn't want people to know.

In retrospect, getting on a long haul flight, my system
full of aspirin, just after I'd had a stroke was a silly thing to
do. But, I had to weigh that risk against me having to spend
months and months in a hospital in Thailand which would
have cost a fortune.

The flight seemed endless and when we landed at Heathrow,
my company manager Roger Bell was there to pick me up
and drive me straight home. Kath was waiting for me there

and drove me over to Morriston Hospital, Swansea, where I was admitted immediately. I had a scan and the specialist confirmed that I'd had a stroke. This was a Friday and I was supposed to start back to work on my two-hour show on Radio Wales the following day.

I phoned Radio Wales and spoke to my producer Angela David, to explain what had happened and where I was. She was horrified. I was also booked to appear at the Tower Hotel on the Saturday night with my band, the Soul Sharks. So I had to phone the band's leader, Mark Roche, to tell him the bad news.

A replacement act had to be found for the Tower Hotel, so Mark phoned comedian Colin Price who agreed to stand in. Of course once Colin knew what had happened to me, the show-biz grapevine began buzzing and the news rapidly spread that Owen Money had suffered a stroke. Loads of performers started making enquiries about me. They wanted to know how I was, when I'd start to get better and, most importantly, were there any more lucrative club dates they could fill in for me? Show-biz people are *so* caring.

I have to say that the treatment I received in Morriston Hospital was second to none. I have to say it in case I ever have to go back there. No, seriously, the consultants, doctors and nurses were excellent. The hospital catering I could have done without, but you can't have everything. Well, where would you put it?

For anyone, having a stroke is terrifying, but for a performer, someone whose job it is to communicate with an audience, it's doubly worrying. If a comedian isn't able to deliver a gag properly because his speech is indistinct, the audience won't get the joke and the comedian won't get the laugh. The comic might be able to get away with one dud or misheard joke, but any more than that and he can easily die the death on stage.

Club audiences can be very unforgiving and if they find

a comedian is failing to tickle their collective funny bone, their mood can change from red-faced jollity to hard-eyed intolerance in an instant. Take it from one who knows. I hope that hasn't put off any aspiring comedians but, boys and girls, you'd better know the truth. And likewise when you're hosting a two-hour radio show, which involves reading out dedications, talking enthusiastically about the music you're playing and sometimes conducting interviews with huge stars, you have to be able to make yourself clearly understood by your listeners – who in my case are Ted and Betty Jones from Ceredigion. Though as I haven't heard from them in a while, they might have moved.

Because my lifestyle had been so relentlessly hectic up that point, the first real chance I had to seriously think about writing my autobiography was when I came out of hospital and sat at home recoop... recoup... rec... getting better. The BBC in Cardiff was inundated with letters, cards and phone calls from hundreds of well-wishers and I have to say my bosses at the BBC were genuinely touched by this outpouring of affection, showing just how much Owen Money meant to the people of Wales. It was definitely worth all that money I spent on stamps.

I took things very easy for the rest of the year and made an effort to lose weight – which I had managed to do many times before – and this time I intended to keep the weight off. However, I had to be realistic about matters. However much my health improved week by week, there was no chance of me appearing in a gruelling touring pantomime during the Owen Money Theatre Production's 2006/7 Christmas season, so my old comedy pal Mike Doyle stepped into my shoes (and striped socks and multi-coloured trousers) for that production and he has become an integral part of my annual pantomimes ever since.

So, during the autumn of 2006, although I was involved with the producing and administration of my up-coming pantomime, I felt quite disappointed that I would have to take a back seat and wouldn't be able to get up there on stage and act the idiot (I do this quite well, apparently) with my fellow artistes for two or sometimes three performances a day.

Then, one cold November morning (I'll tell you how cold it was – I *almost* switched-on the second bar of my electric fire) an official-looking letter arrived at my house, post-marked 'Downing Street'. Yes, Downing Street, where the Prime Minister lives in a house behind a big fence guarded by six policemen with guns... and yet he *still* gets out occasionally.

My immediate thought was it could be something to do with the Merthyr Village project I mentioned earlier. After I discounted that, I thought I might be further behind with my council tax than I realised. There was only one way I was going to find out what was inside the envelope so I looked around for my little letter-opener. His name's Cledwyn, he comes from Gilfach Goch and I found him in the kitchen making a quiche. After he'd opened the envelope, he handed it to me and went back to his quiche. By the way,'quiche' is a French word which, translated into English, means "Aw! Why can't we have chips instead?"

When I read the letter contained within the envelope, I was surprised to read that I was going to be awarded the MBE in the 2007 New Year's Honours. When I say 'surprised' that doesn't really come anywhere near to describing how I felt at that moment. I was elated. Amazed. Thrilled to bits.

Never in a million years did I think I'd ever receive such an award which, the letter informed me, I would be presented with at Buckingham Palace by the Queen. So that was it! The Queen obviously listened to my shows on Radio Wales, was a bit of a fan, had been too shy to write in for a request and this was *her* way of thanking me.

Owen Money. Comedian and broadcaster; previously a betting-office clerk; a fruit and vegetable salesman; 60s recording artiste; factory worker; used-car salesman... was going to be a Member of the British Empire.

Now I've got to be honest with you – and please don't tell her Majesty next time you see her – although it was fantastic to be told I was getting the MBE, I would have *much* preferred to have received a Knighthood. Like Sir Anthony Hopkins. Well it wouldn't have hurt Her Maj to push the boat out a little bit further, would it? She only has to look at a list of names on a piece of paper and put a tick next to them. She wouldn't be the first person to tick me off. "Arise, Sir Owen Money of Merthyr Tydfil and all lands extending down to and including Cardiff Bay, Barry Island and Splott!" does have a nice ring to it, don't you think? And besides, I reckon I'm more than qualified to be a Knight of the Realm. I've encountered more than my fair share of dragons in my time.

After 2006 had started so badly, to be told that I was thought worthy of receiving an MBE was a real pick-me-up. But I couldn't go around telling everyone the good news, because the letter informed me that the Queen's New Year Honours list wouldn't officially be released to the press and the public until... you guessed it... New Year's Day. Or midnight on New Year's Eve to be precise. However, I felt I had to tell my employers at Radio Wales because in many ways my award was a reflection of the faith they'd had in me for so many years. I also told one or two of my closest friends. And several dozen German tourists at a service station on the M4, who had no idea what I was talking about.

In fact I had two reasons to celebrate the day the envelope arrived with the news about my MBE because it was the last Thursday in November, which, any wine connas... connous... coniss... *expert* will tell you, is Beaujolais Nouveau Day. I don't like to boast but I am a bit of a wine expert myself. In fact my 'nose' is so sensitive I can tell a red from a white just by looking at it.

So I headed off for Swansea and, with a knowing smile on

my face and a borrowed fiver in my wallet, I booked myself
in to the very posh Morgans Hotel where I knew they were
celebrating this special day in the wine-lovers' calendar. Now
when I say Morgans is posh, I mean posh! They don't have
'muzak' in the lift. When the lift doors open, Nigel Kennedy's
standing there, belting out Vivaldi on his fiddle. And when
he takes a fag break, Katherine Jenkins stubs out her own
Woodbine and jumps in to impress hotel residents with her
beautiful arias. I hope you're not making up your own jokes
now.

After I checked into my room, I went down to the bar and
tasted my first sample of Beaujolais Nouveau 2006 which
had been rushed all the way from France to Swansea. There
was no real need for them to have rushed it, because I had no
intention of going anywhere for the next 24 hours.

By the time I'd drained my third glass of red wine I still
couldn't decide whether it was a vintage year, so out of
courtesy to the industrious grape pickers and wine makers of
La Belle France, I partook of a fourth glass. Then a fifth. And
then a sixth.

I couldn't say that I was inebriated – basically because
I was much too squiffy to pronounce the word 'inebriated'
– but there was a danger that in my exceedingly happy state
I might accidentally spill the beans about my special letter
from Downing Street and my... ssshhh! Whisper it, MBE.
However, the danger soon passed once I had enjoyed another
glass or two because I felt it was high time for me to take my
leave of my fellow wine-appreciators with whom I'd spent a
convivial evening. So I bid them goodnight and headed for the
lobby despite their heartfelt requests to stay a while longer.
But their pleas fell on deaf ears. I didn't want to be associated
with a bunch of drunks.

I took the lift to my room, not forgetting to drop a shiny fifty-
pence piece into Katherine Jenkins' little tin-box after she'd
serenaded me with a brief selection from *Madam Butterfly*.

The poor girl looked all-in and she told me she wasn't due to finish until midnight because she was covering for Nigel Kennedy who'd had a last-minute booking at Aberystwyth Non-Political Club who were offering him seventy-five quid in readies.

I can't remember how I found my room or managed to get into it, but I vividly remember waking up the next morning in agony, ready to complain to the management about the horribly cramped and uncomfortable bed I'd paid them a small fortune for. It was hard as a rock. There was no give in it. Definitely the worst hotel bed I have ever slept in. As I reached for the phone to make my complaint, it struck me as odd that the phone was so far away from the bed and placed really high-up on the wall. It was only then that I realised why my bed was so hard. I'd fallen asleep on the floor!

I was also ready to complain to the management about the jackhammer that seemed to be operating in the adjoining room. Until I realised the banging and thumping wasn't coming from next door. It was inside my head. I swore there and then that from now on I'd replace Beaujolais Nouveau with Beaujolais Nomore...

But, in the words of that intellectual giant and university lecturer, Jimmy Cricket, "There's more!" When I went down to breakfast – I think it was around teatime – the manager asked me if I'd enjoyed the champagne. "What champagne?" I asked, very quietly, just before I washed down a handful of aspirins with a pint of tea. "We sent up a bottle with our compliments," he replied. I thanked him, again very quietly, but thought he was off his head. I didn't see any champagne in my room. If I had I might have had a glass or two as a nightcap. Well, in for a penny, in for a pounding headache. But sure enough, when I went back to the room, there was an unopened bottle of champers in a big silver bucket, swimming in a small pool of melted ice. And I hadn't even noticed it. As I've always believed in waste-not, want-not, and as there just happened to be a champagne-bottle-sized empty space in my suitcase, I packed it away to be drunk another day. That's *the* bottle that was to be drunk. Not me. I rarely touch the stuff.

Well, I think we're more relaxed in each other's company now than when we started out on Page One so, in Chapter Two, I'm going to be a little more serious and take you right back to the beginning. No, not to Adam and Eve and the Garden of Eden. Just *my* little Garden of Eden. Otherwise known as Merthyr Tydfil...

CHAPTER TWO

MERTHYR TYDFIL. SO GOOD they named it... Merthyr Tydfil. For those of you who don't know, Merthyr isn't just a town in Glamorgan, it's also a county borough, with a population of around 55,000 – 30,000 of whom live in the town itself. And if you go shopping in any Merthyr supermarket on a Friday evening, 9,000 of them will be standing in the check-out queue in front of you.

Merthyr Tydfil was named after Saint Tydfil, a daughter of King Brychan of Brycheiniog – which I wouldn't recommend saying when you've got a mouthful of crisps. Merthyr was originally the Welsh word for 'church', but the more usual and more recent meaning is 'martyr', hence the local football team, Merthyr Tydfil FC are referred to as "The Martyrs" .

I was born Lynn Mittell in Merthyr in 1947 and for anyone who remembers that immediate post-war period or perhaps heard stories about it from their parents or grandparents, it was a very austere time for working-class people. Husbands and sons who had returned from serving in the forces and were looking for any sort of work, wore badly-tailored but serviceable double-breasted 'demob' suits and because food was still scarce, housewives had to go shopping with ration cards, initially issued during the War, which limited the amount of, say, eggs, potatoes or... if you could find it... red meat, they could buy. You've only got to watch any of those old black and white British films made in the late 1940s and early 1950s, usually starring John Mills or Jack Warner, to get a real flavour of how basic and bleak things were back then.

But as most families had very little in terms of possessions – this was long before the big changes of the mid-to-late

1950s when people gradually started to acquire fridges, washing machines and black and white televisions – as children growing up at the time, we didn't feel deprived because we didn't know any different. In fact as my parents ran a pub, the Royal Oak Inn, in Lower High Street, I never seemed to want for much. They'd been in the pub game long before I came along. The Cefn Coed Hotel was their very first one and in fact they were the youngest landlord and landlady in Merthyr at the time.

My Dad was an extraordinary man, an ex-professional football player who could play one-handed piano and who was absolutely hopeless when it came to electrical equipment. There were wires and leads and plugs dangling around all over the place. Which makes it all the more remarkable that the Royal Oak Inn was the first pub in Merthyr to have a microphone which could be used by the entertainers. To this day I don't know if it was actually earthed, but not one pub singer went up in smoke. Mind you, there were one or two whose act would have been improved no end by a sudden shower of sparks and 20,000 volts.

We were also one of the first families in town to own a television set. I think it was one of those huge ten-inch screen models and even in 1953 we had a choice of viewing. The set could either be on... or off. Today, you switch on your telly and the picture appears more or less immediately. Not then. The sets had to 'warm up'. So if you wanted to settle down to watch, for example, an episode of a popular series like *Quatermass* (which the announcer would always warn viewers "is not suitable for children or for those of a nervous disposition") which started at nine-thirty, you had to switch the TV set on some time before. *Like two days before.*

I'm not kidding you, between the time you first switched the telly on and the time the picture eventually arrived, my Mam could cook my tea... bath me... put me in my pyjamas... write a note to the milkman... serve a dozen customers downstairs in the pub... and would still have ten minutes spare to do a bit of hoovering and dusting. There was only one channel – BBC – the same company I would find myself working for many years later. I think there were some programmes for housewives on during the afternoon, followed by *The Children's Hour* at five o'clock. After that, and this will sound unbelievable to anyone who wasn't around then, the BBC stopped broadcasting for an hour... so that parents could get their little ones to bed! Then programmes would resume at seven o'clock until closedown at half-past ten, or, eleven o'clock at weekends. This was called the 'toddlers' truce'.

One of the first programmes I remember watching was *Muffin the Mule* that had an opening song that went...

'We want Muffin, Muffin the Mule.
Dear old Muffin, playing the fool.
We want Muffin, everybody sing.
We want Muffin the Mule!'

Ah, they don't write songs like that any more, except for the Eurovision Song Contest. Muffin was a non-speaking wooden puppet, held up by half-a-dozen strings of such thickness you could use any one of them to secure the *QE2* to the dockside at Southampton. Dear old Muffin used to 'clack' to and fro across the top of a grand piano played by John Mills's sister, Annette. I don't mean she played *the part* of a grand piano, I mean she actually played tunes on the piano and spoke to Muffin in a 'frightfully posh' English accent which sounded so unlike the way we spoke in Merthyr, I thought she must be from some far away foreign land.

Muffin was black and white. Well he could have been green and orange I suppose, but as colour television didn't begin in Britain until 1968, and only then on BBC2, he was black and

26

white to everyone who tuned in to watch him walking around the top of a piano and either nodding or shaking his head as Annette Mills asked him a question. Okay, it was hardly *Mastermind* but we kids loved it.

My best mate at the time was David Delaney, who had an older brother named Malcolm, who became an amateur boxer for Wales. I remember having a pillow-fight with Dai Delaney in his bedroom, in the course of which I accidentally knocked-over a bedside lamp, breaking it. It didn't half annoy his Mam, who went berserk, calling us "little bastards!"

That was the first time I ever heard a woman swear. I was shocked. I'd heard men swearing in the pub and picked up certain bad words as kids do. Not knowing how bad they were, when I was three or four I'd once told my Dad to "F-off!", for which he gave me a battering. But to hear those words come from one of my mates' mother was something else. Malcolm Delaney eventually married my first girlfriend and the first love of my life, Mary Fly. Poor Mary died tragically young at the age of 40.

Growing up in a pub, I got to know many of the local characters: the regulars who came in night after night for their pints. And, of course, the atmosphere would always be thick with tobacco fumes, because everyone seemed to smoke in those days. If they weren't passing their fags around, they were sucking on a pipe. And no-one took a blind bit of notice. Try and light up in a pub now and there'll be police sirens and blue flashing lights within seconds. Luckily the smoking ban doesn't worry me because I gave up years ago. I used those patches. I put one over each eye so I couldn't find my fags. I also visited an acupuncturist. But I didn't like him. He stuck needles in all my ciggies. Finally the only way I could give up smoking was to go cold turkey. If you've ever tried to smoke cigarettes made out of cold turkey, you'd give up too.

One of the regulars at the pub was Stan Thomas, who many years later went on to create, with his brother Peter, Peter's

Savoury Products. After he'd sold that company for seventy-five million pounds in 1987, he started a company called TBI which bought eight airports, including Cardiff International Airport and he has always found time to raise millions of pounds for charity, including the Noah's Ark Appeal. Not bad for someone who started out selling meat pies and pasties to local chip shops! Any chance of a sub, Stanley?

I'm going back to the late 50s now. Stan was older than me – funnily enough, he still is – and he was a bit of a Teddy Boy. He had the DA hairstyle, the drainpipe trousers and crêpe shoes. In fact I remember annoying him once when I pointed out his shoes were crêpe. He said, "That's *your* opinion. I think they're quite smart". Stan was friendly with another Teddy Boy named Roy 'Cherry' Walters and the pair of them were always in the Royal Oak, even though they were always skint.

So now is a good time to let you in on a secret that I've kept to myself for fifty years. In fact it's a sort of confession on behalf of my late father, who passed on many years ago. And as he wasn't the beneficiary of the 'crime' in question, it makes little or no difference now. As I said, Stan and Roy were permanently broke and my dad, who had a heart of gold, always felt sorry for them. One December, as Christmas approached and it was obvious that Stan and Roy were due to have a pretty miserable December 25th, without food, drink or the money to buy presents, Dad did something that I suppose may have been illegal at the time, but he did it in the true spirit of Christmas to benefit the less well off. And Stan and Roy were certainly two of the poorest men in town. I don't know exactly how Dad did it, but when it was time for the Royal Oak Inn's Christmas draw, the two winning tickets taken out of the tin, belonged to... you guessed it... Stan and Roy, who won ten pounds each. When you consider that at that time the average weekly wage was less than ten pounds, it'll give you some idea of how much this win would have meant to Stan and Roy. It made all the difference between a grim Christmas and a great one.

Stan, as I mentioned, is now a very wealthy man, but he has never forgotten my father's kindness that Christmas. As some of you may be aware, I am a mathematical genius and I have worked out, with the aid of a spirit level and a second-hand bicycle pump, that the £20 prize money, with compound interest added over 50 years, is now worth £250,000 and eighty-seven pence. So Stan, on behalf of my old Dad, any time you're ready to repay him, through me, I'm happy to accept a cheque or cash. All joking aside, Stan Thomas was a great friend to my parents and I was very proud to have him as a bearer at their funerals.

The Royal Oak Inn was where I made my show-biz debut, not as Owen Money – I went through several name-changes before I settled on that one – but under my real name, Lynn Mittell, when I was around nine or ten. Members of the Territorial Army used to come down to the pub from their base in Sennybridge and, one night, I started singing one of my favourite songs in front of them. It was Frankie Vaughan's 'Garden of Eden' which became a big hit, even though it was banned by the BBC. I was never sure if the ban was imposed because the BBC radio bosses thought the lyrics were sacrilegious, which they couldn't have been because I don't think Frankie would have recorded the song if they were. Or because there was a rather saucy film doing the rounds of the fleapit picture houses at the time that, co-incidentally, was also called *Garden of Eden* which was one of those disgusting 'nudist' films that were a five-minute wonder in the 1950s.

The 'nudist' films were basically one-hour travelogues, showing pretty girls swimming, playing tennis or working on the meat counter in Tesco's (I made that last bit up – they worked on the cheese counter) – all of them *totally and utterly stark naked*!

Actually you only ever saw their jiggly boobies and their

wobbly backsides. They artfully managed to cover their more exotic 'parts' with newspapers or beach balls. Even so, this was very racy stuff for the time. But here's the thing I could never get my head around. This was the 1950s, when even a glimpse of stocking-top could send a young man crazy with desire. But these 'nudies' weren't given an 'X' certificate, 'for adults only'.

The censor realised that the films, with titles like *Around the World with Nothing On*, *Naughty Naked Nudes of Neath* and *She Took Off Her Vest in Haverfordwest*, were so innocent, so lacking in erotic excitement – and in truth were pretty boring after the initial shock of seeing a forty-foot pair of bazoomas staring at you from the screen – that he passed them with a 'U' certificate! So *anyone* could go and see them. My dad warned me *never* to visit a cinema showing a nudist film, because I might see something that a boy of my age shouldn't. But what eleven-year-old could resist? So I went to see *Naked as Nature Intended* and, sure enough, I did see something I shouldn't – my dad, sitting three rows in front!

Anyway, the song 'Garden of Eden' was also a big hit for me in the Royal Oak Inn because after I'd finished singing it, the lads from the TA had a whip round for me, filled a beer glass with coins and I earned myself seventeen shillings and sixpence – in today's money, around seventy-five pence. My first paid gig!

Some of the other characters that used to frequent my parents' pub were Glyn Davies, also known as Glyn Shag – only he knew why; George Kelly, who was a yodeller; Bernie Murphy, who sang like Bing Crosby; and then there was Ossie, who was married to Pearl. One night he came in late from the pub, and so that their pet budgie wouldn't start squawking and wake up Pearl, he had the bright idea to take a pork chop out of the kitchen and put it in its cage. There was method in his madness because the budgie didn't make a sound. He probably stared at the pork chop for hours, thinking "What the bl**dy hell is this?"

I was an only child – according to my two brothers – so Mum and Dad did tend to spoil me. They didn't see it as such; they just wanted me to have some of the things they never had when they were children. One Christmas morning I came downstairs to our large lounge where Dad had laid out a model railway track, right around the room. No train, just the track. Of course there was a train. And a couple of carriages. But my reaction to seeing what should have been the highlight of any young boy's Christmas wasn't elation. It was disappointment. You see, all my mates had model railways made by well-known firms like Hornby or Triang, but the one my parents bought me (delivered by Santa of course, kiddies!) was nothing like the sleek, shiny model trains my mates owned. The present laid out in front of me that Christmas morning was a huge, and to my eyes, ugly train set made in Germany.

I didn't realise it at the time, but it must have cost my parents a fortune. But I just didn't like it. Children are like that. They know exactly what they want for Christmas or their birthday and if what they're given happens to fall short of their expectations, they can't hide their disappointment. I didn't make any effort to hide *my* disappointment, so I must have come across to my parents as a really ungrateful child.

Despite this, Mam and Dad didn't shout at me for my behaviour, which they were fully entitled to do, but after my dad and my godfather, uncle Alfie Lewis, had played with the train set all day, Dad put it all away and it never saw the light of day again. I don't know what happened to it, but knowing the price that 1950s toys and collectables fetch at auction, especially if they're kept in their original boxes as my German train set would have been, they'd now be worth several thousand pounds.

Here's another Christmas present story, but thankfully

this one has a happier ending. There was a sports shop in Merthyr called Barnes and they stocked the first white leather footballs I'd ever seen. And boy did I want one! Up until then, footballs had always been made of brown leather, so these gleaming white ones looked really fantastic to my young eyes. I suppose I must have hinted to Mam and Dad that I'd like one for Christmas and sure enough, when I woke up on December 25th, Santa had delivered one. I was thrilled to bits with this, not only because it was something I'd set my heart on owning, but also because I knew I was the first boy in the bottom end of town to own a white football.

Now I don't remember it snowing on many Christmas mornings in my lifetime, but it definitely did that day. Despite the cold weather and snow, I couldn't wait to play with my football and I was allowed out with my mates. We took the ball up to a place we called the Mucky Tip at Rhydycar. That was one of the few days it didn't look mucky because it was covered in snow.

We hadn't been up there long and were just having a bit of a kick around when my mate Roger Williams gave the ball a powerful kick... it sailed through the air... and landed in the river Taff! My brand new shiny football which had only been in my possession for a matter of hours... was floating away from me, downstream!

I immediately imagined what Mam and Dad's reaction would be when I told them what had happened – they would go bananas, even though it wasn't me who kicked the ball into the river. I felt so sick I considered running away and leaving the country rather than face my parents. Not that I had a passport. And of course the airports would have been closed Christmas Day. And even if they had been open, there were no buses running to take me to the... well, you know how things go through your mind when you're in a state of panic!

There was no way that I could jump into the icy water

to rescue my ball and as I stood on the bank, watching it heading towards the Bristol Channel and eventually the Atlantic Ocean, I imagined it being washed ashore on some tropical island in six months time and a little Hawaiian kid finding it. I *hated* that little Hawaiian kid. Playing with *my* Christmas present!

All of a sudden I was aware that someone had waded out into the water to rescue my precious present. It was Malcolm Delaney, Dai's older brother. He was much braver than the rest of us and managed to grab the ball and bring it back to me. Talk about relieved. I couldn't thank him enough. When I got back home, I never said a word about the incident to Mam and Dad, just in case they decided not to buy me any more Christmas presents!

So as you can tell, I wasn't a perfect child. In fact as I was growing up I started getting into all sorts of scrapes that tried my parents' patience, like the time when I was eight and the cook at our school, Caedraw Primary, gave me and my mate Michael Flynn some money to go down to Lloyd's Sweet Shop to buy her a packet of twenty Craven 'A' cigarettes and bring them back to the school. That's right. She asked two eight-year olds to buy fags for her! Yes, it *was* a far more innocent age, but Michael and I were far from innocent. We were the youngest smokers in town and with the cook's money in our grubby little hands we knew that she was never going to enjoy her cigarettes.

We sauntered into the shop and I asked for twenty Craven 'A' and a box of matches and nonchalantly handed over the money. The shopkeeper must have assumed I was buying them for a grown-up, as children were always being sent on errands to the shops, because he handed me the ciggies and matches, gave me my change and went to serve the next customer. Michael and I couldn't believe our luck. Instead of taking them back to the school, we ran all the way to the local cemetery, where we knew we could have a smoke without being seen by anyone, laughing out loud at what we'd got away with. We settled ourselves down behind a grave stone, out of sight and, that afternoon, we smoked all twenty cigarettes between us.

Think about that for a moment, we were two naughty little eight-year-old boys in short trousers, puffing our way through ten fags each in a matter of hours! And as all naughty little boys do, we thought we could get away with it.

When I got home from school that day, my Mam looked me up and down, leant forward and sniffed. And then she smacked me right around the head. My breath, clothes and hair must have *reeked* of cigarette smoke. Once again I'd been a naughty boy and she went berserk. I got a right belting.

She used to have the knack of hitting me and speaking to me at the same time, and she'd emphasise certain words to coincide with each blow. It went something like "WHO do YOU THINK you ARE?" or "HOW many TIMES do I have to tell YOU... NOT... TO... SMOKE?" And talking of the things my Mam used to say when she was hitting me, does anyone know where "Kingdom Come" is? The thing is I must have been really resilient or incredibly stupid because a couple of days after I'd had a good smacking, I'd forget all about it and do something else to annoy her and Dad. I suppose I just had mischief running through my blood.

You've heard the saying "Curiosity killed the cat?" Well there was one occasion when my curiosity, if it didn't actually kill me, didn't do my insides a lot of good. Like all kids do at some point, I was having a good old nose around in my parents' bedroom drawers. I have no idea what I was looking for because I wasn't at the age where I had any idea what parents hid in their bedroom drawers. Anyway, I opened one particular drawer and there it was. A great big bar of chocolate. Unopened. Still in the silver foil packaging. And looking very, very tempting.

That was the point where I should have closed the drawer,

left the bedroom and forgotten all about what I'd seen. Because I knew that if I took it, Mam and Dad would obviously know it was me who had stolen it. Who else was around to rifle through their drawers? Nevertheless, I was not even worrying about the punishment they'd mete out when they discovered it was missing. I took the chocolate bar to school, without taking the time to wonder why they'd want to hide a bar of chocolate in their bedroom.

I shared out the chocolate with my mate Dai Delaney and although it didn't taste like the usual chocolate bars we were used to, like Cadbury's or Fry's, we ate it. Chocolate's chocolate, right? Well, not necessarily. Not when it's called Ex-Lax. A bowel-loosening, chocolate-flavoured laxative that constipated people were supposed to eat just two squares of to get themselves... moving. I'm not sure if what I'd found was a 'family size' bar but Dai and I had eaten much more than two squares each.

I'm not going to describe exactly what happened to us a short while after we'd eaten the Ex-Lax , because to do so I'd need to descend into crude lavatorial humour, which is not really my style. All I will say is, if Ex-Lax is still available, let me assure you that a couple of squares with a cup of hot tea are more than sufficient to shift your problem. If you eat half a bar at one sitting (no pun intended) you will not only shift your problem, you will also shift the pizza you had the previous week. Your last Christmas lunch, including the pudding that followed. And a piece of rump steak that's been lying there since 1987.

If you thought the end of *Titanic* was moving, it doesn't come close to how moving the Ex-Lax bar was that day. Dai and me both ruined our underpants... trousers... socks... and any chance of impressing the girls in our class. The stench was appalling. It was so bad, even the Headmaster, who had completely lost his sense of smell after a Japanese sniper shot off the tip of his nose during the War, complained about it. Luckily for Dai and me our 'accident' happened in the classroom and, as you know, classrooms have plenty of paper close to hand. Exercise books. Text books. Drawing paper. Loads of the stuff to choose from. I can't remember what I used, but there was a terrible moment when the teacher nearly passed-out when I reached for the register.

If completely ruining our clothes (believe me, soapsuds and hot water couldn't have freshened them up – they were *way beyond* salvaging) and embarrassing ourselves in front of our classmates wasn't enough, once I got home I had to explain to Mam and Dad what had happened. Although, as they had the entire pub windows open, I think they may have had a pretty good idea of what had occurred when I got within 200 yards of the place. Naturally I got no sympathy from Mam and Dad, just another smacking, a hot bath and an early night with no telly-watching. And just as naturally, despite the humiliation and the battering I suffered, I didn't learn my lesson.

I mentioned that I used to go around singing 'Garden of Eden', which, because it had been banned by the BBC, I must have heard on the only radio station that played pop music in the late 1950s – Radio Luxembourg 208. This station was, obviously, based in Luxembourg, and started around seven in the evening and went on until after midnight. They employed many DJs over the years, including Jimmy Young (after his chart career), Noel Edmonds and Emperor Rosko. The ones I remember from the 1950s were names like Don Moss and the station's chief presenter Barry Aldiss.

Fans of 208 assumed at the time that all the DJs were flown out to the Grand Duchy on a rotation basis, and although the DJs did broadcast from there sometimes, many shows were pre-recorded at the station's London base in Hertford Street. Because 208 was broadcast on Long Wave it meant that the signal wavered all over the place and usually faded completely at the exact moment your favourite tune of the time was being played. But we didn't care, because it was so exciting to listen to pop music pouring out of the family radio along with programmes like *The Ovaltineys* and *Dan Dare*.

And later, when those little transistor radios came out, there was nothing better than snuggling under the bedclothes and listening to the top twenty and all the new releases that the BBC didn't or wouldn't play. I must have been around eleven or twelve when my Mam bought me my first transistor radio and it was something special, because it had an in-built timer. When I went to bed I'd tune it into 208, put the timer on to last thirty minutes and put the radio on my bedside table, enabling me to fall asleep listening to the latest chart hits well within the thirty minutes, after which it switched itself off!

Apart from the pop songs that started coming through from America in the mid-50s, I can remember hearing 'The Dambusters' March', Eric Coates' rousing theme to the 1954 film, on the radio all the time. We naughty kids used to refer to the film as "The Bumdusters"!

Radio Luxembourg was an important influence on young music fan, because when I was growing up in 1950s there were two main BBC radio stations and they were hopeless when it came to pop music. The Home Service, a speech-based station which slowly evolved into Radio Four and The Light Programme, which featured various dance bands and orchestras (I remember Victor Sylvester and his orchestra used to have a regular morning show) which also broadcast hugely popular programmes like *Music While You Work*, *Housewives' Choice* and *Workers' Playtime*. Seems like 100 years ago, doesn't it?

But because the Musicians Union had a tight grip on the number of hours the BBC could and couldn't fill with music *on records*, pop fans had to be grateful for the odd BBC programme that featured new and Top 20 records, like *Jack Jackson's Saturday Spin*. There was an upside to the BBC's 'live' music policy, as shows like *Easy Beat* and *Saturday Club* featured performances by bands like the Rolling Stones, the Hollies, the Kinks and... the Beatles! These BBC versions of their hits were always a little more rough and ready than their carefully produced records but, listening at home, we didn't mind. And because the shows were on tape, they've been preserved so that decades later, music fans can hear bands (or groups as they were then) who could actually sing and play instruments.

Of course many years later the arrival and popularity of the pirate radio stations, (which coincided with the Mersey Beat explosion) made the starchy BBC change their policy on playing records and they created Radios One and Two. While Radio One pumped out the latest hit singles and new releases and made stars of Tony Blackburn and Kenny Everett, for the first few years of its existence, Radio Two still continued the old Light Programme policy of featuring 'live' bands.

I can still remember Joe 'Mr Piano' Henderson used to have a show on the Light Programme every Saturday morning in the 1960s. A two-hour show, featuring some jolly piano music, a couple of guest singers like Marion Ryan and Vince Hill, a handful of records and bit of easy-going chat. Can you imagine Radio Two putting out a show like that now? It still sounds quite entertaining to me. I might try and flog it to Radio Wales...

Around the same time that I was discovering music and starting to sing a bit, I was also introduced to another lifelong passion of mine. No, not Beaujolais Nouveau. The Beautiful Game. Football! And in particular... Merthyr Town FC and their home ground, Penydarren Park, where I saw footballing legends like Harry Lowe and Trevor Richards in action. My Auntie Gwen ran the tea chalet inside the grounds and she used to let me sit on the wall to watch the matches. My Dad used to take me to the home matches and sometimes his mates would give us a lift. Which sounds very nice and friendly, until I tell you that he was the world's worst car passenger.

No matter how competent the driver was, my Dad would sit in the front passenger seat and let out a continuous stream of complaints. "You're much too close to the car in front!" "You nearly hit that pedestrian then!" "Didn't you see him pulling out?" Eventually his mates got used to his criticisms and learned to ignore them for the most part. But one day, on the way to a match at Penydarren Park, Dad was being especially annoying to the driver, Roy 'Cherry' Walters.

He moaned about Roy's driving from the moment the car pulled away from the kerb and didn't stop whinging until we were nearly at the football ground. Instead of letting Dad irritate him, Roy, who had a wicked sense of humour, got him back in his own way. As the car was still moving along the road, Roy removed the steering wheel and, to my Dad's horror, handed it to him, folded his arms and said, "Right. Let's see if you can do any better!" My Dad still complained about the poor quality of people's driving, but he never again did it in Roy's car.

My initial interest in football soon turned into an obsession and I would try and see my local team play as often as I could. The fact that many of the Merthyr Town players used to drink in my parents' pub and I got to know them was an added bonus.

Talking of pubs, it was around that time that Mam and Dad left the Royal Oak Inn, where they'd been tenants, and bought their first pub – The Beehive Inn. Well that was its official name, but the locals liked to refer to it as "The Bucket of Blood" because of all the fights that went on in there. We had some really tough-looking customers at the Beehive and I remember one in particular who had a broken nose, brown teeth, cauliflower ears and a great big bushy moustache that permanently stank of beer and fags. But she had a lovely personality when you got to know her.

CHAPTER THREE

THIS CHAPTER IS MAINLY about some of the misadventures I got involved in during my school days. A famous man once described school as "The happiest days of your life". Obviously this man was either mentally unbalanced or had left school so many years before he came out with that daft statement that he had no clear recollection of what it had really been like. School is alright if you're academically gifted. But once you graduate from the junior school to the 'big school', if you're a thicko or even just an average student who can just about get by, you're facing five years of sheer purgatory. I reckon that being chained next to Ben-Hur in a Roman galley and being forced to row for ten hours a day while some fat, sweaty bloke in a leather skirt smacks you on the back with a whip every twenty minutes is a breeze compared to five years in big school.

We all need a good education. A solid grounding in the things that are necessary to set you up for life in the real world so we can make a decent living. I'm talking about spelling... reading... maths... history... geography... and identity theft. But why do kids have to go to a school every day for lessons? It's the going to *school* that puts kids off education. They'd do much better if lessons were taught in, oh, I don't know, off the top of my head... Morrisons or Sainsbury's. Or your local Multiplex cinema. Yes, if schools were replaced by Cineworlds and Odeons you wouldn't have to drag your kids out of bed in the mornings. They'd be up and out before dawn every day.

As for my education, Mam and Dad always encouraged me to do well, although I don't suppose they'd had much of an education themselves. Nevertheless they were both intelligent, worldly and astute business people. Whether or not they thought I might follow them into the pub game, they wanted me to have a good, solid education. Which just got me remembering something. On my radio shows I must have played thousands of records over the years and, hand on heart, there are very few of them I don't like. But there were a few I absolutely loathed and if you're a regular listener to my shows you'll know the ones I mean. One of my least favourite records is 'Another Brick in the Wall' by Pink Floyd and its monotonous chorus, "We don't need no education". Which is ironic when you think that members of Floyd all went to posh universities and colleges and became millionaires living in country mansions. (Actually I once came *that* close to winning a million pounds on the lottery. *That* close! Yeah, the fellah next door won it.)

But back to my education and, contrary to what a lot of people think, I did go to school for more than one term. In fact when I was 16, I left school with ten O Levels. But the Headmaster made me put them back. Seriously though, through sheer hard work and many hours of revision late into the night, but mostly from bunging every member of the exam board a tenner each, I managed to earn myself two O Levels. One in Art and one in Metalwork. So naturally my first job was painting the Forth Bridge. Yes, the money was good, but it was no fun commuting from Merthyr every day.

The junior school I attended was Caedraw School and my teacher was Mr Beynon. I was quite happy at that school, especially when I played for the school football team. I remember when I was ten, we played a match against Dowlais Catholic School at the GKN Dowlais ground and we beat them 3–0 and all three goals were scored by Kenny Owens.

In the 50s and into the early 60s, when children reached the age of eleven we all had to sit the '11 plus' exam – which was actually a series of exams taken over a couple of days as I recall. Depending on how well you did in the exam, this more or less shaped your educational future. If you passed, you went on to a Grammar School where you would continue your education up to your O Levels and, if you were really clever, on to your A Levels. If you failed, you went to a Secondary Modern School where the standards, so we were told, weren't as high as the Grammar School. I must have been a bright pupil because I passed my '11 plus' without any problem, but my mate Dai Delaney failed his, so when we left the Juniors and went up to 'the big school', we got separated and formed new friendships.

My new 'big school' (and it really was big – eight hundred pupils!) was Quakers Yard Grammar School which was miles from my house. In fact it was so far away I had to take a train to and from school every day – and I don't mean a modern diesel unit. This was one of those old-fashioned steam trains puffing-out billows of white smoke and black soot, a half-a-dozen wooden carriages and a guard's van right at the back. So just getting to school every morning was quite an adventure.

On my first day there I was very nervous because, apart from the new intake of eleven-year-olds that I was part of, everyone seemed so much bigger and tougher than me. School prefects are supposed to make sure everyone obeys the school rules, but there was one particular prefect, named Dai Ishmael, who ignored some of the rules and used to pick on me. I suppose he was a bit of a bully and liked to use his position as prefect to torment little oiks like me. However, I soon had an ally in the shape of Dai Delaney's big brother Malcolm, who, being older than me, had been at Quakers Yard for a few years and he used to look out for me.

In that first term I met lads like Andy Powell, Anthony Parry and Alun Francis who became a French horn player. Odd that he should choose that instrument. He couldn't speak a word of French. Alun came from Troedyrhiw, which reminds me that that was also the home town of a great performer who had many hit records in the 1950s: Malcolm Vaughan, who was born in Abercynon and moved to Troedyrhiw when he was a small child. Coincidentally he went to the same school as me, but as he was born almost 20 years before I entered the world, we were never in the same class. Malcolm was once part of the comedy double-act Earl and Vaughan and then became a solo singer in the mid-50s, having hits like 'You Are My Special Angel' and 'St Theresa of the Roses'. When I was at Quakers Yard School, Malcolm was a big star, always on the telly and radio. In later years he retired and he and his wife Gaye moved to Eastbourne, where he passed away in February 2010 aged 80.

At the big school I got reacquainted with Kenny Owens Griffiths, also known as Kenny Owens, the one who scored three goals against Dowlais Catholic School. He might have been a good soccer player, but I always thought there was something not quite right about him and unfortunately my suspicions were proved right when we were both involved in an unpleasant incident which I'll relate later on.

When you're a young boy of eleven, and your hormones start arriving, ve-ry slow-ly at first, and you begin to get a little bit curious about girls. Well, most boys do. But not *everyone* obviously. As Bertie Bassett says, it takes all sorts. I mean this is the 21st century and if you happen to be a male person of the masculine order who doesn't like... well let me put it this way, if you don't like girls and would rather... oh hell! I'm painting myself into a corner here. You all know what I mean. I don't have to spell it out. What I'm trying to say is, *me*, Lynn Mittell, *I* began to get curious about girls. Well they seemed so much more cuddlier than boys. Not that I'd ever wanted to cuddle a boy. I was just trying to... oh look! Here I am back in this corner with a paint brush in my hand!

There were two female teachers I had a crush on. Miss Flynn... and a more mature teacher who had the biggest pair of boobs I have ever seen. Or had ever seen up to that point. They were always well-hidden beneath her blouse and cardigan, but even so, Mrs Griffiths' boobies were flipping enormous. Like two melons bouncing around in a carrier bag. I couldn't take my eyes off them in the classroom and often used to think of them when I was lying in bed, under the sheets, fiddling with my little transistor radio.

It was when I turned twelve that I really started to get into music, which would have been, for those of you who haven't been paying attention, 1959. What a year for pop music. Although Buddy Holly died in a plane crash, along with Richie Valens and the Big Bopper, on February 3rd, Buddy had recorded a stack of songs for the Coral label, which were released both as 78s and 45s over the next couple of years until 45s completely replaced those easily breakable 78s.

Elvis was a year away from going into the army and was still making great films like *King Creole* and *Jailhouse Rock*. The charts were full of American stars like the Everly Brothers, Brook Benton, Connie Francis, Pat Boone, the Platters and Bobby Darin. Mind you we also had our own home-grown stars too, like Cliff Richard, Billy Fury, Marty Wilde, Mark Wynter and Wee Willie Harris with his bright red hair.

Although we young music fans were starved of hearing pop acts on the radio, we were able to see many of them on television thanks, amazingly, to the BBC. In 1957 they'd created a series called *Six-Five Special*, so called because it started at five past six, on Saturday evenings, just after they got rid of their toddlers' truce hour. The show was a bit of a mish-mash really, but I used to love it because it regularly featured pop singers, as well as traditional jazz, crooners and comedy. So although it wasn't Britain's first true all-pop music television show, because of its mixed content, it was hugely popular family entertainment. The show was hosted by broadcaster and actor Pete (sometimes Peter) Murray and Jo Douglas, who later went on to become a successful film producer. Pete's catch phrase was "It's time to jive on the old six-five!" – what a memory I've got. Actor and singer Jim Dale was also a regular on the show long before he starred in the Carry On films and became a success on Broadway. As they say, it's not where you start… it's where you finish. I'm writing this in a garden shed in Aberbeeg.

Comedy was provided by ex-boxer Freddie Mills and Bernie Winters, who wasn't a boxer but some years later he did go on to own a large St Bernard named Schnorbitz. See what I did there? Boxer? St Bernard? I bet you're doubled-up with laughter right now. It's the way I write 'em.

Six-Five Special was a bit hit-or-miss (like *Juke Box Jury*!) because for every Lonnie Donegan or Terry Dene who appeared, there'd be a more middle-of-the-road act like Joan Regan or Cleo Laine who appealed more to the Mams and Dads watching. But that was the nature of TV variety shows. You'd have your favourites who you were eager to see, and there'd also be some acts that sent you out of the room to make a cup of tea. In fact, now that variety shows have vanished from our screens, apart from the annual *Royal Variety Performance*, I find that many of the shows that replaced them – featuring chefs, gardeners, interior designers, antique collectors, DIY experts and 'fly on the wall' documentaries that make 'stars' out of ordinary people (for ten minutes) – don't just make me want to leave the room; they make me want to leave the country!

The resident band on *Six-Five Special* was Don Lang and his Frantic Five. They were British musicians who adopted an American image. They all wore American-style college jackets with big letters on the back, something us British kids in our drab, short grey trousers and navy mackintoshes, had never seen before. Jovial Don sang and played the trombone, quite often at the same time and the band had a hit with the novelty song 'Witchdoctor'. You know how the song goes. "Ooo – eee! Ooo – ahah! Ding Dong, Walla Walla Bing Bang!" which was one of Andrew Lloyd Webber's earliest efforts.

The producer of the show was Jack Good, who became a bit of a controversial personality and years later I found out there was a very rude joke going around about him at the time. I'm not sure whether my publishers will allow it to go into the book, but as it's based on a double entendre, you can either take it one way or the other. As the bishop said to the actress. No... that's not the joke. Here it is:

> *Jack Good and actress Kim Novak are going to become a double-act known as... Novak and Good.*

> *Then next year, they will be joined by Tommy Steele to form a trio called... Steele , Novak and Good.*

And if you don't get the joke, maybe it's just as well.

Jack was a big rock-and-roll fan and argued with the BBC that the kids at home didn't want comedy and tradition. They wanted a whole hour of rock-and-roll without interruptions by Chris Barber's Jazz Band or Anne Shelton belting out 'Lay Down Your Arms'. But in the grand tradition of the BBC they adopted a 'we know best' attitude and told Jack, the man who had given them this hit format, that the mix of performers would stay exactly the same.

Did you hear that sound? That loud bang? It was the BBC shooting themselves in the foot. Jack Good left *Six-Five Special* and went to ITV, created a brand new fast-moving show absolutely packed with pop stars like Cliff, Marty, Joe Brown, Dickie Pride, Cuddly Dudley and so many more up-and-coming rock and rollers.

When this new show *Oh Boy!* went out at six o'clock on Saturday nights it totally thrashed the *Six-Five Special* in the ratings. And not long after, the BBC announced that the *Six-Five Special* had come to the end of the line and would be shunted off to a remote siding where it would be left to rust. So the 21st century rivalry between *The X Factor* and *Strictly Come Dancing* is nothing new.

Once I'd settled into Quakers Yard, and because I had a railway season ticket to get me to and from school, it was easy for me to 'bunk off' lessons from time to time. We called it 'mitching'. But whatever you called it, if you ever got caught out, it meant big trouble from the school *and* your parents. One of my favourite 'diversions' from the normal school day was for a gang of us to stay on the train after most of our fellow pupils had got off at Quakers Yard Station and continue on to Cardiff General Station where the journey terminated. This could have been a potential problem because our season tickets only covered us from Merthyr to Quakers Yard, but we managed to bluff our way through.

Just a short walk across from the station was the still fairly new Empire Pool, which stood next to the River Taff and had been built for the British Empire and Commonwealth Games in 1958. It only cost us sixpence to get in and we could stay there for hours, having hidden our swimming costumes in our school bags. If we'd left for school with towels rolled-up under our arms that just might have given the game away, so we must have hired our towels for the day. The Empire Pool was at the time one of the most modern-looking buildings in Cardiff and for us kids it was a wonderful place to swim. Sadly it was demolished in 1998 to make way for the Millennium Stadium.

But back in 1959 the boys from Quakers Yard made full and regular use of its facilities. The only down side to our fun was that we knew that we had to get back on the train to Merthyr and make sure we all got home 'from school' at the same time as we normally would. Timing isn't just important for comedy! As our season ticket wouldn't cover the return journey, and also because we were hardly drowning in money, when we got back to Cardiff Station we'd all buy tuppenny platform tickets. They were scrapped years ago, but they used to allow people onto the station platform to bid farewell to relations and friends going on a train journey or if you wanted to meet someone off a train. What they weren't supposed to do was allow anyone onto a train...

So we'd jump on the train that would get us to Quakers Yard at the exact time that all the other kids – the good ones who had been to school all day – would be waiting on the platform to take them back to Merthyr and the other towns along the line. Those days we spent 'mitching off' took a lot of meticulous planning and ingenuity and in later years I've often reflected that if we'd channelled all that brainpower into our lessons and passing exams, we would have ended up as politicians, surgeons or barristers and earning a fortune.

Inevitably, our day trips to Cardiff came to an abrupt end when Mam and Dad found out what I'd been up to. I'm not sure how my little secret was discovered. It could have been the unmistakeable smell of chlorine that surrounded me when I walked in through the door. Or perhaps it was the sight of my bathing costume drying on the line, when we hadn't been down to Barry or Porthcawl the day before. I got another beating for that. But I thought it was worth it for all the fun my mates and I had and, to be honest, if I'd gone to school on the days when I 'mitched off' I don't think it would have made a blind bit of difference to my education.

As a non-smoker, it's strange that so many of my childhood scrapes involved cigarettes. I told you about Michael Flynn and I getting through a packet of 20 Craven 'A' when we were 8. Well there was an incident some years later which illustrates that even as a little lad, I was a budding entrepran... entrepron... entreprin... businessman.

Mam and Dad sold cigarettes in their pub and kept them on a shelf behind the bar, out of reach of little fingers. I don't mean kids. No, several of our customers were dwarves and they were heavy smokers. Perhaps if they'd quit smoking they might have grown a bit more. I don't know. It's not for me to say. Anyway, my fingers weren't that little because I used them to steal the odd packet of cigarettes, thinking no-one would notice. I did tell you that I never learned my lesson. I'd take the packets to school and sell the ciggies individually to my mates for two and a half pence each. It was a great little business for a while, until one of the teachers found out about it. He was livid, quite understandably. He'd been selling ciggies to the kids for three pence each and I was taking away all his business. That was a joke by the way. Mam and Dad did find out that I'd been stealing cigarettes and I got another beating. No wonder my least favourite colours are black and blue!

I also got into the habit of eating my lunch at the Station Café in Merthyr and I'd always have the same three-course meal. Meat pie... brown sauce... and a Woodbine. Even after all these years, I can still smell that unmistakeable acrid, burning odour. Those meat pies were horrible.

Along with all the many scrapes and misadventures I got involved in, there were other times when life wasn't so light-hearted. Like the day Kenny Owens, the lad in my school who didn't seem quite right, tried to kill me! We were 'mitching off' school together and started walking along a local viaduct, which was easily two-hundred feet high. When you're a kid you have no real sense of danger or a fear of heights. I thought *Vertigo* was just a Hitchcock film starring Kim Novak. Yes the same Kim Novak who formed a double-act with Jack Good. See how I'm interconnecting all these little stories? This book wasn't just thrown together in a fortnight, you know; it took nearly ten days.

So with no fear of what might happen to me if I slipped, I casually started walking along the parapet of the viaduct, looking down at the valley far below. I'd walked about twenty yards or so when I felt something small and hard hit me on my back. It was a stone. Then another stone, a bigger one this time, hit me on the back of the head and it bloody-well hurt. I looked around and saw Kenny, standing there with a handful of stones, laughing. He threw a couple more at me with such force that I almost lost my balance and then I realised this boy was deliberately trying to make me stumble and fall off the viaduct.

Like a lot of cruel, vindictive kids – they're still around, you only have to read the papers – he had no real concept of what would have happened if he'd succeeded in killing me. He'd have been sent to Borstal and when he'd be older, moved on to prison. His life would be in ruins and any hope of having a decent career, shattered. He'd be shunned by the people of Merthyr. And the whole incident would have a deep effect on both our families for years to come. All because he thought it would be funny to see me topple off the viaduct. And this was long before *You've Been Framed* paid viewers for their video tapes of people falling over.

I quickly jumped down from the parapet (onto the viaduct side, not down into the valley!) and had a right go at Kenny for his stupid behaviour. As you can imagine, I used some colourful language to describe what I thought of him. You know the sort of earthy, Anglo-Saxon words normally used by rough-hewn workmen on building sites, alternative comedians and the Archbishop of Canterbury whenever he forgets to take his mitre off before taking a shower. I'm talking about words like "You silly bounder!" and "What the fippin' heck do you think you're doing, you daft perisher?" Not that it had any effect on Kenny. He wasn't scared of anyone. He even sneered when I called him "A rotten spoilsport!" How can you deal with people like that?

Kenny really was a strange one. Despite his homicidal tendencies, he was quite intelligent and once he set his mind on something, he'd achieve it. In our first year at Quakers Yard we were in the same class and at the end of term, just before we broke up for the long summer holidays, he was fourth from the bottom of the class – and there were a lot of kids in our class – well over forty. Instead of being upset at his failure, he said to me, "Next year, I'm going to be top of the class!"

That wasn't just empty bravado on his part, because twelve months later he came top of the class. Whether this was through hard work or simply his innate intelligence which he hadn't bothered to call upon in the first year, I don't know. What does it matter? He did what he said he would and that was a hell of an achievement. However, despite his academic gifts, he was definitely a troubled soul. I can't say I liked him. There was something dangerous and unpredictable about him. All school kids are capable of switching from being your best mate one minute, to being a right pain in the backside who wants to punch you or steal your belongings, but I learned that it was best to keep away from Kenny. Which isn't easy to do when you're in the same class, even if you're surrounded by forty other boys.

Why he was like he was, I can't tell you. Perhaps his odd behaviour was created by problems at home which today would have been investigated by Social Services. What I do know is, in later years he spent time in mental institutions and eventually committed suicide in one of the most horrible ways imaginable. He poured a can of petrol over himself, struck a match and...

A terrible end to a troubled life.

CHAPTER FOUR

AH, SO YOU'RE STILL with me! Thank heavens for that. I thought I might have lost you after that last grim story. But it just goes to show that no-one's life is untouched by tragedy, not even a comedian's. Like everyone else, entertainers have to go through the bad times as well as the good times. It's what makes us and shapes us into what we are. A right load of misery-guts!

Which reminds me of a true story. Every performer who tries to get a laugh, whether it's a sharp-suited comedian telling gags or a red-nosed circus clown getting soaked with water, owes a debt to the 'King of Clowns', Joseph Grimaldi. The odds are you might never have heard of him but, up until recently, before 'alternative' comedy took over, the sort of quick-fire gags that mainstream comedians cracked nineteen-to-the-dozen were called 'Joey-Joeys' after Grimaldi. And circus clowns are still known as 'Joeys'.

Grimaldi lived from 1778 to 1837. So even though he never worked for BBC Wales Television, some of my older fans might still remember him. Especially *you*, Doreen Hopkins of Neath. There were comedians 'clowning around' on stage before he came along, but Joseph Grimaldi was the first clown to be given *the leading role in a pantomime*. Before that they took comedy parts that were secondary to the plot. Grimaldi changed all that. He took centre stage. He was also the first comedian to dress up as a dame, starting a tradition that has 'dragged on' from decade to decade.

What I've been doing in my own pantomimes – and before that in the many pantomimes I appeared in at the Grand Theatre, Swansea, and the New Theatre, Cardiff, 'clowning around' in brightly-coloured costumes, acting daft, falling about and getting cream pies in my face for two fast and furious hours, isn't a lot different to what Grimaldi was doing several centuries ago. In fact I still use some of his gags in my act!

For years he was acknowledged as the 'King of Clowns'. Hugely popular, he regularly packed-out Sadler's Wells and the 2,500 seater Theatre Royal, Covent Garden, throughout his long pantomime seasons. Two and a half thousand people at every performance! Two shows a day, six days a week. Imagine how much money he made just from the ice creams and flashing fairy wands. He was a true super-star, centuries before that much-overused word was invented.

So, to the true story. Around that time a man went to his doctor complaining of depression. Nothing he could do could raise his spirits. Every day was the same as the next and he couldn't get out of this depressed state of mind.

The doctor listened sympathetically to the man, who looked ashen, completely worn out and at the end of his tether and said, "My dear sir, you're dangerously close to a complete mental breakdown. You need to pull yourself out of this terrible rut you're in and enjoy life. Cheer yourself up. Go along to Sadler's Wells and see the great Grimaldi!" The man's shoulders sagged a little; he sighed and in a tired, world-weary voice replied, "I *am* Grimaldi!"

When I was a young teenager in Merthyr, I hadn't even heard of Joseph Stalin let alone Joseph Grimaldi. I had no idea that one day I would be a professional comedian, standing on a stage in front of a crowd of 20,000 people who all thought I was the funniest man they had ever seen. I had no idea then… and I still haven't.

As a 'veteran' of the pub trade and the owner of a very successful public house, my Dad was heavily involved with the Licensed Victuallers Association. Try saying that with a new set of dentures. You'll spray everyone within a half-mile radius. Those of you who are old enough to remember have probably forgotten that in the late 1950s, pubs in Wales weren't allowed to open on Sundays, although social and working-men's clubs could. My Dad thought this was unfair and campaigned long and hard to change the outdated Sunday licensing laws.

Naturally there was a lot of opposition from church and chapel organisations who believed the Sabbath should be kept special. Dad's argument was this. There was nothing stopping anyone going to church or chapel in the morning and having a drink at lunchtime too. The one activity didn't have to interfere with the other. It took several years to change things but, eventually, county by county, under pressure from licensees and their customers – amongst whom of course were many influential councillors, magistrates and MPs who weren't averse to enjoying a pint on a Sunday – the local authorities granted that pubs could open on Sundays.

The process was so slow that quite often, people who lived in counties where Sunday opening was still banned (known as 'dry' counties), would pop over to the nearest neighbouring county where the pubs were open and partake of a tipple or two. Unlike today, pub opening hours were restricted on Sunday, usually from noon to three o'clock, when the landlord would lock up and have his Sunday lunch. And they'd re-open at seven until closing time at ten-thirty. It all sounds a bit quaint and old-fashioned in this era of 24-hour drinking, doesn't it? I don't know about you, but I'm not a big fan of 24-hour drinking. The longest I ever lasted was just under 22 hours and then I passed out.

So, now it's 1960 and I'm into my early teens. I have no concept of fashion sense, my hormones are raging, my hair is greasy and my skin has so many spots you could play join-the-dots with them and end up with a picture of Windsor Castle at twilight. Despite all this, I managed to get myself a girlfriend. Her name was Dorothy Edwards. Yes, I was once a friend of Dorothy.

But that wasn't a real romance. How could it be? She didn't have proper boobs, unlike the next girl I went out with, Susan Morgan. I used to watch her in the swimming pool and stare at her boobies bouncing around inside her bathing costume. They were nothing like the size of Mrs Griffiths' massive mammaries. In fact *one* of them would have been roughly the same size as Susan Morgan. But beggars can't be choosers. Which reminds me of the time Keith Chegwin publicly announced that he was giving up alcohol for good. And I remember thinking, "So it's true. Cheggers can't be boozers!"

I got friendly with Gaynor Powell and her boyfriend James Hooper, who not only bought me a white tie which I thought was fantastic (I told you I had no concept of fashion sense) but they also bought me my first Elvis record, *The Girl of my Best Friend* on the RCA Victor label.

Every year at Quakers Yard they took a school photograph. Why they took a photo of the school every twelve months I really don't know. The building always looked the same. But they *also* took an annual photo of the pupils and on the day that all 800 of us were lined-up to pose for the photo, yours truly wasn't wearing his school tie. He was wearing the gift from Gaynor and James. My trendy new white tie. A few weeks later when the school photos were handed out to everyone, I looked at mine and saw straight away that amongst the school ties worn by the other 799 kids around me, my white tie looked like… a white tie!

I knew for certain that if I took the photo home as it was, my Mam and Dad would have wiped the floor with me, so I came up with a brilliant idea. I took out some coloured pencils and using my artistic skills, I subtly changed my white tie into a school tie. When I took the photo home, my parents couldn't have looked too closely at it because I didn't end up with a clip around the ear. Taking into account all the times I misbehaved as a youngster – although I didn't see it as misbehaving, I was just having fun – the odds were bound to fall in my favour once in a while.

It was around that time I joined my first group. Time for a quick clarification. We used to call them groups in the 60s, but sometime around the early-70s, when progressive rock and heavy metal musicians started taking their music and themselves very seriously, they preferred to be called a 'band'. The word has since replaced 'group' to describe any and every sort of musical combo from the Beatles to Take That and Metallica. In fact even The Band, who were once a group, became a band. Still with me?

The first group... sorry... *band*... I was in had me on vocals, Clifton Price on lead guitar, Tony Bevan on rhythm guitar, Rob Edwards on drums and George Snare on bass. We were called the Night Riders, but then changed it to the Crescendos.

We learnt the usual songs that all the other bands were playing, mostly chart hits and Chuck Berry tunes, and started playing at High Street Youth Club. We must have become competent pretty quickly, because when the legendary American rock and roller Gene Vincent came to play a gig at a local dance hall, we were asked to support him.

Even though I was now well into my teens I was still causing my parents grief on occasions. The guitar I was playing was alright, but I really needed a new one that looked and sounded much more professional. Mam and Dad knew this and bought me a smashing new blonde Hofner 50 electric guitar from Boosey and Hawkes in London – which was very generous of them. The problem was, they bought it as a Christmas present and I couldn't have it until December 25th. But you know me by now, I found out they'd hidden it behind their wardrobe and whenever they weren't around, I'd take it out and practice on it. When I'd finished with it, I'd put it back where I found it. No harm done. Until...

The band entered a talent competition at the Theatre

Royal and I desperately wanted to play my new guitar, which wouldn't officially be my new guitar, at the contest. Knowing the consequences if I got found out, I took the Hofner from its hiding place and played it at the contest, which we won! That night I replaced it behind the wardrobe without Mam and Dad knowing and, to all intents and purposes, I got away with it. Well, until the following day, when the band's picture was on the front page of our local paper as the winners of the talent contest and there I was, smiling like the cat that got the cream, holding the guitar that wasn't 'officially' mine. As I couldn't afford to buy up every copy of the paper and destroy them all before my parents saw their son caught bang to rights with the 'stolen goods', I was in big trouble. Once again Mam went mad. I can't even remember if she gave me a hiding for that one. I had so many they seemed to meld together in one long smack around the head.

As is often the case with semi-pro bands, the personnel changed from time to time when other priorities took over for various members or a tempting offer came in from another band. The first change we went through was when Clive John replaced Tony Bevan on rhythm guitar. Clive hadn't been with us very long when we had a gig at Bedlinog Conservative Club, which was all fine and dandy, except that the gig was on a Sunday night and Clive's father was a lay preacher at the Market Square Chapel and didn't approve of people being entertained on the Sabbath. Whether the audience at Bedlinog Conservative Club would actually *be* entertained by us was another matter.

We were all too young to drive so whenever we had a gig, we either used to get a lift to the venue or catch the bus. That's right, we'd get on a bus with our instruments and equipment – well we could hardly walk to the gig! So on this particular Sunday evening we all climbed on board the bus that went past Bedlinog Conservative Club. The problem for Clive was, the bus also went past his father's chapel and, as we passed it, there was his dad, standing outside the building. All we could do was quickly duck out of sight and hope he hadn't seen us.

But our problems didn't end there. Once we got off the bus with all our gear, the club was at the top of a steep hill, which we had to climb, carrying guitars, drums and amps and we sweated under their weight! Thank goodness I don't have to do that now. These days, now that I'm semi-famous, I make sure I only ever work clubs that have a bus stop right outside the front door!

Mind you it was worth the climb that Sunday night, because we got paid two pounds in cash and, as an added bonus, because the audience liked us so much, a bunch of them helped us take our equipment back down the hill to the bus stop. We played loads of gigs and the more we played the better and slicker and more popular we became. Our money started going up and for one Sunday gig, at Merthyr Ex-Serviceman's, we got paid six guineas!

Clive left when one of those tempting offers from another band came in, but that wasn't the last I saw of him, because one Sunday night (we did gigs on *other* nights too!) The Crescendos were playing a gig at some club and after we'd finished playing and were packing up our gear, I was approached by Micky Jones and Clive, who asked me to join their band The Rebels.

At that point, The Rebels' full line-up was Clive and Micky, plus Jeff Jones and Ray Williams. And within a day or so, they had one more member. Me! Because of this personnel change we felt we needed a change of name, so we called ourselves The Mystery Men. I've no idea why. It's a mystery. We liked that name so much we decided we'd stick with it no matter what happened. And this is what happened. We changed it to The Bystanders.

The growing success that we were enjoying was mainly due to our harmonies and because of our unique sound we offered the audiences something different to the usual repertoire of cover versions of chart hits and Chuck Berry standards, although we could do those too. You have to remember that there were lots of bands around in the early sixties. I mean there were thousands.

On any given Saturday you could walk down any street in any town in the country and you'd hear at least one band rehearsing through an open window. There were some fine guitarists, drummers and singers around but when it came to close harmonies nobody could touch us. We'd listen to the Four Seasons songs over and over until we could copy their fantastic sound. It helped that we invested some of the money from our gigs into new equipment and one of our best investments were the Vox column speakers that enhanced our vocals.

After a gig at the Empress Ballroom (where we'd supported a very popular band from Pontypridd, Tommy Scott and the Senators), someone thought that as I was the lead vocalist, then, like Tommy Scott, it would be a good idea for my name to be incorporated into our band's name. I'm not sure if this decision was unanom... unanem... unanerm... *agreed by everybody* in the band, but I was rechristened 'Jerry Braden' and we became Jerry Braden and the Bystanders.

The history of pop music has practically ignored Jerry Braden, but a few years later Tommy Scott became a big star, sold millions of records and had huge success in America, where he's lived on and off for many years. Don't tell me you've never heard of Tommy Scott? Of course you have. He packs out arenas wherever he tours and in many ways he's more popular now than he was in the 1960s when he changed his name to Tom Jones.

Our band was still only semi-professional because we all had full-time jobs. Since I'd left school I'd been working in Arthur Parker's betting shop and although I may have harboured thoughts about becoming a professional musician from time to time, it was just a wild dream. I had money coming in from my day job and a little more coming in from the gigs, so I was quite content to be Lynn Mittell by day and Jerry Braden by night.

We continued to play gigs, supporting stars that were touring dance halls, like Wes Sands, with whom we appeared at the Palace Ballroom. He was managed by the legendary Joe Meek, and although he was making records, Wes didn't have any chart success, even when he changed his name to *Clive* Sands. I wonder what made anyone think he'd be more successful as a Clive than as a Wes? In any event, he had to wait until 1976 to achieve his one and only hit, a cover of the Hoagy Carmichael song, 'My Resistance Is Low', which he recorded under his real name – Robin Starstedt. Pop trivia fans amongst you will know he comes from a musical family, as his two brothers are Peter 'Where do you go to my lovely?' Starstedt and Richard Starstedt, who changed *his* name to Eden Kane. Still awake?

One band we supported, Brian Poole and the Tremeloes, had a big influence on our image. We were all appearing at the Ritz ballroom in Llanelli and when The Tremeloes came on stage they looked like real pop stars, because they were playing fantastic-looking powder-blue Fender guitars! We immediately wanted guitars just like them and, as it happened, Clive John worked in Gamlin's music shop in Cardiff and he managed to get us identical powder-blue Fenders. We had our first publicity photo taken with these guitars and with Jeff Jones sat behind his new Ludwig drum kit, which he still owns to this day. Well you know what they say about a decent drum kit. It can't be beat.

With our new guitars and drums and our brilliant blend of harmonies, there was no stopping us. We started a regular gig at the Tower Ballroom in Swansea, managed by Ron Bateman. The Searchers had played there to an audience of 800 people and got paid £50 for their night's work. So we went on that first night to the same sort of crowd and raised the roof off the place. The crowd loved us. In a matter of weeks we were playing to crowds of a 1,000 people. We were treated like real pop stars and even got mobbed by fans.

With the enthusiastic audience reaction and screaming girls chasing us we felt we were experiencing what the Beatles were going through every time they appeared in public. It was around this time that I had my first serious relationship with a girl. Her name was Jennifer Hill and she was the grand-daughter of publican Bert Moss. Most couples used to go to the pictures on their first date. Not us. We went to see Acker Bilk and his Paramount Jazz Band. I didn't even like jazz, but he was a big star and had achieved a unique musical success when his record 'Stranger on the Shore' simultaneously reached the top of the UK and American charts in 1961. When someone like that turned up near your town, you had to go and see him.

I had been out with other girls before, but I hadn't 'gone all the way' with any of them. Jennifer Hill was the one I lost my virginity to. I'm not going to make any jokes or light-hearted remarks about this, because as a result of our sexual fumbling, Jennifer became pregnant. What happened next has to be examined against the background of the early 1960s. No-one talked about sex, except in the pages of *The News of the World* every Sunday; 'good girls' weren't supposed to let their boyfriends have their way with them and, crucially, you couldn't freely buy condoms at every retail outlet from Spar to Sainsbury's like you can today. Having a baby at such a young age would have completely ruined Jennifer's life. She knew I had no intention of marrying her, even if I'd been old enough. So she had an abortion, which must have been a terrifying ordeal for her. You won't be surprised to hear that Jennifer's mother absolutely hated me and I can understand why.

While Lynn Mittell continued working in the betting shop, during 1962 Jerry Braden and the Bystanders became massively popular. We played anywhere and everywhere, from the Tivoli, Mumbles to Clydach Town Hall. Despite what had happened to Jennifer, when the sexually voracious groupies made clear what they wanted, I didn't disappoint any of them.

After one of our gigs we were approached by a man named Wyn David who was a hairdresser and a record producer. It didn't seem odd that he had two jobs, because so did we. What's weirder than being a pop singer and a betting office clerk at the same time?

Wyn loved the band and told us he could take us to the next level. So as we hadn't received any better offers, we put ourselves in his hands. He either had plenty of useful contacts or plenty of brass nerve, because the next thing we knew, he'd arranged for us to have an audition at the famous Marquee Club in London's Wardour Street. It's an audition I will never forget because while we sat in the club, waiting to do our stuff, who should walk in but Paul Jones and Tom McGuinness from Manfred Mann and two of the world's greatest guitar players, Jeff Beck and Eric Clapton. Knowing that they were all in the place where we were auditioning didn't do much for our nerves.

But, we must have come across okay because out of that audition we were offered management deals by some of the biggest agents in what was then known as 'Tin Pan Alley', better known these days as Denmark Street, off Charing Cross Road. We were approached by Tito Burns, Dick Katz, Kennedy Street Enterprises and the one we eventually signed with, George Cooper.

One of the bookings he got us was at the Lyric Theatre, Carmarthen, a venue I've been back to many, many times since. It's a lovely theatre, but unfortunately our gig there was in January 1963. For those of you not old enough to remember, this was the month of the Big Freeze. The snow came down so fast and so thick, the entire country came to a standstill for the best part of two weeks. Cars and buses couldn't move. Trains couldn't run. Schools and workplaces had to close because there was no way to get coal and anthracite from the mines to the depots and out to the public. Not many houses had central heating then, so how we all didn't freeze to death is down to luck and plenty of hot tea.

We played a great gig at the Lyric that night and as we started packing away our gear we noticed that it had been snowing hard while we'd been inside all night. The road out of Carmarthen looked a bit dodgy but that wasn't the problem for us. Our van broke down! We didn't have enough money to book into a hotel or bed and breakfast so we had no alternative but to stay in the Lyric theatre... for five days. But we weren't lonely because other bands that had been playing in the area and had found themselves stranded joined us also.

I remember the Wild Ones were there. And then there was the Swansea band, The Iveys, who later became Badfinger. I can't remember if the place was heated or what but we managed for food to keep us going for five days, but I do remember promising myself that in future, whenever I was booked to play a gig more than an hour from home, I'd make sure I took at least one change of underpants, a clean shirt and a toothbrush. We must have all been stinking after spending five days and nights wearing the same clothes. Then eventually the big thaw started around the same time as our little van and we were able to drive home.

We were always having trouble with vans. We played the Masonic Hall in Milford Haven and after the gig we hadn't driven a few yards when the van broke down. At that time of night there were no garages open, so we would have had to sleep in the van if the caretaker of the Masonic Hall hadn't offered to let us sleep on the Hall's wooden benches. It wasn't very comfortable but it was better than being outside in the van overnight. Well, that's what we thought. But we didn't get much sleep because the place had a sprung dance floor, which of course people had been dancing on all evening.

As we were starting to nod off, the springs, which had been squashed down by all the dancers' bodies 'bopping' to our music, started to bounce back into shape. Every time one of the under-floor springs snapped back into position, it did so with a loud 'Bang!' Just what you want to hear at two in the morning. Then again at five past two. Ten past two. And for the rest of the night. There were 352 springs under that dance floor. I know, because I counted them. We'd have had a more restful night in the van.

Wyn David was always looking for ways to push our career ever upwards and he thought we were now at a standard where we should be making records. Using either his influential contacts or his bare-faced cheek again, he booked us a recording session in a studio in Portland Place, right opposite Broadcasting House. We were in one studio recording a song called 'That's the End' and, down the corridor, The Yardbirds were in another studio recording the Graham Gouldman song 'For your Love' with bongos, a stand-up bass and then session-player Brian Auger on harpsichord.

It was so different to the driving, guitar-led rhythm-and-blues material they were known for, but it gave them a Number Three hit in the summer of 1965 and a Number Six in the United States. The only downside for the band was, between the time they recorded 'For your Love' and it's release date, Eric Clapton left the band. But I don't think he's done too badly since.

Wyn David called his record label Pylot after his company Pylot Promotions and I have to say, he was very good at promoting us. He even managed to persuade the local ITV channel TWW to film us at the Qualiton Record Factory as copies of our single were being pressed. It was a very exciting time for us and although 'That's the End' didn't get into the Top Twenty... or even the Top Fifty, we had enough local fans to ensure it sold over 1,000 copies in Wales. I have 999 copies at the back of my garage if anyone's interested?

We had our feet firmly on the pop music ladder to success, so I thought, and we were now touring with big name groups, like The Spencer Davis Group, featuring their brilliant vocalist Stevie Winwood and Johnny Kidd &The Pirates. And the always-busy Sounds Incorporated, a band who, along with The Mike Cotton Sound, seemed to be part of every pop-package tour in the 60s – and there were a lot of them going round the country. Often featuring anything up to eight acts on the bill (usually all signed to one record label or management company), those pop-package tours were certainly great value for money, even though some of the acts on the bill were strange bedfellows. I remember one tour that played Sophia Gardens, Cardiff, which featured, amongst others, Engelbert Humperdinck and Jimi Hendrix! I wonder if they duetted on 'Purple Haze' at any point in the show?

So with all that touring and a record under our belt, I was more than happy to be part of the Bystanders – we'd dropped the 'Jerry Braden &' title by then – and I thought my position with the band was pretty solid. I mean how could they manage without me?

If you look up the word 'overconfident' in the dictionary, you'll find that the definition is 'Owen Money aka Lynn Mittell *just before* he was sacked by the Bystanders...'

CHAPTER FIVE

ONE SUNDAY, TOTALLY OUT of the blue, Clive John called me to a meeting with the rest of the band at Jeff Jones' house to tell me that I was sacked. I was stunned. I'd been part of the line-up that had taken us to the foothills of the charts and if we kept going, we could have gone all the way. But Jeff told me that it was nothing personal. The uniqueness of the Bystanders was their close harmonies and Jeff didn't think I was strong enough vocally. They replaced me with a new singer named Vic Oakley and sometime later when I heard him sing, any resentment I'd felt at being elbowed out of the band disappeared. His voice was much better than mine.

When the Bystanders eventually broke up and merged into one of Wales's greatest rock bands, Man, Micky Jones became an internationally respected guitarist. When they broke up, he continued to play in various bands almost up to the time of his far-too early death on the 10th of March 2010.

When it was officially announced – well we had quite a fan base by now who wanted to know what was going on – that I was leaving the Bystanders, the official reason given was 'illness'. I wasn't ill but I was in a bit of a daze for a while after, although amazingly I didn't feel any real bitterness at being sacked from one of Wales's top bands after we'd come through thick and thin. I wasn't resentful because I was young and resilient and I just knew that there was *some* area of show business I might be able to shine in one day. It might sound a bit big-headed to you, but I was just a starry-eyed teenager from Merthyr with a positive attitude, eager to get on, who hadn't yet had his dreams crushed by some of the harsh realities of show business.

Doors did start opening for me. Especially at Cardiff

Airport where they'd just had those automatic ones installed. I told you there were loads of bands around and, having gained a reputation with the Bystanders, it didn't take me long to join one of them. They were called the Cheatin' Hearts, named after a Hank Williams song. Well it could have been worse. Another one of his songs was 'My Son Calls Another Man Daddy' which is too long and miserable for a band's name. By the way the song is long and miserable too. The Cheatin' Hearts line-up included Alan Crompton on guitar, Jeff 'Jethro' Lewis on bass, Gerald Williams on organ and a sax player named Vic Winnan.

With that line-up of instruments, our sound was a lot funkier and soulful than The Bystanders and we were one of the few bands around who could cover the Tamla Motown and Stax hits of the time and give it that authentic American sound. There was one Welsh band that came close to our style, the Amen Corner, and we often played the same venues as them. They went on to have many chart hits and when they broke-up, their lead singer, Andy Fairweather-Low, went to great solo success and he's still recording and touring today with his band the Low Riders. He's also a pal of Eric Clapton and has recorded and toured with Eric many times, including the now classic 'Unplugged' session. And to think he started out playing the same dance halls as me. Mind you, he can't tell a joke to save his life!

The Cheatin' Hearts were still a semi-pro band and we all had day jobs, although I'd left the betting shop by now and was working in a much more glamorous environment – Aberdare Car Sales. Well at least I wasn't cooped-up behind the counter all day. I was able to wander around the showroom and talk to potential customers and once I had the hang of things, my outgoing personality helped me to become a pretty good salesman.

But when 1966 came around, my life went through a big transformation. I was 19 and anxious to make something of myself in the music business. The years were going by and I didn't want to end up as a fifty-year-old car salesman sitting at home watching famous singers and bands on my TV set, thinking, "If only I'd had the courage to turn professional. Who knows what might have happened?"

The decision on the future of the Cheatin' Hearts was decided in February 1966 after we'd auditioned for the Kennedy Street Agency in London, who were looking for acts to tour Germany. When we arrived at the audition venue there were fifty acts waiting to impress the bookers and agents, but they had the usual line-up of lead, rhythm and bass guitars plus drums. We were the only band there who had brass and a keyboard. Our audition number was the Mamas and Papas hit 'California Dreamin'' and it impressed a German promoter who booked us into his club in a place called Trier in southern Germany, not far from the border with Luxembourg.

Thrilled at getting the chance to travel abroad and get paid for it, we merrily signed all the contracts, but as none of us spoke German, we had no idea what we had agreed to. What was clear as day, however, was that we couldn't work in Germany for several months and expect our bosses to keep our day jobs open for us. So we all made the decision to go full-time. It was a huge gamble and we were very much aware of the possibility that one day we might have to come back to our old bosses with our tails between our legs, asking for our jobs back. But the chance to turn professional was just too tempting.

The German residency wasn't due to start until May, so in the interim we decided that, as we were now professional musicians, if we wanted to be taken seriously and really be part of the scene, we had to move to London. Moving from your home town and moving to London is something thousands of people have done and, these days, with motorways and fast trains (two hours from Cardiff to London Paddington) it's not a big deal.

But in February 1966, leaving Merthyr to travel 'all the way to London' was looked upon by many people in the Valleys as either a great adventure or (certainly by the older generation) an act of sheer madness which would end in drink, drugs and debauchery, depending on your outlook. Or whether you were familiar with the story of Dylan Thomas's life. To be honest with you, I was never that keen on drink and drugs, but I was really looking forward to the chance of some debauchery. No, seriously, I'd read all about it in the Sunday papers, but could never find any within a ten-mile radius of Merthyr, so if it meant trekking all the way to London town for some, I was more than prepared to make that sacrifice.

The distance between the Welsh Valleys and London was of course a geographical as well as a cultural one. At the beginning of 1966 the Severn Bridge – that's the original bridge – was still under construction and wouldn't be officially opened by the Queen until the 9th of September of that year, so to travel by road to London took a lot longer than it does now. In fact the road that took you around Gloucester added an extra sixty miles to the journey.

There was a car ferry named *The Severn Princess* that would take you across the river Severn from Beachley near Chepstow to Aust on the Somerset side, but by the time you'd queued for your turn to get on board, you could have been half-way to Gloucester. However, the biggest problem about the ferry was the huge tidal range of the river, which made it notoriously unreliable. It obviously couldn't function at low-tide and it was also unable to function in very high tides. So there were only a few hours every day when it was safe for it to chug across that incredibly fast-running river, carrying cars and people. Give a thought to that old Beachley/Aust ferry next time you 'whiz' across either of the two Severn crossings in under five minutes.

So off we went to London to start our new lives in the glamorous world of show business. Or as we knew it –

Hammersmith, where we all shared a flat in Welja Road. We were never famous enough for the Heritage people to place a 'The Cheatin' Hearts Live Here' blue plaque on the wall of our block of flats. But the man who invented toothpaste once lived around the corner and there is a plaque outside his house. By a strange coincidence, the man who invented mouth-wash was born just across the street – but he hasn't got any plaque!

The band played in clubs in and around London, including The 400 Club and we got to know many musicians, who would often come back to our flat to crash out for the night – and the following day. We also started going out with London girls, who had a different attitude to life than the girls I'd known in Merthyr. Not so much sophisticated as worldly, especially the four girls we all went out with, who were nurses. 'My' nurse was Barbara and her family owned a farm in Lincolnshire, where we spent one enjoyable weekend. I was certainly seeing the world! It was an exciting time for us and although we weren't getting rich, we were earning enough to pay the rent and have a good time. 1966 was 'the' year when London was officially declared to be 'Swinging'. Although you wouldn't have thought so from Roger Miller's song 'England Swings', the first line of which was...

England swings like a pendulum do
Bobbies on bicycles, two by two...!

Which makes the place sound like London policemen have to ride around in groups of four for protection. Living and working there, it really did feel that London was the centre of the universe for a short while. It was the time of Carnaby Street and Biba and Lord John and discotheques like the Bag o'Nails and Tramp. The Beatles were still together and making records and I can still remember how we felt when we heard the first radio play of their latest single. I suppose that's how today's kids feel when they hear a new song by their current pop idols. I would have named one there, but by the time this book comes out they might have disappeared back into obscurity!

Before we knew it, May had rolled around and we set off for Germany and the town of Trier. I do love a Trier, don't you? The journey through Europe was pretty uneventful, apart from when we travelled through Luxembourg. For the entire time we were in that country, every time we spoke, our voices would start fading away... then start getting louder... then fade away again.

When we got to the German border, the guards (Hans Zupp and Heinrich Manouvre) who checked our passports, noticed that Jeff was under 18. With their legendary, laid-back, Germanic charm, they told us bluntly that Jeff wouldn't be allowed into the country. Which meant that our journey had been a waste of time. And petrol. After all it was five bob a gallon! I tried to reason with the guards and pointed out they probably had a few people under 18 living in their country, so one more wouldn't make much difference, but with their legendary, laid back, Germanic charm one of the guards called me an "English Dumbkoff". I wasn't having any of that. I looked him straight in the eye and said, "Get it right, Fritz. I'm a Welsh dumbkoff, if you don't mind!"

The guards told us to go back to the British Consulate in Luxembourg and ask their advice, so with the first gig of our German contract only a day or so away, we turned the van around. When we explained our predicament to one of the staff at the British Consulate, his official response was, "I'm very sorry, but the Germans are very strict about this sort of thing. Jeff is under 18 so he simply cannot be allowed into Germany." While their unofficial advice was, "Hide him in the back of your van and try and smuggle him in!" guess which advice we took?

The club in Trier was called the Café Wilelmshol, which

was up a mountain in a German castle, which they call a 'schloss'. No, I've no idea why. Stop interrupting.

Now while it was a wonderful break for the Cheatin' Hearts to get a residency in Germany so soon after turning professional, as is often the case in show business, the day-to-day reality of the work was less exciting than we'd anticipated. The up-side was that the audiences loved us. With our organ and tenor sax in the line-up, we gave an authentic American feel to R&B and soul standards like Wilson Pickett's 'The Midnight Hour'. There was an American army base nearby and the club would be full of GIs shouting out requests like, "Play 'Land of 1,000 Dances'" and we would always oblige. We had plenty of opportunity to. Which is where we come to the downside...

In British dance halls and clubs we were used to playing two forty-five minute sets, although there were times when we played for longer. The Germans are known for their strong work ethic and in Trier we were expected to play not two, not four, not six... but *nine* forty-five minute sets every day. That's... let me see... forty-five... times nine... equals... four hundred and five minutes... which in pounds, shillings and pence... is... six and three-quarter hours every day.

Apparently this gruelling schedule was mentioned in the contract we all signed, but none of us had noticed it. That was our first big lesson in professional show business. Always check the contract, because as sure as eggs are eggs, it'll be weighted in the promoter's favour. I'll be the first to admit it's more fun than working in a factory or a betting office (both of which I've done) or working down a mine (which I haven't done, but never say never, eh?). But singing and playing and making sure everyone was enjoying themselves for almost seven hours a day was very tiring.

I felt a bit like an always-smiling Butlins Redcoat, singing and playing at the same time. But the audiences loved us, so their enthusiasm kept us going. Unfortunately, the owner of the club wasn't so enthusiastic about our music. Despite the fact that we worked hard to keep the customers entertained and gave them what they wanted, he made it plain that he would have preferred the usual three guitarists and a drummer line-up to our funky, organ-based sound.

One special member of our appreciative audience was a beautiful blonde German girl I started going out with. And I stayed in with her sometimes too. Her name was Angelica and she was a real looker, a blonde German beauty who reminded me of Kim Novak. You remember her? The one who joined Jack Good for that double-act which became a trio when Tommy Steele joined them?

We managed to keep on the musical conveyor belt, playing nine sessions a day, for two weeks and then... the pressure suddenly took its toll. Because of our long working hours, as well as a rubbish diet of *wiener schnitzel* and strong lager, our keyboard player, Gerald – the man whose playing largely defined our sound – collapsed from exhaustion. He was in such a bad way that he was never going to get better in Trier, so we had to send him back home. We kept the van, so he had to make his own way back to our London flat and it's a long way from Germany to London. But we figured the walk would do him good. In fact he didn't do too badly out of the episode, because when he got back to our flat in Hammersmith, he started going out with my old girlfriend, Barbara the nurse. She must have given him plenty of TLC – not to mention TCP – because they eventually moved into their own place together.

The owner of the Café Wilelmshol used Gerald's departure as an excuse to wave a not-so-fond farewell to the rest of us and we moved on to another club residency, this time in a town in northern Germany, where the clientèle were rough seamen who were more interested in fighting and drinking than listening to a bunch of British lads singing Tamla Motown covers.

Thankfully my mind has wiped both the name of the town and the club we played in from my memory. It was a real dive. I mean the absolute pits. To get into the place you had to walk down two steps, physically and socially. The doorman used to stop customers on the way in and ask if they had any weapons. If they didn't, he provided them. I'm telling you this club was so rough, six weeks before we arrived, the manager, a tall, bald bloke built like a brick ship-yard, got into an argument with a drunken customer, who went berserk and buried an axe in his head. And when we turned up, he still hadn't bothered to remove it!

I'm exaggerating, only just a little, but it really was the scummiest venue I have ever played in. And I have appeared in some real khazis in my time. So one evening around seven o'clock, without telling anyone at the club about our intentions, we piled our instruments and equipment in the van and did a runner.

We drove right through the night and decided to head back to Merthyr. Our old van had served us well and we'd probably travelled hundreds if not thousands of miles in it. I know this is going to sound like I made it up, but I swear on my mother-in-law's life that this is absolutely true. We got back to Merthyr and parked the van outside my father's pub. A moment after we'd taken all the gear out of the back of the van, the engine suddenly burst into flames. It happened so quickly there was nothing we could do about it. Apart from stand there and feel the heat of the twisted metal and twisted plastic. It was like the van was saying to us, "That's it, boys. I've taken you to Germany and back. You've had more than your money's worth out of me. I'm checking out! Tarra!"

So, there I was. Back in my home town after six months of trying to make a career for myself in the music business. It hadn't worked out, but it wasn't due to our lack of talent or musicianship. Various circumstances – the crummy venues we were booked into; Gerald collapsing – had prevented me and the rest of the band from reaching the big time and Merthyr had brought me back like a giant magnet. Mam and Dad were pleased to see me of course and I moved back into my old room, while I planned what to do next.

Not long after I got back to Merthyr I started seeing a girl named Wendy Probert. Her father Ivor owned a fruit and vegetable retail business, which he ran with his wife Kitty and their two sons, Kerry and Phillip, and Wendy's two sisters, Judy and Nicola. They were obviously quite well-to-do and Wendy owned a Vauxhall Cresta which she used to pick me up in. I had started playing again in local bands and still had dreams of being a successful professional musician. But I learned not to reveal too many of them to Wendy because it soon became obvious that she strongly disapproved of anyone (me in particular) wanting to become a professional entertainer.

She thought that I should settle down and get a 'proper job' in Merthyr. Because I liked her, despite her strong, negative feelings towards something that I was passionate about and wanted to dedicate my life to, and because we weren't at that time in a serious relationship, her attitude towards my ambitions didn't really worry me.

As the summer turned to autumn, I still hadn't really decided what to do next. I played some local gigs and I went out with Wendy. But only occasionally. We wouldn't become a serious 'item' for a while yet.

Then at half-past nine on the morning of Friday the 21st of October 1966, I was sat in the Queen's Café in Merthyr when I heard that something terrible had happened in the village of Aberfan, just down the valley from Merthyr Tydfil.

CHAPTER SIX

THE ABERFAN DISASTER, as it became known, began at 9.15 a.m. on the 21st of October when torrential rain, which had lasted for days, caused a huge tip of coal waste to slide down the mountainside towards Aberfan. There was also a thick mist which covered the whole of the village. Even at that stage, it might have been possible for the gang in charge of the tip to phone the emergency services and warn them of the impending disaster. Had they been able to do so, it might possibly have saved lives. We'll never know, because the gang weren't able to make that call. Overnight, someone had stolen the telephone cable.

It was ten long minutes later, at 9.25 a.m. that the first emergency call was received by Merthyr Tydfil police, "I have been asked to inform you that there has been a landslide at Pantglas. The tip has come down on the school."

During those ten minutes, a mountain of black slurry had slid down the mountainside, first destroying a farm cottage, killing the occupants. Relentless and unstoppable, it rapidly moved on towards Pantglas Junior School where, on the last day before the half-term break, the children had just returned to their classrooms after singing 'All things bright and beautiful' at morning assembly in the school hall. Anyone even remotely familiar with this appalling tragedy will be aware of what happened next.

Over the decades there have been many books written and documentaries made about the Aberfan disaster, all of which explain the sequence of events much more eloquently than I could ever attempt. But not all the writers and film-makers were there just after it happened and witnessed the horrors that I did.

You might wonder why I am devoting so many pages to the Aberfan Disaster in this book and I've got three reasons. The first one is, I'm a Welshman; it happened right on my doorstep and I was one of the thousands of volunteers who made their way to the school to do whatever they could to help. How could I not mention it in my book? Secondly, I think people should be reminded of it from time to time, out of respect to the children and adults who died and the families who have had to live with their grief.

So many other tragedies have happened since 1966 and, rightly or wrongly, as we get older, some of them fade in our memories. Which is not to say we should obsess about the terrible things that go on in the world on a daily basis – we'd all be manic depressives. The fact they fade from the memory is a good thing in some respect. But just think for a minute about the tragedies that we've lived through just in the last 30 years.

Apart from the IRA bombings of the 70s and 80s and at least three major train crashes, there was the Zeebrugge ferry disaster in 1987; the Marchioness disaster on the river Thames in 1989; the terrorist attacks on the Twin Towers in September 2001; the tsunami which took so many lives in Thailand on Boxing Day 2004; and, closer to home, the flash floods which threatened to destroy the Cornish town of Boscastle in August 2004. Despite the fact that these incidents happened in your lifetime and you saw them on your TV screens in colour, you might possibly have forgotten about some of them. Which is exactly the point I'm making. Because the Aberfan disaster happened over forty years ago and a generation has grown up in Wales knowing very little, if anything, about it. And I think they should.

And the third reason I'm writing about it is because it was one of the most traumatic experiences that I and all the people in the Merthyr area who volunteered to help have ever lived through. No-one who arrived at the disaster scene and took in the scale of the tragedy could ever forget their emotions at the time. I saw things that will stay with me forever, as I will explain in a moment. Just before I do, I'd like you to read the words of one of the teachers who was in one of the classrooms at Pantglas Junior School when the black slurry smashed into the building:

> I was standing in front of the class. Workmen had been repairing the roof and I thought I heard some slates dropping off. I looked up through the fog and I saw this enormous spinning boulder and there was a black line alongside it. I looked at the class and, as I did, the boulder crashed into the room at the speed of a jet plane and I was hurled from the centre of the room to the corner by the door.

> The room was shaking and was filling up with muck and rubble. Then it stopped and there was an eerie silence. I was trapped up to my waist in desks and goodness knows what else. The children were all trapped amongst their desks but mercifully no-one was injured badly.

The children in that particular classroom were incredibly lucky. It didn't take the full force of the impact. Here is what two pupils from another class witnessed:

> I remember being thrown across the classroom when the stuff hit us and then I blacked out. I woke up to the sound of the rescuers breaking a window and then I saw my friend. I will never forget the sight. There was blood coming out of his nose and I knew he was dead. If I close my eyes his face is as plain as that moment.

> I was trapped for an hour and a half until the fire brigade found us. My desk was jammed into my stomach and my leg was under the radiator. The little girl next to me was dead and her head was resting on my shoulder.

A schoolboy of 14, not a pupil at Pantglas, gave some idea of the size and scale of the black slurry mountain that enveloped the school in his description of what he saw:

> I was walking up the hill and saw a big wave of muck coming over the railway embankment. It was coming straight at me... and as I ran I saw trams, trees, bricks and boulders in it.

As soon as I heard what had happened in Aberfan I drove to Merthyr Vale in my mini-van, even though I was banned from driving at the time. From Merthyr Vale I walked the rest of the way to Aberfan to join the hundreds of other people who had turned up to dig people out of the slurry. Many were miners who had either just come off the nightshift or had just started work, as this miner explained:

> I went to work, changed, went down the pit and I hadn't been down there ten minutes when they sent for everybody to come up because the tip had slid. Well, we came up. I couldn't fathom it out. I'd never seen anything like it. The front of the school was there, but there was no back. We went there and we dug and dug all day.

When I got there at 9.50, the slurry and muck were still sliding down and at 10.30, according to the Chief Constable of Merthyr, "... a large quantity of water was still pouring into the disaster area, and I was informed it was coming from the mountain springs and two large water mains which had fractured when the disused canal and railway embankment had broken".

Most of us didn't have shovels or tools. We just used our bare hands to pull away the rubble and muck hoping we could bring people out alive. It was an impossible task but we all felt we had to try. If the same thing, God forbid, happened in your town tomorrow, wouldn't you do the same thing? You couldn't just stand back and hope someone else would do it. I saw terrible, unforgettable sights around me. Dozens of panic-stricken parents, clawing at the rubble, desperately looking for their children, calling out their names, hoping they might still be alive.

Despite the fact that the slurry had buried so much of the school, some pupils and teachers were found and rescued. But, again in the words of the Chief Constable of Merthyr, "No-one was brought out alive after 11 o'clock".

In less than two hours, the black slurry mountain had claimed 144 lives – 116 of them children. My old teacher, Mr Beynon, was found dead, with his arms around two children as he tried to protect them from the slurry.

But hundreds and hundreds of us, now joined by the rescue services, kept looking. I don't know what kept us all going. Adrenaline and that faint hope that we might just find one more child alive, I suppose.

We also had a constant supply of hot drinks, provided by the WVRS, the Salvation Army and the Red Cross. I stayed there all through the Friday, all Friday night, and the Saturday morning. I eventually went home at Saturday lunchtime, feeling totally drained. I was supposed to be playing at a gig that night and even though I wasn't really in any condition to entertain people, I got washed and changed, put my gear in my mini-van (that I wasn't supposed to drive because of my ban) and headed for the gig.

More than likely, as so many were that weekend, the gig would have been cancelled out of respect. But I didn't get to the venue to find out. Everything I had seen and heard and touched and smelt the day before was still with me. I turned the van around and drove back to Aberfan to see if there was anything else I could do; there were an estimated two and a half thousand volunteers there. People started getting anxious because it had started raining heavily at half-past two and there was a real fear that the tip would start sliding again and engulf the rescuers.

In the following months, throughout Wales, many fundraising events were held to help create the Aberfan Disaster fund, which was launched by the Mayor of Merthyr, to help the survivors and the bereaved. Over 90,000 contributions came in from all over the world and when the fund was closed the following year, the total amount was £1,750,000.

Apart from donating money to help the bereaved, the fund went towards house repairs, a community hall, and holidays for the villagers and a permanent memorial. The only sour note was that both the National Coal Board and the Treasury refused to accept full financial responsibility for the disaster. There were still coal-waste tips on the mountain above the village which needed to be taken away to avoid further tragedies and to get this done, unbelievably, the fund had to hand over £150,000 to the NCB; donors, villagers and the local MP were furious and the people of Aberfan have never forgotten this, even though the money was eventually paid back in 1997 – thirty one years after the event. And now, forty-four years later, I still can't drive past Aberfan without remembering that Friday in October 1966.

After eighteen months of 'courting', Wendy Probert became my first wife. Our love was a match made in Heaven. And her wedding ring was made in Hong Kong. She was working in B&Q when I met her. It was a chip-board romance. No, seriously, she was coming out of the NatWest bank the first time I saw her and I knew straight away that girl had something very special to offer me. A cheque book.

I did mention that Wendy didn't approve of my musical ambitions, so because I was now a married man of 19 and not making any real headway with my pop career, when she made it plain she wanted me to pack-in the music business permanently and get a proper job, I did as she asked.

Wendy persuaded her dad, Ivor Probert, to take me on in his fruit and vegetable business, and Ivor turned out to be the biggest influence on my life up until that point – far greater than my parents. I'd already had some sales experience working at Aberdare Car Sales and I was pretty good at dealing with the public, but Ivor *really* taught me how to sell and how to get my point across to customers. Ivor was a superb teacher and an even better salesman. That man could buy a load of cheap bananas that were well on the turn and sell them without any problem. He had what they refer to these days as a 'strong work ethic'. Which meant that he worked bloody hard and was good at his job. He was never that keen on taking holidays and would work long hours every day.

My first job with the Proberts was driving Kerry Probert's van, delivering fruit and vegetables while Wendy was the manageress of the shop. The family all lived in a house called Beechwood which was so big they actually employed a housekeeper to look after it. A family with a housekeeper – in Merthyr! I have very happy memories of that house. It was always filled with music. There was always a 45 or an album playing on the record player. In the summer of that year, 1967, the Beatles brought out their weird and wonderful *Sergeant Pepper's Lonely Hearts Club Band* album, with its fascinating cover, gate-fold sleeve and cardboard cut-out badges and moustaches! We'd never seen (or heard) anything like it.

Wendy and I listened to it over and over. I would have loved to have formed a new band and covered some of the Sergeant Pepper songs, which were very complicated, musically. But, knowing how much she loathed the idea of me ever playing again, I felt I had to keep my dreams to myself.

I know that happens in many marriages. Couples have to make sacrifices, big and small, in order to maintain the relationship. And by agreeing to forget about my musical past and drop any plans for any musical future I might have had, I'd sacrificed a huge part of myself for the love of a woman.

I forgot to mention that when Wendy and I got married we flew by BOAC to our honeymoon destination. Rhyl! No... get this, we flew to *Nassau*. Yes the one in the Bahamas! Blue skies, white sands, emerald seas, cocktails on the veranda as a cool evening breeze rustles the leaves on the palm trees. Sounds romantic, right? Well, as romantic as a honeymoon can be when you're staying in the same hotel as your in-laws, your brother-in-law and my father-in-law's brother-in-law. It was less a honeymoon, more like a two-week wedding reception where the guests won't leave. But I'm not really complaining, because Ivor and Kitty paid for it all.

We moved into our own house, Number Two, The Walk, which was bought for us by Ivor and my Dad, for the sum of £2,000! Today, because of its association with Owen Money, it's worth an entirely different sum. £500! It was fantastic to have our own house at such a young age. In the sixties, most newly-weds had to move in with their in-laws for a couple of years while they saved for a deposit on a house. It made economic sense, but young married couples living with, usually, the brides' parents, had little or no privacy and this led to small niggles and minor rows on a daily basis which could often snowball into major confrontations, mostly with the mother-in-law. Hence, the mother-in-law joke, which was already sixty or seventy years old in the 1960s, was still alive and well.

If any young comedians are reading this and think mother-in-law jokes should be consigned to the dustbin of humour-history, you should remember that they served a useful purpose, a blessed release if you like, during an era when the mother-in-law was a much-feared figure who held on to any influence she might still have over her daughter with an iron grip! As it happens, I had a wonderful relationship with my in-laws Ivor and Kitty, who always treated me well. But then Wendy and I didn't live with them, we had a place of our own!

Mind you, the house needed a tremendous amount of work done to it. For example, when we opened an old cupboard in the kitchen, we found a load of rot. The previous owner had left behind the entire works of Jeffrey Archer in there. I remember Wendy and I spending an entire Bank Holiday weekend, scraping-off what seemed like inch-thick anaglypta wallpaper room by room. It absolutely creased us. Our arms and backs were aching for weeks after. I still say to this day we should have used wallpaper scrapers instead of our fingers.

We were like any young married couple bringing two wage packets into the house. We spent a bit and saved a bit, which enabled us to take the odd holiday. New wallpaper and fresh paint in every room meant our house was looking how we wanted it, with Wendy always adding that feminine touch. But while she was a great home-maker, she made it quite plain from the off that there was no chance of the patter of tiny feet being heard around the house. She didn't want children. Well, not with me, anyway!

When my father-in-law Ivor thought I was ready, he promoted me from a delivery driver to a salesman. That really tested my salesmanship at times, never more so than the Christmas Eve when Ivor realised he had far too many unsold Christmas trees left over. And once the shops shut on Christmas Eve afternoon, no matter how good a salesman you are, no-one is going to buy a Christmas tree off you.

So he sent me off in the van to travel around the streets of Merthyr, knocking on doors, asking people "Merry Christmas! Would you like to buy a Christmas tree?" You can imagine some of the answers I got.

But most of the time, I enjoyed working for Ivor and I threw myself into the work and got up every morning at four to drive down to the fruit and vegetable wholesale market in Bessemer Road, Cardiff, to collect fresh produce for the shop.

As for Wendy and me, things weren't so great. I was still friendly with some of the lads I'd played with in bands. Merthyr is hardly a sprawling metropa… metropi… metrope… big city, so I'd often bump into some of my old band mates, which Wendy wasn't happy about, even though I'd done what she'd asked and packed in playing.

Although I was no longer in a band, I was still interested in show business and I remember going to see, and thoroughly enjoying, a concert party called The Bee Jays which was organised by a man called Warren Watkins. My fascination with show business continued to irritate Wendy and the cracks started to appear in our relationship. It was around that time that a few things happened that would affect both our marriage and my (far off) future career as a comedian. That's what I am, by the way. A comedian. I thought I ought to remind you...

The first incident happened when we went to the Pant Social Club together for a night out and there was a comedian on the bill I'd never seen before. His name was Colin Price. In later years, Colin would go on to become a big name in Wales and a good friend of mine. He continues to work the clubs today and is on better form now than ever. Go and see him if ever you get the chance.

But, back to the first time I saw him perform, at the Pant Social Club. Before that night, I had no ambitions to be a comedian. It never entered my head. I was an ex-pop singer who had never told a joke on stage. Well, Colin's performance just blew me away. He looked like he was in charge and sounded assured and in complete control of the audience.

I may well have watched other club comics before I saw Colin, but he was the one who had the most impact on me. He came out with joke after joke after joke, and every one of them was a belter. The crowd loved him and I laughed out loud at each and every gag, which isn't easy when you're trying to write them all down on the back of a beer mat. I had no idea at the time but that night would turn out to be a massive turning point in my life.

When Colin Price finished his act and walked off to loud applause and huge cheers, I wiped the tears of laughter from my eyes, turned to Wendy and said, "That's what I want to do with my life. I'm going to be a comedian." It was only then that I realised it might have been better to have kept my thoughts to myself. They say one picture is worth a thousand words. That night, Wendy's cool, silent, grim-faced reaction to my enthusiasm was the equivalent to a bound edition of *War and Peace*. That was the first incident that put the wobblers under our marriage.

The second one happened one Boxing Night, when we went to a local club where my old band the Cheatin' Hearts were playing and they invited me up on stage, for old times' sake, to sing a number with them – the Bee Gees song, 'Massachusetts'. As soon as I stepped up on the stage, Wendy turned on her heels and stormed out of the club. Her behaviour was bizarre. I'm not sure if there was some sort of jealousy hidden inside her or if she was immature or what, but it was obvious she couldn't cope with the thought of me being on stage, entertaining people. I'd willingly had to lock my ambitions away to please her, but it was obvious that the 'spectre' of show business was hanging over us the whole time we were married and any interest that I showed in it, or it showed in me, would provoke the same reaction in Wendy. Anger.

So that Boxing night, it was all over between us.

She went back to live with Ivor and Kitty and I moved back in with my parents... again! Mam and Dad had moved by then, to number 26, Crab Apple Close, which sounds like it should be a little country cottage with roses all around the door and a little stream flowing past the front gate. But the house was actually up on the Gurnos Estate – sometimes referred to by its posher residents as '*The Gurnois*' – and the only stream that ever flowed past our front door was on a Saturday night when the locals staggered back from the pub and couldn't wait until they got home to relieve themselves.

With Wendy gone, I no longer had any restrictions on my ambitions. But with regard to me becoming a stand-up comedian, I didn't have the first idea where to begin. So I started going along to clubs to watch comedians working. I'm not talking about purpose-built comedy clubs that most towns and cities have these days, like Jongleurs or the Glee Club. They didn't exist 40 years ago.

The clubs I went to were working-men's clubs or social clubs. There was nothing glamorous about them. But working-class people flocked to them for a drink and some entertainment. Forget glitz and glamour. They were more spit and sawdust. And that was just in the meat pies.

I went to see comics like Hayden 'Wit' Munday and Lennie Leyton, not just for a night out, but to try and learn 'how they did it'. Because I didn't have a clue how someone could go on stage for half an hour or longer, and remember all those jokes! I also went back to see Colin Price, time and time again, and although he always made me laugh, I started noticing the technical side of being a comedian. The timing... the pauses... the phrasing... the emphasis on certain words... and the importance of that killer punch-line which should leave the audience helpless with laughter. I also noticed that he didn't change his act all that much. He would always throw in a couple of new ones, but the bulk of it was almost set in stone. No, not stone – more like solid gold, because his material got the audiences howling with laughter every time.

I liked his laid-back style of delivering his gags, never chasing the laughs. When I first saw him working in 1967, his material was squeaky clean. Not one mucky joke amongst it. However I've noticed when I've seen him work recently that he's started putting in jokes that aren't just 'near the knuckle', they're more 'well past the elbow'.

Mind you, compared to what some of the young comedians get away with on late-night TV and their live shows, Colin's gags could have been written by Enid Blyton. But it's a sign of the times that his club audiences now willingly accept and probably demand much stronger material than would have been allowed in the 60s and 70s. I'm not making any judgement on this, it's just an observation. And I'm sure Colin, who's been a friend of mine for years and appeared as a guest on my ITV One Wales series, *A Night Out with Money*, knows exactly where to draw the line.

I'll admit that I do include *some* saucy material and double entendres in my act, because innuendo has always been a staple of comedy. Though to be honest, before I got into comedy I thought 'innuendo' was an Italian suppository. Mild sex jokes (usually about the lack of getting 'it'), is a universal subject for comedy that all adults can relate to. Look at the continuing popularity of the Carry On films, all packed with innuendo and double entendres, long after they stopped making them.

I don't care if you're a street sweeper or a solicitor, a plumber or professor, a smile will always appear on your face when you hear certain 'rude' words like 'knickers', 'drawers' and 'bum'! Especially whenever the Prime Minister throws them in at Question Time in the House of Commons.

Telling gags on stage is second-nature to me now, but at the time Wendy and I went our separate ways, I was barely into my 20s and the art of being funny in front of an appreciative audience seemed to be way out of my grasp. Comedians I went to watch seemed to be members of a very exclusive club I could only aspire to join one day. In fact I sent the membership form in well over 20 years ago and I'm still waiting for a reply.

But a career in stand-up comedy was only a vague dream then and I had a living to earn. It might sound odd to you that even though Wendy and I had gone our separate ways, I was still working for my father-in-law. But it says something about the sort of generous, warm-hearted people Ivor and Kitty Probert were, that even though I was no longer living with their daughter, they didn't treat me any differently. Most in-laws might have sided with their daughter and treated me like some sort of outcast –working for them would be out of the question. But they continued to employ me quite happily and I was really grateful to them.

However, with my estranged wife still working in the shop every day, this couldn't continue indefinitely, so I started looking around for another job. Remember this was the mid 1960s, when jobs were plentiful. If you were unhappy or unfulfilled in your job, it was relatively easy to walk away from it and walk into another, better paid one. So, a little reluctantly, because I had enjoyed working for him, I told Ivor Probert I thought it might be for the best if I moved on. Ivor understood of course, and wished me luck.

I took a couple of days to decide what direction I should take, career wise. Working for Ivor, driving around in the van, delivering fruit and vegetables, I'd basically been my own boss. I had the freedom of the road and enjoyed being out and about in the fresh air. So naturally I chose to take a job in a factory. I started work at Merthyr's once-famous Hoover factory, which closed down in 2009.

I started work there the same day as Brian Wallage and the first thing they gave me to do was so horrible; it made me pine for the glamorous world of fruit and vegetables I had so foolishly left behind. I was a stripper. No, not that sort of stripper. That would have revealed my shortcomings. No, they put me in the Paint Stripping Department, which involved dipping machinery parts covered in paint, into acid. Ve-ry care-ful-ly...

The acid would eat away at the paint and take the parts back to the bare metal. It was hazardous work so they kitted me out with state-of-the-art protective clothing. A pinafore and rubber gloves. It doesn't sound very practical I know, but it came in handy whenever they wanted an extra pair of hands to help with the washing-up in the works canteen.

I'd only been working there five weeks when I made my second television appearance. Remember my first one? When the Bystanders and I were filmed at the opening of Qualiton Records? Tch! How soon you forget. That first telly appearance was a carefully arranged affair, which I was prepared for. Not so with my second appearance. I didn't even have make-up on. Which was unusual because it was a Tuesday.

A dispute began between the management and the employees and it got to the point where negotiations reached a stalemate. A stalemate isn't, in case you wondered, a friend of yours who doesn't shower very often and hasn't heard of deodorant. Negotiations broke down and all the workers were called to a union meeting in the canteen: (a) because the union convenor wanted to talk to the workforce and (b) because chicken curry and chips were on the lunch menu.

So everyone, to a man, downed tools. Even people who didn't normally use tools in the course of their job, picked up tools and put them down again, just to prove a point. I made my way to the meeting in the canteen along with hundreds of my workmates, having first removed my pinafore and rubber gloves. I knew that if everyone had the chicken curry and chips, there'd be a giant pile of greasy washing-up to do afterwards and I just wasn't in the mood to help out. I was just about to go the canteen when I suddenly had to answer a call of nature and nipped into the loo for a quick wee, fully intending to attend the meeting as soon as I'd finished and washed my hands!

Well what followed was either the shortest union meeting of all time or the longest quick wee of all time, because when I came out of the loo, the union convenor had called a mass walk-out. We were on strike. Which worried me because I'd never been on strike before. I hadn't had any training in being on strike. If only I'd had the foresight I could have done a course in being-on-strike at night school. But I'd been too busy going out enjoying myself.

So, there I was. Standing outside the gents toilet, with my little rule book in my hand, as two thousand angry workers stormed out through the canteen doors and started making their way to the exit, which meant they had to pass right by me. Rather than get trodden into the ground by four thousand pairs of heavy work boots, I decided to get out of the building before the mad rush.

Someone must have tipped off the press and the local BBC and ITV news programmes that something was going to happen at Hoover because when I ran out of the building I was confronted by a small army of journalists, photographers and TV cameramen. Which is how I ended up on the evening news and on the front pages of several local papers as 'The man who led 2,500 Hoover workers out on strike'. And I hadn't even been present when the strike was called.

The Hoover workers' strike went on for 12 weeks, during which time, none of us got any pay. Even if an employee wanted to work he couldn't, because the factory gates were guarded by gangs of union pickets, twenty four hours a day. I was single and living with my parents and I soon started suffering financially. How the married men with children managed all those weeks I can't imagine. So when good old Ivor Probert came to my rescue and offered me a temporary job, delivering fruit and vegetables again, I jumped at the chance to earn some money.

Unfortunately, Merthyr Tydfil was much smaller then than it is now (the same could be said about me I suppose) so when I was driving around in the van, my route would often take me past the Hoover factory. This meant there was a real chance that I might be spotted by the pickets at the gate and be labelled a black-leg for working while they were still on strike. I don't think for one moment I was the only Hoover employee earning some money on the side but, nevertheless, every time I passed the factory, I used to duck down in my seat in case anyone recognised me.

I might have left the music scene behind, but I was still crazy about my other passion – football. On Saturdays I always made the effort to watch Merthyr Town play and I was playing for Hoover's own football team on Sunday mornings. The manager was Billy Williams and some of my team mates included Gareth Thomas, Kenny Clements, Ken Harris and Brian Hamer.

When the Hoover strike was settled, I left my delivery job with Ivor Probert and returned to the factory. Not long after, Ivor and Kitty took Wendy on a world cruise. It seems to me that most people of a certain age go on cruises today, as there are always last-minute bargains on offer, even the ones that sail around the Caribbean. In the 1960s, to go on a world cruise was quite something and must have cost a packet. But no-one deserved a luxury holiday more than hard-working Ivor.

It's true you know. Fate does work in mysterious ways. I'd had nothing to do with bands since I married Wendy, for reasons you'll remember. But while Wendy was cruising around the world, I heard that Warren Watkins was looking for a bass player for his band Good News. As I had no-one to stop me from doing so, I told Warren he needn't look any further. I was back in the music business.

CHAPTER SEVEN

BEING BACK ON STAGE with a band gave me a chance to try out my budding skills as a comedian. I wasn't ready to do a full comedy act all by myself, but Warren did a lot of impressions which involved him running off stage to make a quick costume and wig change. So while he was changing characters, I started slipping in a few jokes.

I'm not saying I was as funny or as quick-witted as Bob Monkhouse, but I didn't do too badly. I'd watched loads of comedians by then and remembered plenty of their gags. I'd also learned how to sell myself, how to be outspoken and confident when I was selling fruit and vegetables. I started putting more and more gags into the act and I'd get big laughs which, of course, gave me more confidence.

We started a residency at the Merthyr Labour Club every Tuesday night. The regular customers used to refer to it as the 'Quaker's Dance' – once around the dance floor and outside for your oats! And I must admit that I helped myself to the occasional bowlful. When two years had gone by and it was obvious to all concerned that there was no chance that Wendy and I would get back together again, it was decided that our marital home, number 2, The Walk, should be sold.

But as I've said already, never say 'never', because after those two years had passed, something totally unexpected happened. I had to call around to Ivor Probert's fruit and vegetable shop one day for some potatoes and Ivor said, "I've got to pop out for half an hour. Do me a favour and look after the shop for me?" which I was happy to do even though I was the only person serving in the shop. It didn't worry me because it was a place I knew very well. And Ivor trusted me with the money I might take over the counter.

The phone rang, I picked it up and on the other end of the line... was Wendy. Naturally she was surprised to hear my voice and I was equally surprised when I noticed she sounded much friendlier than she had during our last few conversations. In fact by the end of the conversation she'd agreed to come out for a drink with me and hadn't made any conditions like, "I'll come out with you if you promise to lock your guitar away for a fortnight". So, as arranged, I met Wendy for a drink and we got on so well, it led to us enjoying what might be termed 'an intimate reconciliation', during which it was impossible for me not to notice that she'd learned a lot since we'd been together.

In two years, Wendy had matured beyond belief. And the weird thing was I wasn't jealous. Why would I be? I was reaping the benefit of her experience. In fact, we had such a wild, enjoyable time that first night, we decided to have another go. No. Not another go at *that*. At our marriage! We told both our parents, who of course were delighted. They were like most parents; all they wanted for their children was for them to be happy.

With number 2, The Walk, sold, we had to move in with her parents, which was fine because Beechwood House had loads of room. It seemed that Wendy and I were back on course. Wrong!

We really did try and make a go of things second time around, but we were now two entirely different people. Yes the sex was fantastic, especially when she was there, but outside the bedroom, the old niggles and petty jealousies began to rise to the surface again. After we'd been back together for around three months I did what you might call 'a moonlight flit'. It was a Tuesday night and the phone rang at Ivor and Kitty's house. It was Warren Watkins, asking me if I'd like to re-join Good News.

It took me less than ten minutes to pack my clothes, grab my guitar and leave through the back door. I was gone for good. Wendy and I eventually got divorced in 1973 and she met a man named Paul Reardon and had a baby. Wendy and I didn't speak for many years after that, but when Ivor Probert died, I wrote a letter to Wendy, expressing how I felt about this great, big-hearted man and how his guidance had helped me in so many areas of my life. I also mentioned that I appreciated that he'd always treated me with respect, even when my marriage to his daughter fell apart. Ivor Probert was one of the very few people I've met in my life who I could honestly describe as an exceptional human being.

I attended his funeral – nothing would have kept me away – and the church was packed to the rafters with family, friends and his many customers. After the service, as the whole family came down the aisle, they saw me and came over to hug me. That meant more to me than they'll ever know. When I had my stroke in 2006, Wendy phoned me to make sure I was okay and in the course of our conversation she mentioned that she still had that letter I'd sent her after her father passed away. Time does indeed heal wounds...

I was still playing with Good News, although only on a semi-professional basis. But I was much more than a musician. I was also the van driver and the man who bought the cigarettes. When I think of the smoking that went on in that van, I'm amazed the windows weren't tinted a nicotine colour.

It was around this time, but before my divorce from Wendy, that I met a young lady named Kath O'Brien who was to become the second Mrs Lynn Mittell. It was her brother-in-law Kelvin who fixed-up our first date, but because she came from a big Catholic family, and because, technically, I was still married, her father didn't approve of me. However, when he realised I was serious about his daughter and she wasn't just another girlfriend, he eventually got to like me (well who wouldn't?) and became a big help and a good friend to me. Kath O'Brien became Kath Mittell on January 12th 1974. It was a white wedding. It snowed all day.

We bought our first house in Lower Thomas Street, Merthyr, and although I was playing in Warren Watkins' band, I was working for Sterling's Fruit and Vegetable Wholesalers. I moved on from there to Pentrebaen Car Sales, where my boss was Gary Thomas. My experience at Aberdare Car Sales was invaluable as were my years in the fruit and vegetable trade. I was a damned good car salesman and shifted a lot of cars. I was earning five to six hundred pounds a week! If I'd stayed there longer the sky would have been the limit for me. I might have ended up running my own used-car showroom and could now be retired in some style in Marbella or Portugal. But if I had, I doubt very much if anyone would have asked me to write my autobiography. And Owen Money would never have existed.

I was approached by Jeff 'Jethro' Lewis who asked me to join his comedy show-band. The other members were Tony Prosser and Gary Shag. Both Tony and Jethro were great vocalists, and wowed the audience when they sang 'My eyes adored you'. We went through a few name changes and eventually settled on Tomfoolery.

Our mix of comedy and music was unique at the time. There were the Barron Knights of course, but they rarely appeared in Merthyr! And northern cabaret show-bands like the Grumbleweeds and the Black Abbots (in which the great Russ Abbot served his comedy apprenticeship) wouldn't appear on the national scene for a few more years. As our reputation grew, we became the top comedy show-band in Wales.

Tomfoolery played a showcase in Neath in front of agents and bookers and although we didn't know whether or not they'd find us funny, we decided to impress them with our powder-blue suits, so at least they'd remember us as being very stylish! The bookers and agents loved us and from that one show we got twelve months' work! Four or five gigs a week... for an entire year! We were thrilled to bits.

But even so, we couldn't make that leap to being professional musicians and so we hung on to our day jobs. With the money I was making from selling cars and the money I was making from the gigs – even deducting petrol money, agents' commission and after splitting it between us – financially I was doing very well for a young man in his 20s.

This made it difficult, certainly in my case, to think about giving up our day job, as the drop in our earnings would have been too great. We even turned down an offer of work in the clubs of the north-east of England.

But every band, whether they're semi-pro or professional, no matter how much success they might achieve, are made up of individuals with their own personalities and ambitions and egos. And it's easy to rub each other up the wrong way. Remember the 1970 film *Let It Be* which showed the disintegration of the Beatles during a long period in the recording studio? The cameras caught the little sideways looks and off-hand gestures that showed that their relationships and musical collaborations were coming to an end.

If it can happen to the Beatles, with the prospect of the band's potential future earnings – which would have been in the tens of millions by now – hanging in the balance, it can certainly happen to a comedy show-band from Merthyr who hadn't even turned pro. Even the best of friends fall out occasionally and there were nights when one of us felt we had been 'ganged-up' on by the others, or were seething with anger because insults had been exchanged in the van on the way to the gig. Or we might be unhappy about a band mate's performance. These things can create resentment, jealousy even and lead to a full-blown argument.

A bit like the time we were playing a gig at the Abergavenny Social Club. I'm not sure how it started. Either Tony said something that Jethro didn't like or Jethro said something that got right up Tony's nose and they started hitting seven bells out of each other. I stepped in to stop the fight and tried to calm them down, but in the meantime someone had called the police. When they turned up they were ready to throw Tony and Jethro into the back of a police van and treat them to a night in the cells, but once again Lynn 'The Mediator' Mittell stepped in to explain that it was just a minor flare-up. And it wouldn't happen again. The police accepted my explanation and, when they left, we got up on stage and played as if nothing had happened.

Two hours later Tony and Jethro resumed their fight, the police were called again and even my brilliant negotiation skills couldn't prevent my two band mates from feeling the strong arm of the law. That night signalled the beginning of the end for the first line-up of Tomfoolery, but I was still friendly with Jethro and we decided that as the band had worked hard to create a great reputation, it made sense to try and keep it going.

We recruited a couple of new members, namely drummer Jeff Jones and guitarist Robert Hyde, who happened to be my wife's cousin. I've always said there's nothing wrong with nepotism, provided you keep it in the family. Which reminds me about the article I recently saw in the paper about the corrupt Prime Minister of a small Caribbean island, who filled all the important positions in his cabinet with his three sisters, eight brothers, eleven cousins and seventeen nephews. Last week he retired so he could spend *less* time with his family...

It wasn't long before the line-up of Tomfoolery changed again. Jethro and Robert left and in came Jeff Davies, Mike Jones, Scott Goulbourne and David (Tom) Blower. As I was the only one left from the original Tomfoolery, we obviously couldn't call ourselves by the same name. So, with stunning originality, we re-named ourselves... pause for half-a-minute for dramatic effect like they do on The X Fracture and Strictly Dumb Prancing... ready for this... *New* Tomfoolery!

We are now into 1975 and New Tomfoolery auditioned at the Meadow Vale Country Club for one of UK's biggest agents – Robert Holmes of the Forrester George Agency. Luckily our blend of comedy and pop songs impressed him and he offered to sign us up.

There were all sorts of lucrative jobs mentioned to us, *if* we turned professional, but that was out of the question for me because, on the 30th of March, I became a father for the first time, when Kath gave birth to our son Matthew. By now I was working as the steward of the Merthyr Labour Club and the money I was earning was consistently good, so with Kath at home looking after Matthew, there was no way I could jack-in my day job and live on the money I earned from the band. We needed both incomes and I was happy to continue living this sort of split existence as I'd done for some years. I was doing my duty as a husband and father by paying all the household bills and when I played with the band and threw in lots of jokes and bits of comedy 'business' that got the audience roaring with laughter, it was the outlet I needed for my creative side.

Things got very 'rock and roll' for us when we took on Brian Wallage and Big Norman as our two roadies, to lug all our equipment around. We needed them too, because apart from our guitars and drums and amps and microphone stands, we were acquiring more and more comedy props and costumes and wigs for our act. We went from strength to strength and, a year or so later, history repeated itself (although geography *never* does, have you noticed that?) when, in 1978, we were offered work in Europe and we had to decide whether to leave our day jobs and go full-time.

It was a lot harder for me to take the gamble this time around. If we took up the offer of work in Europe we'd be earning pretty good money and with our profile raised there was every chance our earnings would increase. We might even become famous. Who was to say that that wasn't possible? On the other hand, for me to walk away from a steady job that was paying me anything up to six hundred pounds a week, I'd have to be completely crazy.

Say hello to Lynn Mittell. He's completely crazy.

We took our comedy and music act to Italy and Germany and they loved us. When we got back, David Blower left the band and Jethro rejoined. It was getting to the point where we thought about having the van fitted with revolving doors!

The London agent Alan Blackburn was looking for acts to play hotel-lounges in Las Vegas, so as our act was pretty slick and audiences liked us in other places that began with 'L' like Llanelli and Llanfrechfa, we thought it was worth going along to audition. We thought it went okay, but you can never tell. When we were told they'd get in touch in due course to let us know, we weren't sure whether they liked us. But we didn't have time to ponder about it because we had a gig lined up in London's West End. Well, the west end of Wembley, anyway. The venue was the String of Pearls club, where the annoyingly talented Brian Conley was the compere. He could sing, dance, tell jokes, perform magic tricks, do fire eating and do impressions. He was a little comedy firecracker. The audience loved him. And the bugger was only sixteen!!

I heard a great story about Brian which he won't mind me telling you, because like all great performers, he often tells this against himself. When he took over the role of Bill Snibson from Robert Lindsay in *Me and My Girl* at the Adelphi Theatre in the Strand, the show was already a smash hit. It had been running for a couple of years and tickets were selling like hot cakes. They were baked in the oven and were covered in currants.

As is usual when a West End show is such a success, other performers wanted to see it and almost every evening, after the curtain came down, Brian would welcome stars of stage and screen to his dressing room. Then one afternoon the cast were told that the legendary Hollywood star **Bob Hope**, who would have been in his mid-80s at that time, would be in that night and that he wanted to meet the cast. However, as Bob had a late supper engagement, he would be coming around backstage during the interval. So far, so good.

The first half of the show went well and when the safety curtain came down during the interval, the entire cast assembled on stage to meet the great man. Bob, accompanied by his wife Dolores, smiled and nodded to the principals but didn't engage in any conversation. When he came to Brian Conley, he looked him up and down and, with that famous Hope half-smile, half-sneer playing on his lips, he said, "Kid… you've got it all!" A magical moment for any young British entertainer.

But then Brian made the mistake of saying, "Mr Hope, on behalf of the entire company, I'd like to thank you for taking the time to come and see us and I hope you enjoy the rest of the show". Hope looked at Brian for a moment, then turned to Dolores and, with one hand cupped over his ear so he could hear her reply said, "Waddidee say?" It was immediately apparent to Brian and the company that the reason Bob Hope hadn't engaged any of them in a two-way conversation was because he was stone deaf!

We were then contacted by Alan Blackburn, who wanted us to attend a second audition for the Las Vegas residency. We were still in with a chance! We went to the audition and did a chunk of our act, songs, gags, impressions, quick costume changes. Alan Blackburn got the works. It must have been the moment when he saw us taking the mickey out of 'The Human Zeppelin', Demis Roussos, singing 'Ever and Ever', that he thought, "These boys are far too sophisticated for the Las Vegas audiences". Because we didn't get the job.

I haven't got many regrets in life, but I would have liked the chance to play Vegas, even a hotel lounge, which are nothing like the hotel lounges we have over here. They're more like miniature night clubs where, for no entrance fee, other than the price of a couple of drinks, you can sit back and be entertained by 'unknown' American singers and bands, who are ten times more talented than some of our biggest manufactured stars. However, as the old saying goes, as one door closes another one slams shut on your hand, two of your fingers are broken and you have to be taken to casualty for minor surgery.

We missed out on Las Vegas. But we were offered something *almost* as tasty. A long summer season in Blackpool. Isn't it strange that if the British call Blackpool "The Vegas of the North" but not one American... not *one*... has ever referred to Las Vegas as "The Blackpool of Nevada"? Why *is* that?

Our summer season in Blackpool was at the South Pier and when I say 'summer' season, it actually started in the spring of 1979, went through the summer and ended when the autumn leaves were falling. If we'd carried on into the winter, we could have changed our name from New Tomfoolery to the New Four Seasons. The South Pier line-up was: top of the bill, the follically-challenged but fantastically funny Mick Miller, New Tomfoolery, JJ Stewart, comedy musicians Nuts & Bolts and three girl singers who called themselves The Angels, but who most definitely weren't.

Blackpool's changed a lot over the last 30 years and the remaining theatres like The Grand and the North Pier no longer put on spring to autumn summer seasons with a half-dozen acts and a big star topping the bill, mostly because there aren't that many star performers left, 'names' if you like, who could fill one of the theatres from April to October. The venues now tend to break the week up and have say, Freddie Starr on for two nights, Joe Pasquale on for two nights, Billy Pearce on for two nights and a 'That'll be the day' type tribute show on for one night. This gives holidaymakers a much greater choice of course, if they can afford to see more than one show.

And that's the thing. People tend to go to Blackpool for a couple of days now, rather than for two weeks. Add to that the fact it's got itself a reputation as a stag and hen night weekend destination, which would obviously deter families and older people from being around the town on a Friday and Saturday night, and you can see that it bears little resemblance now to the summer that I was there with New Tomfoolery.

In 1979 the town was buzzing with stars 'off the telly'. A very young Les Dennis; The Black Abbots comedy showband, featuring Russ Abbot on drums; Ian and Janet Krankie; ventriloquist Neville King and his bad-tempered and dishevelled Grand-dad doll; and Little and Large packing them in (twice nightly!) at the Opera House.

When you're in a long summer season, about four or five weeks in, with autumn a long way off, it's easy to start getting bored. Being in the theatre and performing in the evenings is always great fun, but unless you're the type who likes to cover yourself with sun cream and lay on the beach (which is not always an option in Blackpool), the days can seem endless.

This is why, going back to the early days of variety, that comedians became associated with the game of golf. It was something to get them out of bed in the mornings; allowed them to get a few hours of fresh air and gentle exercise; and, as they usually played with fellow comedians it gave them the chance to swap jokes, which is why I started playing golf and often paired-up with Les Dennis and members of the Black Abbots.

Our prop man, Brian Wallage, was with us, as was our roadie Big Norman, and because there were too many of us to spend five months living together in one house, we rented two houses for the season. This enabled us to invite family and friends to visit from time to time. Kath came up to join me, with Matthew who was now four.

I still harboured thoughts about being a solo stand-up comedian one day, and whenever I got the opportunity I'd go and see comedians working in the dozens of hotels, clubs and bars around town. It was a comedy paradise! I'd go to the Viking Bar, the Leyton Institute, the Norbreck Castle... so much choice it was mind-boggling. I'd watch the comedians and listen and learn... and nicked all their best jokes and used them myself with New Tomfoolery.

We then managed to pass an audition for a new BBC television talent series called *Rising Stars* produced by Barney Colehan who had created and produced the long-running show *The Good Old Days*. We appeared on the show, singing 'Lovely to see you again', along with ventriloquist Adam Daye, the Julie Byrne Country Band (which included a then-unknown Cheryl Baker as a backing singer) and singer Jacqui Scott.

There was also a larger-than-life magician on the show who called himself the Great Soprendo, who spoke in a nervous, high-pitched Spanish accent and his catch phrase, which he used every time he performed a trick, was "Piff! Paff! Poof!" which I don't think he'd get away with today. This 'Spanish' gentleman was Geoffrey Durham who was from East Molesey in Surrey and some years later married Victoria Wood, although they're now no longer together.

If any professional or budding performers reading this get, understandably, despondent whenever they get turned down for a job or are paid-off or fail audition after audition, they should know that Geoffrey Durham almost gave up the business after he failed to win his edition of *Rising Stars*, thinking he didn't have the talent to make a career in show business.

But something made him carry on, as the Great Soprendo, and he took any job that came along, even bookings in northern working men's clubs, which he confessed later that he hated. These years of performing to tough audiences enabled him to hone his skills and his stage-craft. In 1990 he dropped his stage name and as Geoffrey Durham he is now one of the most respected magicians in the business. He's hosted several television entertainment series (in the days when television was entertaining), he's a member of the Inner Magic Circle and he's in great demand for corporate functions and as a magic adviser. So it just goes to show where sheer perseverance and self-belief can take you.

I know what you're thinking. If the Great Soprendo didn't win the show, who did? Well it wasn't New Tomfoolery. Even though in the week between our show and the next one we spent a fortune on postcards and stamps (this was the era of postal votes for talent shows) voting for ourselves. Despite our efforts, all we achieved was fourth place... and writer's cramp. The winner was Jacqui Scott, who later became Mrs Keith Harris, although their marriage didn't last very long. Perhaps it was because he didn't give her Cuddles?

New Tomfoolery began rehearsals for a pantomime at Swansea's Grand Theatre. This was my very first pantomime and, several years later, when I'd become Owen Money, I became closely associated with the Grand, appearing in several spectacular pantomimes in that beautiful old theatre, which I'll be dealing with in a separate chapter. That first pantomime, with New Tomfoolery, was *Robinson Crusoe* which starred Welsh comedian Kenny Smiles and Barry Howard, who later became famous for playing Maplins Holiday Camp's prissy dance instructor Barry Stuart-Hargreaves in the classic BBC sitcom *Hi-De-Hi!* He also appeared in the Christmas 2009 *Dr Who* special, which of course was made in Cardiff by BBC Wales. See how everything seems to come back to Wales eventually?

As for Swansea-born Kenny Smiles, he started performing on cruise ships and was a big hit with the Americans, who dubbed him "The Mad Welshman"! He's so popular with American audiences that he moved to the USA and settled down in the spectacular Ozark Mountains in the state of Arkansas. On one of his trips back to Wales he appeared on my Thursday afternoon show on BBC Radio Wales. He was terrific fun and I enjoyed his jokes so much, I only stole half of them! He now spends weeks at a time cruising the warm waters of the Caribbean. But don't feel too sorry for him.

Talking of ships and cruises brings me back to that first pantomime. The band and I played the captain and the crew of the ship that Robinson Crusoe and his girlfriend Alice Fitzwarren sail away on in search of treasure. It was during this long pantomime run that the unrest that had already started in the band got so much worse. Despite the bad atmosphere between us, I tried to black-out all the negative feelings and back-biting and saw the show as a massive learning experience – another step towards that seemingly unobtainable goal of being a stand-up comedian.

Working in a theatre production was very different from playing with the band at a gig. We were performing twice, sometimes three times a day. We were working with actors who expected us to behave in a disciplined way. But unfortunately Scott Goulbourne was totally undisciplined, which was the cause of much bad feeling between us. The discipline that was expected of us extended to seemingly basic things like making sure we were at the theatre well before the curtain went up and memorising the entire script, so that we didn't just learn our lines, but also knew the other actors' words too.

But despite the back-stage bickering, when we were on stage we did what we were being paid to do. We made the audiences laugh. And there was one occasion they roared with laughter so loud, the tiles on the roof of the theatre were in real danger of falling off.

You've heard it said that certain performers 'stopped the show', meaning the audience were so overwhelmed, their enthusiastic applause and shouts and whistles held up the show for a while? Well one night at the Grand Theatre, New Tomfoolery stopped the show... literally.

In pantomime, no matter what the story is and who the stars are it must have a beginning, middle and a happy ending. Provided the children in the audience are having a good time and know when to cheer the hero and boo the baddie, pretty much anything can happen during the two hours or so the show runs. Which is why New Tomfoolery was booked to appear at the Grand and why, half-way through the show, we found ourselves 'shipwrecked' on a desert island, and discovered our guitars, drums and amps had been safely washed ashore. And even though the story took place in the 19th century and there wouldn't be any electricity on a desert island, blissfully ignoring these facts, we just plugged-in, started playing and went into our daft impressions.

I have a theory that this suspension of logic, always completely accepted by the audience, is why Harold Pinter never wrote a pantomime.

The highlight of our little comedy spot in the show, was our take-off of the popular Greek-Egyptian singer Demis Roussos, singing 'Forever and Ever' (the vocals for which got progressively 'higher and higher') which had always gone down well in the clubs and in our Blackpool season. This was something we'd become quite well-known for in club-land, especially in Wales and when we put it in the panto act, the reaction was just as appreciative.

Demis Roussos was a hugely overweight singer who always wore a floor-length kaftan and seemed to float around the stage as he sang. Add to that comic image a straggly beard and a high singing voice and you have someone who was ripe for parody. It took two people to carry this impersonation off. As a couple of band members played the melody, Scott, who had just run into the wings to change, came back on dressed as Demis, singing 'Forever and Ever', which was funny enough. But what the audience was unaware of was that Scott was sitting on the shoulders of our roadie Big Norman who was crouched down under the kaftan. We may have used a large cape rather than an authentic kaftan, but you get the picture.

Then as Scott glided around the stage with Big Norman still hiding under the cape, I would come on doing an impression of Norman Wisdom, in which I pretended that one of the microphone stands was a pump. Every time I pressed down on the stand, Big Norman (reacting to a cue from Scott) would stand up a little bit more and 'do the lift', so as Scott's voice got higher and higher, he would also get taller and taller. The more I 'pumped' on the microphone stand, the higher he got, until he was eleven or twelve feet high. It looked hilarious and was one of the best visual gags I have ever seen. We had plenty of headroom in the theatre, but there were occasions in the clubs where the stage area was much smaller and lower, when Scott's head would disappear through the ceiling tiles. Which of course would create even more audience laughter.

This routine always received a great reaction in the panto, but the laughs were never bigger than on a night when our props man Brian Wallage had to replace Big Norman, who was ill. We couldn't leave out the best part of our act, so we told Brian that he'd have to 'do the lift' until Big Norman was back. Brian was a lovely man (like Big Norman and Scott, he is sadly no longer with us) but he was a props man, not a performer. That said, he was keen to help out and assured us he could do it.

He knew the routine back to front, but I still talked him through it step-by-step to minimise the possibility of anything going wrong. I took him out onto the stage and pointed to a white line marked on the boards. I said, "You'll be under the cape, with Scott on your shoulders and you'll look down at that white line and follow it to the middle of the stage and then stop. You then face to the left and Scott will then be facing the audience. He'll give you the cue when to start lifting him up and when the song is finished you turn left again and follow the white line off stage."

A piece of cake. Well it is if you can manage to follow a white line that you can barely see because you're in the dark, while at the same time you're carrying someone on your shoulders who is singing to 900 people. And provided you don't mix up your left with your right. Hats off to him, he did it perfectly for a couple of performances, without any calamities. Until the Saturday night.

Brian and Scott came on, with Brian hiding beneath the cape and Scott on his shoulders, belting out 'Forever and Ever' and I was 'pumping' the microphone stand to make Demis Roussos grow taller, as I impersonated Norman Wisdom with loads of "Mr Grimsdales!" thrown in. As usual the routine was getting big laughs... and then it was time for Brian to carry Scott off stage. For reasons we never did find out, instead of turning left, as he'd done in previous performances, he walked straight on – into the orchestra pit. On top of the drummer, with Scott on his shoulders still singing away as if nothing out of the ordinary had happened.

The audience was in hysterics. Martin Yates, the show's musical director, who went on to work in many West End shows, stared open-mouthed at the chaos in front of him. Two of the backstage crew, 'Splinter' and Rob, pulled Scott up onto the stage, and in doing so revealed to the audience that both Brian Wallage and the drummer were lying in the orchestra pit unconscious. The children in the audience thought it was fantastic and their shrieks of laughter echoed around the auditorium. The show came to a halt as the St John's Ambulance volunteers, who attended each performance, put Brian and the drummer on stretchers and carried them out to cheers from the audience.

That was one of the lighter moments in what was for me a miserable period in my life. Although I enjoyed being part of a pantomime company, I wasn't at all happy with certain members of the band like Scott, for example who, for all his talent, continued with his undisciplined behaviour. So

I suggested to Geoff and Mike that, to make sure that New Tomfoolery could have a future, we needed to have a shake-up in personnel. They agreed something needed to be done, but unfortunately for me, *I* was the one they and the rest of the band thought should leave.

So, I went from being the 'revolutionary' to becoming the 'deposed leader' which was ironic as I'd been invited to join New Tomfoolery because I'd been part of the original Tomfoolery – and now they were getting rid of me! I don't regret the years I spent with the band because I learned so much about comedy during that time. But we weren't some semi-pro band who could change members without any repercussions. They didn't have the power to fire me and I couldn't just walk away.

We were still under contract with the Forrester George Agency and when the office learned about this dissent in the band, John Chilvers and Bob Holmes, who worked for the agency, came down to see us to find out what was going on. I told them straight that because of the bad feelings the rest of the band felt towards me, I wanted to leave. However, it would have been unprofessional to have just left them in the lurch and I suggested to John and Bob the name of the person who would be my ideal replacement. Brian Conley.

I knew he'd always liked the band and the type of comedy we delivered and having seen him perform I knew he would fit in perfectly. I phoned Brian, explained the situation and he agreed to come down to discuss things. I booked him in the Glengariff Hotel and he and the boys in the band had a meeting in which he was offered a place in New Tomfoolery. He said 'yes' and the rest is history.

And as far as the band was concerned, so was I.

CHAPTER EIGHT

I NEEDED WORK AND money, so I phoned my mates Tony Prosser and Richie Powell who were both good singers, and we discussed forming a new band featuring three-part harmonies with a bit of comedy thrown in. Richie was a painter and decorator, while Tony played with the resident band in the Baverstock Hotel on the Heads of the Valleys Road. The building is still there but it's a retirement home now. Anyway, one day when we were rehearsing for this new trio, Tony, who knew I was interested in comedy said, "We have cabaret acts at Baverstock's on Saturdays. You ought to come up one night."

So because I always do what I'm told (!), Kath and I went there the following Saturday and the place was full with people, all ready to have a good laugh. Now while I wouldn't say that I was dressed scruffily – they wouldn't have let me in if I was – I wasn't properly dressed for what was about to happen.

Tony came up to me with a panicky look in his eyes and said, "Lynn! You've got to help us out. The comedian hasn't turned up!" I didn't know what he meant at first. Then he said, "This lot have come here to see a comic tonight and won't be very happy if they find out there isn't one. You know loads of jokes. Fancy going on? I'll give you thirty-five quid!"

Now you have to remember this was the early 1980s and even when I was with the band I was only getting twenty quid a night. Thirty-five pounds would get Kath and me out of a financial hole, because at that point I had no income and no prospects. Thirty-five quid then would be worth a hundred and fifty quid today, maybe more. I said, "Okay, I'll do it."

This was the moment when all those hours I'd spent watching comedians working was about to pay off. I'd observed and absorbed Mick Miller's act in Blackpool for five months. I knew it back to front. But I decided not to do it back to front otherwise the audience would hear the end of the joke before the beginning, which is never a good thing for a comic. I'd watched Frank Carson and knew all his jokes. I'd watched Colin Price loads of times. I'd seen dozens of pub comics and club comics and comedy impressionists. I had hundreds of jokes embedded in my brain. But now it was *me* who was being asked to get up on stage, all by myself without the safety-net of other band members around me, to make people laugh. Would I remember the jokes once I had the microphone in my hand? Could I put them into some sort of act? Would the audience like me? I only had twenty minutes to get my head together and risked making a fool of myself in front of a large roomful of people expecting a professional comedian.

First impressions count. I was at Baverstock's for a relaxed night out. I wasn't dressed like an entertainer – although compared to how some of today's comedians appear, I was the essence of sartorial elegance – so I had to cobble together something decent to wear on stage. I knew that the resident drummer Robert Edwards was the same size as me and I borrowed a spare pair of trousers from him. So far, so tasteful. Then, someone produced a shiny red shirt with frills all down the front. I said, "I thought you wanted a comedian, not a Liberace tribute act!" But that was the best they could do at such short notice. God knows what I must have looked like. Actually I do know. I looked like a terrified bloke in a red shiny shirt with frills all down the front who was ready to run out through the exit any minute. I said, "How long do you want me to do?" and they said, "Do as long as you can!" I said, "Right then. I'll do a song to get me on and some rock and roll at the end, maybe three or four songs. So I should

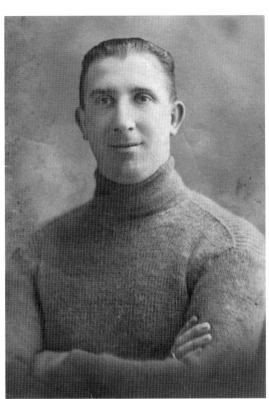

My dad when he played
football for Birmingham City
in 1933.

My grandmother and Aunty
Gwen in the 1940s.

My dad (in the middle) with my godfather Alfie Lewis and Roy 'Cherry' Walters on the right, at Weston-super-Mare in 1958.

With my friend Alan Crompton (left) in 1966.

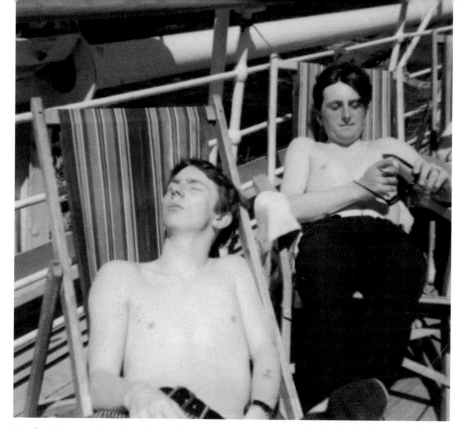

Sunbathing with ex-brother-in-law Kerry Probert on a cruise ship in 1967.

With my mother and son Matthew in 1977.

With my daughter Katie in Majorca in 1982.

Family fun in Majorca with Tom David, Kelvin Davies and Chris Beecher.

Kath and I celebrating our 25th wedding anniversary with our son and daughter and my best friend Roger Parsons.

Having a laugh with my mate and mentor, Colin Price.

My mother in May 1992.

My daughter competing at the Winter Gardens, Blackpool in 1998.

Winning the Park Cup with my son at the Swansea Bay Golf Club.

The Bystanders in 1963.

Publicity shot taken outside Cardiff Recording Studios in 1963.

The Cheatin' Hearts photographed in front of Merthyr Tydfil parish church in 1965.

On a dance hall stage with Jeff 'Jethro' Lewis on guitar.

Tomfoolery publicity photo taken in 1977.

In panto at Swansea's Grand Theatre in 1979.

Standing on the zebra crossing outside the BBC's Llandaff studios in 1990, mimicking the Beatles' *Abbey Road* album cover.

About to start recording a Radio Wales roadshow.

In action at a Radio Wales roadshow in Ynysangharad Park, Pontypridd.

Radio Wales roadshow in Colwyn Bay.

The roadshows generate a great atmosphere...

The current line up of Owen Money and the Soul Sharks.

be able to do about ten, fifteen minutes of comedy in the middle. Half an hour at most"

I stood on the side of stage waiting to be introduced and got distracted by the sound of someone knocking on the wall next to me. Then I realised the knocking was coming from my knees. A voice said, "Please welcome tonight's comedian... Lynn Mittell" and I was on stage and into my opening song 'On a clear day'.

The song over, I went straight into my first joke, which got a big laugh. My second joke got an even bigger laugh. And then I was away. Joke after joke after joke. Every one scoring a ten out of ten. It was unbelievable. I didn't want to come off. It felt as if I'd been doing stand-up comedy on my own for years. It seemed natural to me. I was absolutely amazed at the response I was getting from the audience. Gags I'd heard hundreds of times during that summer season were getting huge laughs because, unless some audience members had holidayed in Blackpool, nobody in Wales had heard them before.

I told so many jokes I didn't have time to do the rock and roll songs. Instead of half-an-hour I did fifty minutes and they'd flown by. I came off to a standing ovation. It was a truly memorable night for me. When I went back to the dressing room to change into my own clothes, Tony and the rest of the resident band ran in and said, "That was fantastic!" I was stunned. In fact I admitted that if I had to go on again, I wouldn't have a clue what to do. Minutes after I came off stage I couldn't remember what jokes I'd told and in what order I'd told them.

It hadn't really been an act. I'd just told a succession of very funny jokes which I knew they'd understand, because the audience were the same sort of working-class people who had packed the theatre in Blackpool. My sort of people. I leapt from one subject to another, unlike today where I'll do a routine, about say, holidays or growing up, then move onto another routine, with a quick gag or funny comment thrown in to bridge them.

I wasn't capable of ad-libbing that night at Baverstock's because it was my first real attempt at solo stand-up. But as your confidence as a comedian grows, if you spot someone getting up and going to the toilet or someone in the audience is bald or short or fat or thin, you can come out of your set routine, make a comment about the person you've spotted and maybe come up with a joke or two about him or her, before slipping back into the routine. To be able to do this, you have to remember exactly what your last line had been and keep that in the back of your mind even while you're picking on that audience member. It's a skill and it takes a long time for a comedian to develop it to the point where he's confident that he can go off at a tangent, knowing exactly how and where to pick up where he left off, maybe five minutes later.

I sat in the dressing room, shell-shocked by the experience. I'd just entertained an audience for nearly an hour simply by being myself and telling jokes. If I had any doubts about where my future lay, they were immediately cast aside when the lady who was in charge of artiste fees came in and handed me fifty pounds! She said, "We're paying you fifteen pounds extra because you were so good" and before I could thank her she said, "What are you doing Christmas Eve, Boxing Day and New Year's Eve?"

I thought she was inviting me and Kath to three parties, but she was offering me three bookings. And although I didn't know it then, entertainers can charge higher fees for that time of the year, especially New Year's Eve. It was a little bit awkward because Tony Prosser was still in the dressing room and we'd only just started rehearsing with Richie Powell in the hope we could get some bookings with our trio... on Christmas Eve, Boxing Day and New Year's Eve.

When I got back to my seat, Kath was very proud of me and told me I was marvellous. Her approval of what I'd done was crucial. I decided that if I was going to take the route of becoming a stand-up comedian, I had to get an agent. I don't mean a personal manager, I mean a booking agent who knew the club scene and who could book me into them. One of the biggest agents in Wales was Joan England who lived in Birchgrove, Cardiff, and I phoned her up and told her that I was a comedian and would like her to find me some work. She asked me how long my act was and I said, "Around 45 minutes" and she told me that wasn't enough. The acts that she booked into the clubs were expected to do two, half-hour spots.

However, she took a chance on me and offered me a booking the following Saturday at Penwaun Welfare Club in Aberdare. I'd be on the bill with a 'name' performer and my fee was going to be fifty pounds, less her commission, which I think was ten per cent. When I walked into the club, I could see from the poster on the wall that the star I was supporting was a singer named Oscar, who is more famous now as the father of Kelly Jones of the Stereophonics.

Oscar was a big name in club land and I'd known him years before when he was with a band called the Kingfishers. The place was heaving, you couldn't have got one more body in. They'd all come to see Oscar and because this was my first club gig on my own, no-one knew me. And I was going on *after* Oscar. As someone once said, "I wouldn't have given that spot to a leopard!"

Oscar went on and stormed the place. And I had to follow him. But amazingly, I got the same response at the Penwaun Welfare as I had at Baverstock's on the previous Saturday. I was elated. Two shows in a week and not only had I earned a hundred pounds, I had proved that my first appearance hadn't been a fluke. I was a stand-up comedian. I no longer had to be in a band to entertain people. The following day I phoned Tony Prosser and told him that I was pursuing a solo comedy career and that meant I couldn't be part of the new three-piece band. Tony had seen how well I'd done at Baverstock's and backed me completely, but I don't think Richie Powell was that happy about it.

There was an agent in Cardiff at that time named Don Tyra, who had been very successful but who was now in the autumn of his career. He was diabetic, drank too much and was a very abrasive character, which made him disliked by many people. But he and I got on great. And although Joan England was correct in saying working men's clubs expected the comedians they booked to do an hour, split into two half-hours, Don managed to get me loads of thirty-minute bookings.

Apart from his work as an agent, Don also owned a 'pro digs' in Cardiff, a bed and breakfast establishment for performers working in the area. Loads of comedians and singers stayed there. In fact that's where I first met my good friend Roy Walker when he was staying there and he still talks about Don Tyra to this day.

As much as I liked Don, he wasn't very well organised. He did terrible things, like the time he realised he'd booked me into two different clubs on the same Saturday night. Instead of phoning the club where I wasn't going to appear to explain what had happened and offer them a replacement, without telling me he was doing this, he'd ring up and tell them I wouldn't be able to appear because I'd been to a rugby international at Cardiff Arms Park that afternoon and got so drunk I was incapable of standing up, let alone performing! This was an outrageous lie, because not only had I never been to the Arms Park, I had never been to watch a rugby match *anywhere*!

He was a real character and his party piece was something that shocked a lot of people, including me the first time. Although by the *twenty*-first time I witnessed it I didn't bat an eyelid. If anyone asked him the time, instead of looking at his wristwatch, he would unzip his flies, take out his willie, look at it and say, "It's half-past two", put it away and zip up again, all in a couple of seconds. To be fair, he never did this when he was sober, only when he'd had a few. And as he drank like a fish, it happened a lot.

Despite the fact he was a drunk and an exhibitionist, we got on okay and he was instrumental in pushing me forward. I can't honestly say that I had a career as such, but I was working and learning and honing my comedy skills. I started taking time to plan the order of my jokes. I still sang a couple of songs at the start and end of my act, 'On a clear day' to get on and Charles Aznavour's 'She' to get off and, because we didn't have backing tapes or mini-disks or whatever electrical gadget they use to get musical accompaniment today, I got someone to write musical arrangements for me. In this business we call show-musical arrangements 'dots', referring to the musical notes on the paper.

So as soon as I got to a club I would hand my dots to the resident 'band', usually a keyboard and drums duo and explain what I wanted them to play and when they should start and stop. Some of these club musicians were great, but there were some who were so truly terrible, so incredibly cloth-eared they would have sounded much more musical if they'd switched places and the drummer had hit the keyboard with his sticks while the keyboard player repeatedly bashed his head on the hi-hat cymbal.

One of the finest keyboard players I encountered in the clubs was the resident organist at the Pantside Social Club in Newbridge – a man who became my best mate, Mr Roger Parsons. There you are, Roger. I said you'd get a mention. You can either send me a cheque for the agreed amount or I'll have it in readies.

The Pantside Club was very popular with entertainers, not because of the audience who were often less than enthusiastic, but because of the excellent musical accompaniment provided by Roger on the organ and John on the drums. I remember Brian James and Mal, the resident duo at the Gurnos Club, Merthyr, they were good too. But first-class musicians were the exception; most of them just 'busked' the tunes, and they'd pretend they could read the dots, often getting quite close to the melody but not quite on it – which is off-putting when you're trying to sing a heart-rending ballad. They just couldn't handle anything that was even slightly complicated. When Richard Harris brought out his famous seven-minute single 'MacArthur Park' in 1968 (a Number One in Britain and a Number Two in America!) and singers started bringing their own arrangements of the song to clubs, half the organ and drum duos in club-land held up a white flag and retired.

By the way, if you like pop trivia, here's something you might like to know. When he recorded 'MacArthur Park' – and it took him several takes as you can imagine because it's a monster of a song – Richard Harris kept referring to it as 'MacArthur's Park', even though the composer and arranger Jimmy Webb kept correcting him. For some reason Harris couldn't stop putting an 's' on the end of MacArthur, so eventually Jimmy Webb just let him get on with it, as you'll hear quite clearly (now that I've pointed it out) next time you hear it on the radio. Not that you'll hear it on any of my shows, because I can't stand the song. My act was coming together and some nights it went so well and the audience reaction was so warm, I didn't have to finish on a song.

I now had about an hour of material; that's a lot of jokes. And although the core of my act didn't change much, I was always adding new material. If I heard a great gag, I'd put it in the act. And if you watch a lot of comedians, like I used to do, you can always take one good gag from each of them. This used to go on all the time, even among the comedy élite – the big names who had their own television series and topped the bill in summer season. They often had their own writers who penned new gags for them every day, but on top of these newly-minted gags, they'd also drop in a line that they'd heard one of their fellow superstars get a big laugh with. I'm not saying it's right, I'm just saying it went on.

This sort of thing is frowned upon by modern comedians, who get very uptight and often consult their solicitors if they find out a fellow comic is using one of their lines – which says a lot about their insecurity. Not that most of them tell *jokes* in the accepted sense. They refer to their acts as 'sets', a phrase taken from the jazz world.

They have rambling, surreal routines which can go on for eight or nine minutes without a laugh, as they hammer home a point. They're all very intelligent, usually have a degree of some sort and have a much greater grasp of the business side of comedy than I ever did at their age. They make fortunes by selling-out stadiums and arenas and going around the country in six-month long theatre tours, at the end of which they have their act filmed for a DVD release, which will then be bought by the thousands of fans who had already paid to see them performing 'live'! Now that's what I call putting the *business* into show business.

I realise that many 21st century comedians probably dismiss my style of comedy – tell joke, wait for laugh, get laugh, pause and carry on – as prehistoric and think I'm just an old fart for my jaundiced view of much of (but not all) modern comedy. That's fair enough. But then I wouldn't go on stage in ripped jeans and an unironed tee shirt and start telling a crude routine which relied on a torrent of sexual swear words to get a laugh. I'm totally aware that there's a huge appetite out there for that sort of comedy and it's a multi-million pound industry these days. I also know that even popular comedians who are perceived as 'old school' like Peter Kay, occasionally insert the f-word into their acts, but it just doesn't appeal to me.

I'll freely admit that I swear far too much in everyday life. A lot of things happen in everyday life to make anyone swear. But here's what I think. True comedy icons like Eric and Ernie, Tommy Cooper, Benny Hill, Max Miller, Syd Field, Frankie Howerd, Arthur Askey, Tony Hancock, Norman Wisdom, Stanley Baxter, Laurel and Hardy, Eric Sykes, Jack Benny, Bob Hope, Jerry Lewis and The Two Ronnies might well have sworn like troupers in their dressing room. In fact many of them did. But they never *once* swore on stage or on television in order to get a laugh and they will be fondly remembered for decades to come. I rest my case.

To be honest, I was surprised at my new-found success as a stand-up comedian, because until that Blackpool season with New Tomfoolery, I hadn't really been that interested in comedy or thought about going on stage on my own to tell jokes. I'd seen loads of comedians on television, like Bob Monkhouse, Jimmy Wheeler, Max Wall, Jimmy Tarbuck, Charlie Drake, Tommy Trinder, Dave King, Jimmy James, Ken Dodd, Dickie Henderson... there were so many great comics around when I was growing up. But the thought of following in their footsteps never entered my head.

But once I started making in-roads into comedy, I made a point of seeing comedians working all over the place, and not just in Wales. I'd go to London, Birmingham... I even went back to Blackpool. I saw dozens of comedians and usually found one gag in each act that I could 'borrow'.

I decided that my new career demanded a new name. I was now Jimmy Lyons, partly because I thought it sounded like a comedian's name, but mainly because I started arriving at clubs where 'Lynn Mittell' had been booked to appear and the audience were expecting a girl singer. Perhaps it was the fault of my publicity photos that the agents used to send to a club in advance. The long blonde hair... the glittery dress... the enormous breast implants... all very misleading.

It was while I was working under the name Jimmy Lyons that I got paid off for the one and only time in Wales... so far. It was at the Llynfi Valley Constitutional Club in Maesteg, which is now called Beethoven's. Why anyone would think it was a good idea to name a place of entertainment after a deaf composer is beyond me. If you're going to name a club after a classical composer, bearing in mind it's a licensed premise, why not choose something more appropriate... like 'Brahms and Lizst'?

Brian Wallage, the man who fell into the orchestra pit in the pantomime, came with me as my roadie. It's always good for a comedian to have someone with them at a gig, riding shotgun. And that night I needed all the friends I could get.

The booking had been arranged by an agent named Chris Farr, who'd worked with me at Hoover's – not as an agent, obviously. He'd told me that the Llynfi Valley was a 'nice little club'. After that night I never believed another word he said.

I turned up at the club and the place was full. The entertainment that night was to be provided by the club's resident organ and drums duo... and me. I'd done a lot of gigs by now, so I walked on stage feeling pretty confident. I told a few, what I thought were, sure-fire gags, but they were met by silence. So I did what I still do to this day, which is to have a pop at people in the room. I wasn't the only comedian who did this. In fact Kenny Smiles' entire act used to be (and might still be) based around the people he spotted in the audience and he could get the audience doubled-up with laughter, without actually telling a joke.

But this particular audience obviously weren't used to this sort of comedy. I might as well have been quoting Shakespeare in Russian. I was getting nothing from them. It turned into a staring contest. And although the room was packed with warm bodies, the temperature dropped way below zero when I glanced at the organist and drummer who were sat with their arms folded, looking like they wished they were at home on the sofa watching the telly and so I made this comment. "Look at that drummer. He's stinking. I bet they hide the money under the soap in his house." Not a titter.

I came off feeling terrible. I'd died a million deaths... and I still had a second spot to do later on. How the hell was I going to get through that and come out alive? As I sat there wondering what had gone wrong and how I could face the audience again, the club secretary stormed into the dressing room with a face like a bulldog chewing a wasp and said, "We were told your act was guitar/vocal and comedy. You haven't even got a guitar with you. And I thought it was terrible the way you picked on that poor drummer." I said, "It was just a joke." He said, "Well no-one here thought it was funny. Here's twenty pound for your expenses. Now get out of here; we don't want to see you again!"

So while Brian Wallage and I are in the dressing room, packing away my gear, we could hear the club secretary talking to the audience. "You'll be glad to know that we won't be having the artiste back on. We'll be playing another five hands of bingo instead!" The cheer that came from the audience when they heard this could have been heard ten miles away.

Bingo fans take the game very seriously, whether there's four pounds, four hundred or forty thousand pounds at stake and they like to be able to hear the numbers being called out loud and clear. My 'walk of shame' with Brian, from the dressing room to the front door of the club, took me right through the middle of the club, where everyone was concentrating, eyes down, pens at the ready to tick the numbers off their bingo tickets as the caller shouted out the numbers. The last thing they wanted was any interruptions, which is why I interrupted them.

Brian and I, holding speakers and leads, pushed our way past the tables and chairs, saying as loud as possible, so we could drown out the bingo caller's voice, "Excuse me! Coming through! Out the way, please! Mind your backs!" and, when we got to the front door, "All the best, you miserable bunch of bastards!" and then we were in the car and gone!

That happened many years ago, but every time I've driven past there since, I'm always reminded that it was the only place where I was paid off. And the strange thing is I've now got more fans around that area, than I have in any other part of Wales. I think there were 23 at the last count; if you include the late Gladys Llewellyn.

That night at the Llynfi Valley Constitutional Club was a turning point in my career. The business of picking on people was something that came naturally to me, something I did every time I performed. But while other audiences would go with it and have a good laugh at what I was doing, which was never done maliciously, that particular crowd took offence. From that night I tailored my act so that if I did make a comment about someone in the audience, only the most sensitive of souls could possibly take offence. And you don't get that many sensitive souls on a night out in a working men's club. Also, I occasionally used material which couldn't in all honesty be described as blue. But it did have a little tinge of blue around it. Not filthy stuff, but the sort of gags that I would have used with Tomfoolery; I decided to stick to jokes that wouldn't offend.

I still wasn't sure that Jimmy Lyons was the best choice of names and one night I was working a club in Ebbw Vale and I started writing some alternative names down and one of them, Owen Money, seemed to leap off the page at me. I was a big fan of Liverpool Football Club and Richard Money used to play for them. I took his surname and then thought of adding Owen, which is a Welsh name, to create Owen Money. I wasn't a hundred per cent sure I was doing the right thing by changing my stage name again (remember I'd been Jerry Braden for a time too) so I drove home from Ebbw Vale via Tredegar and stopped off at the Dukestown Club where some friends of mine – Stan and Peggy, better known as Yorkie and Taff – were appearing.

If you finished your act around ten o'clock, if you timed it right, you could generally drop into a club and catch another performer. And most of the acts knew each other and enjoyed meeting up. There was a time when Stan and Peggy wanted me to join them, to form a comedy trio called Yorkie, Taff and Bwt. Well it's no worse than Steele, Novak and Good. But that never happened.

I told them I was thinking of changing my name. Peggy looked a bit doubtful and said "To what?" Well I think that's what she said. I replied, "Owen Money!" Her eyes lit up and she said, "That's fantastic. The best name for a comic I've ever heard." I needed to tell people in the business about my change of name and the first person I phoned was an agent I knew in Musselborough named Andy Green. I said, "Hello, Andy. It's Jimmy Lyons here. I've just changed my name to Owen Money!" He roared down the phone, "Owen Money! What a 'bleeping' great name that is! Have you got any free dates?" He wanted to book me purely on the strength of my new name. I knew I'd made the right decision. From now on, Lynn Mittell, Jerry Braden and Jimmy Lyons had to make way for Owen Money.

CHAPTER NINE

So NOW IT'S 1981 and the newly-named Owen Money has started playing the clubs in Scotland and even though I may say so myself, he did very well with those tough audiences. Although I had no sole agent or personal manager, I signed with the agency AIR in Spennymoor, County Durham, who acted as my agents in the north-east of England. They got me lots of work in that area and I even worked Sunday lunchtimes, often sharing the bill with a stripper or, as they liked to be called, 'an exotic dancer'. And some of them were very, very exotic. I realise that a young lady taking all her clothes off in a room full of randy men, isn't everyone's idea of entertainment on a Sunday morning, as I said to the organiser of one particular Sunday strip show, Father Patrick O'Flanagan. But Sunday strippers were a bit of a tradition in the working men's clubs back then and it was all treated light-heartedly.

A memory from that time has just come back to me. In one club I played on a Sunday lunchtime, my dressing room was right next door to the one being used by a tall, blonde stripper with a forty-three inch bust. I noticed that there was a hole in the wall between us, about three inches round. Out of decency I felt I ought to cover it up, but then I thought, "If she wants to look, let her look!"

I was doing quite well in the north-east, learning what gags would work with certain audiences, not rushing to the punch line and not talking too fast in my Welsh accent. AIR approached me and said that they were going to 'sell me' to another agency, Beverley Artistes, for one week. They weren't so much selling me as 'renting me out' which was quite a common practice between agencies. The week they 'sold' me for was in July of 1981, the week of the Royal Wedding between His Royal Highness The Prince of Wales and Lady Diana Spencer.

I was booked in for a week's stay in what were probably the best 'pro digs' in the north-east, the South Lodge at Roker, run by Carol Marshall who provided fantastic breakfasts. I knew the place well, because I'd stayed there when I was with Tomfoolery and had met and got to know many of the other guests, performers on the club scene like Bob Carolgees and bands like the Dooleys and Sight n' Sound.

Beverly Artistes had booked me into a different club every night of the week starting on the Monday. But on the previous weekend I had two gigs to do for AIR. On the Saturday, I was at the Simonside Social Club where I had a really good night. The next morning, it was another Sunday lunchtime show, this time at the Houghton Manor Social Club in Hartlepool. It was the biggest club in the area and was known as the comic's graveyard.

As I mentioned earlier, I had decided to stop doing dirty jokes. My act was now so clean, so devoid of anything remotely resembling filth, I used to get letters from Mary Whitehouse begging me to leave in the one about the Bishop, the Beverly Sisters and the bowl of blue blancmange. When you're working to a Sunday lunchtime all-male crowd, all desperate to see the stripper who's going to follow you, it's damned hard not to slip in a few jokes of questionable taste in order to win them over.

I'll hold my hand up and admit that, prior to my decision to dump any material that might offend people, like many comedians of that era, there were a few gags in my act that would today raise a few eyebrows with the Campaign for Racial Equality. I'm not proud of it and I'm not defending it. This was thirty years ago and attitudes to comedy and race have changed in leaps and bounds and when I think of some of the gags with a racial slant that comedians were telling at the time and that audiences were laughing at, I cringe.

So at the Houghton Manor Social Club, Hartlepool, that Sunday lunchtime I went on determined not to tell any rude jokes. I just wanted to be so funny that the audience wouldn't even notice my act wasn't the usual mix of racial and sexual gags. And I absolutely stormed the place. It was a great feeling, knowing I'd got big laughs with clean material. Earlier that morning, some of my fellow guests at the South Lodge wanted to come to see my lunchtime gig, but I was so worried about trying out my new act, and so I wouldn't tell them where I was working. Six months later, I went back to the Houghton Manor, took a load of friends with me... and died on my arse!

On the Monday night of the week for which Beverly Artistes had bought me, I was booked into the Ivy Leaf Club where, before the 'turn' came on, they were having a general knowledge quiz. So I thought I'd have a go myself. Everyone else was split into teams of three or four and I was sat in the corner by myself. Well guess what happened? I'm not sure whether the members of the Ivy Leaf Club were thick or if I was a genius, but I won the quiz. And the members all looked at me as if I'd robbed a charity box off the bar.

I got up to do my act and I immediately felt the blast of their icy-cold hate, oozing out of them, crawling across the floor and slapping me right in the face. Okay, perhaps I shouldn't have opened my act by smiling and boasting, "Hey!! Who won the quiz then?" When it got to the point where I couldn't hear myself telling jokes above the cries of "Get off!" as there were more of them than there was of me, I took their advice and left the stage. My first booking with the very influential Beverly Artistes and I was paid off. I was handed half my fee, which I think was twenty or thirty pounds, and showed me the door. As I walked out I heard the club secretary say, "Right. The artiste has gone so we can play some extra games of bingo!" which earned him a big cheer and a round of applause. It was the Llynfi Valley club all over again. I was earning more money for the bingo industry than I was for myself. The following night, Tuesday, I played a different club and exactly the same thing happened. The audience took a dislike to me, I struggled and I got paid off.

After two disasters, you can imagine how much I was looking forward to the Wednesday night, because I was doing a double-booking. My early show was at Wingate Constitutional Club, followed by a late spot at Coasters in Tynemouth. This was the day of the Royal Wedding, which had been declared a Bank Holiday, so millions of Britons were in high spirits, enjoying their day off, watching the wedding on television or taking part in the thousands of street parties that were held from Lands End to John O'Groats, not forgetting Aberdare. A mate of mine went to a street party on the outside lane of the M4. He said it was alright, but it all went very fast.

When I arrived at the Wingate club, I walked into what can best be described as alcoholic-fuelled mayhem. Despite the fact that the following day was a normal working day, the club members were knocking back the booze as if it was New Year's Eve in the Klondike. In fact I did see two fur-trappers and a Mountie sat in one corner, playing shove-ha'penny.

As well as this very funny man from Merthyr, the club had also booked a girl singer, who bravely went on before me. Well, she didn't have a chance, did she? The audience had been drinking since before breakfast time and even if she'd been Madonna they wouldn't have given her much attention. She sang four songs and the club secretary came up to me and said, "Get ready to go on, Owen. We're going to pay her off. She's crap!" to which I replied, "How dare you interrupt this game of shove-ha'penny with my new fur-trapper friends. I've already won three beaver pelts and a stuffed grizzly bear!"

The poor girl singer – I can't remember her name, but I think she was from Scotland – came off stage in tears, completely demoralised and she was paid off. They don't mess around in the working men's clubs. If they like you, they're very loyal and wonderful audiences to play to. If they don't take to you, you could be as good as Shirley Bassey and they'll sit on their hands after every song.

You might have thought that after two terrible nights, my confidence would have drained away and I'd be dreading going on. But a comedian cannot afford to show fear or weakness. If he does, the audience will eat him alive and spit out the bones. He's the man with the microphone and he has to be seen to be in complete charge of the room he's playing to. I walked on, started my act and I didn't get one laugh. Not one. They were well-behaved and didn't heckle or shout 'Get off!' All they did was listen and give me the occasional ripple of applause. I would have got the same reaction if I'd been reading out a joke-free, formal speech of thanks. To quote Frankie Howerd – "I was completely titter-less".

I decided to sing a song, which got another polite ripple of applause and instead of doing the sensible thing and quitting while I was behind, I thought I'd give them a few more gags. I had just finished telling another joke which they found about as funny as having a wisdom tooth removed without anaesthetic when, in front of the whole audience, one of the club officials walked up to me and said, "Sing another song and come off!" As usual I did what I was told, and went back to the dressing room, where the female singer was still sobbing over the sink. I said, "Do me a favour and move over. It's my turn to cry now!"

I then moved on to Coasters in Tynemouth, where I arrived earlier than expected. The club secretary said, "You're early, man," and I said, "I know. I was paid off at the Wingate Club". He said, "Don't worry, lad. As you're early, you can go on now. We've got a great crowd in tonight. You'll do okay here." I said, "That would make a change." And he said, "Yes, we've got 250 in from the Ivy Leaf Club!"

The same club I'd died in on the previous Monday night, after winning the pub quiz!

I thought I'd show them what sort of comedian I am. I'll make the so and sos laugh tonight! And I swear that in the thirty seconds it took me to walk across the floor of the club to the microphone stand, all 250 visiting members of the Ivy Leaf Club got up, walked out and went to the disco upstairs! I think there were about thirty or forty people left and they might as well not have been there. It was another grim night for Owen Money. And from the expressions on their faces, I don't suppose it was much fun for the audience. When I got back to the digs there was a party still going on to celebrate the Royal Wedding, but I really didn't feel like putting on a funny hat and dancing 'til dawn. I was miles from home, I'd had a run of bad shows and I felt lousy.

Next morning, came the phone call I was expecting. I picked up the phone and I hear, "Hello, Owen. It's Bob Gladwyn, from Beverly Artistes." I said, "Hiya, Bob. It's not working out for us, is it?" Bob said, "You came highly recommended by AIR, but you don't seem to be suiting my venues", which was a polite way of saying no-one thought I was funny. He then went on, "As you know, you're booked into the Felling Social Club tonight, and I've been trying to find someone to replace you". News that didn't surprise me. He went on, "However, I can't get anyone at such short notice, so you'll have to honour the booking. It's a big charity show and there are four acts on the bill, so you'll only have to do a ten minute spot." That sounded okay to me, until he said, "But whatever you do, don't tell any jokes. Cut the comedy and just sing a couple of songs! I'll be down the club tomorrow night and I'll give you a hundred quid so you can at least go home with something!" So in effect he was offering me one hundred pounds *not* to tell jokes! If anyone reading this ever wants me *not* to tell jokes for ten minutes, one hundred pounds is still the going rate.

My total fee for the ten days that I was working for Beverly Artistes was supposed to be £500 and after less than a week I was being virtually paid off with a fifth of that.

As I arrived at the Felling Social Club, the entertainments' secretary met me and he was all sweetness and light. He said, "Nice to meet you, Owen. You're from Wales aren't you? I know Wales very well. Now, as you know, tonight we're having a charity show, you're on first and we only need you to do half an hour of material." So, suddenly, the quick 'on-and-off' ten minutes with no jokes that Bob Gladwyn told me that I'd be doing at the club had been extended to thirty minutes of stand-up comedy. It didn't particularly worry me because I already knew that in the comedy business you have to be prepared to adapt to whatever's asked of you. Sometimes they'll want you to cut your act; sometimes they'll want you to stretch it. But if you call yourself a comedian, you'd better have *some* sort of act.

I remember seeing Ricky Gervais get caught out on a big 'live' music event that was televised a couple of years back. To be fair, he only came on to introduce an act and wasn't expecting to do a turn, but he should have at least come up with a couple of funnies or carefully prepared adlibs. After all, his stand-up act, with which he tours vast arenas, lasts around two hours. When he walked on stage, to huge applause, the next act he was there to introduce were taking much longer than anticipated to get ready. A clearly nervous Gervais was then asked to fill in for a few minutes and this talented man, who has done what many British comedians have failed to do and made it in Hollywood, had *nothing*.

He was standing there in front of thousands of people at

the venue and millions watching at home, totally unprepared. After an embarrassing pause, he did the only thing he knew which would make the audience laugh – the silly David Brent dance from *The Office*. He won them over basically because of who he is and the audience's affection for his David Brent persona, but I don't think he would ever take on a gig like that again without a script. If the Scouts' motto is "Be Prepared", the Comedians' motto should be "Be Prepared – always have a load of gags up your sleeve".

That night at the Felling Social Club I was well prepared. I decided I might as well go out in a blaze of glory, give them their full thirty minutes and after Bob Gladwyn came down to the Felling Social Club to pay me my one hundred pounds – and probably to make sure I left the area at the same time – that would be the end of my career in the north-east.

I went on, did exactly half an hour and – as we sometimes say in the business – I tore the b*ll*cks of the place. They loved me. I went on at eight o'clock and came off at half-past to a standing ovation. Before I got back to my dressing room, the entertainments' secretary cornered me and treated me as if I was his saviour. He had a broad grin on his face and squeezed my hand and said, "You're the best comic we've ever had here. Where are you tomorrow night?" I said, "Back home in Wales I think." He said, "That's a shame. Well, next time you're coming up this way, be sure to let us know!"

So I left him and walked into my dressing room, where Bob Gladwyn was nonchalantly sitting on a radiator, hands thrust into his trouser pockets with a bemused expression on his face. I didn't know whether he'd seen my act or not, so I was half-expecting him to hand me my hundred quid 'pay off' money and escort me to my car. Instead he looked up at me and said, "Owen, I nearly made the biggest mistake of my life by paying you off! You're fantastic!"

And from that day on, until I made the decision to stop working in the north-east, I had loads of work up there. This illustrates the elusive nature of what people find funny. I told the same jokes that night at the Felling as I'd told on all the previous nights and the reaction I got was entirely different. Whether the Felling audience were in a better frame of mind or I wasn't trying too hard for the laughs I don't know. But it was one hell of a learning curve for me and was a real confidence booster.

The gigs began to pour in for me and I started earning reasonable money for working seven nights a week. My work schedule was this. I did two weeks in the south Wales clubs, then two weeks in Scotland, followed by two weeks in the north-east. This was okay for a while but I grew to dislike working away from home for a month at a time as it meant Kath was on her own with young Matthew for weeks at a time back in our home in Merthyr. So I gradually began to do less and less work out of Wales. If an agent called and offered me work in the north-east or north of the border, I'd try and get out of it by telling them I couldn't possibly do it for less than £1,200 a week! I was well aware that, unless you were a major star with your own TV series, this sort of figure was unheard of. Most club comedians were earning around £70 a night, and maybe working four, five nights a week if they were lucky. Naturally, some of the clubs weren't prepared to pay those sort of fees, but there were some who *would* pay, and that made it worth my while travelling back 'oop north' occasionally.

Because I was now mostly working in Wales, Kath and I decided to sell the house and buy a pub with living accommodation upstairs, in Dowlais. It had once been called the Prince Llewellyn Arms but when we bought it, it was called the Silver Slipper, which the locals referred to as the Slipper. I suppose that was because the rough, tough men who made up most of its clientele didn't want to be heard saying, "I'm going to have a drink in the Silver Slipper tonight". It doesn't sound very macho, does it?

My idea of running the pub with Kath and doing the odd comedy gig as and when, started to go out of the window because I was inundated with offers of work. Kath was working part-time as a nurse as well as working behind the bar, so income-wise, we were doing okay especially when I started to introduce live music acts to the pub, which brought in more customers. We were tenants at the Silver Slipper which was owned by Whitbread Brewery who, having noted the success we'd had with the Slipper, offered us the only pub in Swansea that had a music licence, the Hafod Inn. We jumped at the chance and moved lock, stock and several beer barrels to the Hafod.

We made some great friends in that pub, which everyone used to call the LA, which stood for 'Lower 'Afod' and in the early 1980s it became *the* pub in Swansea to go and see live music acts. There were a couple of other Swansea pubs who put on live acts but, unlike us, they weren't licensed for it. The place was always packed and that meant the brewery were as happy as Larry. That said, I have no idea who Larry was or why he was so happy all the time. But I'm glad in a way that I never met him, because I don't think I could handle someone who went around with a great big permanent smile on his face. It's the sort of behaviour that would make me miserable.

It was tough for me to keep the comedy career going and run a very successful pub. I had mid-week gigs as well as regular work at weekends and I would try and balance out my comedy work with helping Kath, who was now pregnant with our daughter Katie, in the Hafod. Well we may have been rushed off our feet most of the time, but we did have the occasional hour to ourselves!

A comedian friend of mine, Robb Duncan, asked me if I'd like go along with him to the Dragon Hotel, Swansea, where he was auditioning for a new HTV Wales television talent show called *Showbiz* which was going to be produced by Colin Stevens. It sounded interesting so I agreed to go with him. I suppose I thought there might be an opportunity for me to audition as well, although I knew that Robb, like all the other auditionees, had a pre-booked slot in the day's schedules which had been organised weeks before. But, nevertheless, when we got to the Dragon Hotel and I found out that there were very few comics among the crowd waiting to be seen, I thought it was worth a shot.

I asked one of the production team if there was any chance that I could do a quick audition and he told me they'd try and fit me in at the end of the day, if there was time. As it turned out they did manage to find time for me, I did an audition... and I stank. I mean I was just *terrible*. Despite all my experience and all those gigs I had under my belt and all those club audiences who had to be rushed to casualty because they'd split their sides laughing at my act... I tanked.

Colin Stevens, acting like a true professional should, didn't tell me I was rubbish and instead he politely thanked me for my time and asked me to leave my telephone number with his assistant, even though the only phone number I was interested in at that point was the one you need to dial the Samaritans. By the way, my mate Robb didn't get picked either, which was no comfort to me.

Fast forward to four weeks later when I was contacted by an agency called Artists Anonymous. It didn't really occur to me then that no performer in their right mind would have anything to do with an agency who were dull enough to call themselves Artists Anonymous. It hardly inspires confidence, does it? I can just imagine this conversation between two comedians who meet in the street:

"So, which agency are you with?"

(Loudly and proudly) "I'm with the 'We Guarantee to Let the World Know Your Name So You Become Incredibly Rich and Famous and We Can Justify Taking Twenty Per Cent of Your Vast Earnings' office."

"Oh!"

"Which agency are you with, then?"

(Barely above a whisper) "Artists Anonymous."

"Artists... *Anonymous*? Are you nuts?"

Perhaps I wasn't in my right mind, because when Artists Anonymous contacted me to tell me about a possible career opportunity, I didn't slam the phone down. They told me that they had arranged an audition for me at the then-famous Double Diamond Club in Caerphilly for a new HTV Wales television talent show called *Showbiz* which was going to be produced by Colin Stevens!

I couldn't tell them I'd already auditioned – and failed miserably – for the same show in Swansea, so I agreed to go along. But this audition was going to be a lot different to the first one, where I'd told my jokes in a cold hotel function room to five or six people who didn't laugh once. There was going to be a live audience in the Double Diamond Club – and you thought *The X Factor* was the first show to audition acts in front of a wild crowd!

Kath came along with me, taking a rare night off from the pub. I don't know how many months Kath was gone but she was 'heavy with child' at the time. When we got to the Double Diamond the place was packed. There must have been eight hundred people in there. And I stormed it! I had them rolling in the aisles. Well, when I say aisles, I mean those narrow spaces between the tables they used to have at the Double Diamond, which that night worked wonders for me, I can tell you!

Colin Stevens was there, obviously, and when he came up to me afterwards, what he said was almost word for word what Bob Gladwyn had said to me a couple of years before. "Based on your original audition in Swansea I wasn't going to choose you for the show, which would have been the biggest mistake of my life. Tonight, you were fantastic!" He went on, "We've learned something tonight. Comedians can't audition in a hotel room in front of a couple of people. They have to play to a live audience", which was something I already knew. But I was too polite to say it.

Colin was the producer, but above him was the Executive Producer, Peter Elias Jones. I think he was called the Executive Producer because he wore a suit and tie and Colin wore a sports jacket and slacks.

Peter and Colin told me that they wanted me to appear on the series which was going to be recorded at the Double Diamond Club over four nights. I was only going to be there for one night but as the series went out on television over six weeks, each show would feature a small chunk of each performer's act.

I turned up for rehearsals, hoping there wouldn't be too many comedians on the same bill. Have a guess who was on the show with me? Go on. No... not Frank Sinatra. Don't be childish. And no, it wasn't Two-Ton Tessie O'Shea. I wish it had been. I could have hidden behind her when I walked into the club and saw Tomfoolery rehearsing on stage with their new front man, Brian Conley!

With all the acts that were doing the rounds of the clubs, what were the chances I'd be on the same bill as the band who'd elbowed me out, all those years before? It beggars belief. But as I watched them, I was reminded of Jeff Davies's parting words to me as they sacked me, "Sorry, Lynn. But you haven't got it anymore!"

As luck would have it, on the night, I was on the bill before them. I realised that when the show went out a few weeks later on TV, there was no guarantee in what order we'd be seen, and that we might not even be seen on the same show, but it was incredibly important for me to go out there in front of a live audience and do well, before my old band, who had thought so little of me, did *their* act.

I checked with Colin Stevens on how long he wanted me to do on the show and he said, "Just keep going until I tell you to stop. I won't cut you off mid-joke. But when you see me making this sign" and he made a circle in the air with his hand, "that'll be the point at which I'll want you to 'wind-up' your act, so you'll have time to finish the gag, say goodnight and come off!"

There were a thousand people crammed into the Double Diamond Club that night. It was roofed. The opening act was a singer, who did okay and then it was my turn. It was, up to that point, the biggest night of my professional life. I went on, told my first gag, it got a great reaction and I was away. The crowd were just perfect. They laughed at all my gags and really seemed to like me. I was on for about forty minutes and then I saw Colin give me the wind-up sign. I finished the gag I was telling, said goodnight and came off to a rousing cheer. It couldn't have gone any better if I'd slipped every member of the audience a tenner.

As I walked off the stage, Jeff Davies was walking on with his guitar, to get ready for his performance with Tomfoolery. I'd gone down incredibly well and he knew it. That should have been enough, but I still needed to say *something,* not out of spite or petty revenge, but simply to let him know that I had never forgotten the words he'd used to dismiss me as some sort of washed-up, no-hoper. As Jeff and I passed each other I said, "Not bad for someone who hasn't got it anymore!" and kept on walking.

CHAPTER TEN

WHEN *SHOWBIZ* EVENTUALLY WENT out on HTV Wales, I was included on *five* of the six shows. I would have been featured on all six, but there'd been a terrible plane crash the day before and by one of those coincidences no-one can account for, the segment of my act they'd chosen to include on the show that night was a routine about flying, so it was, quite understandably, cut out of the show.

While this television exposure didn't send my career up into the stratosphere, it did help to make my name and to get me recognised. People started coming up to me, saying, "I saw you on the telly last night! I really enjoyed you," and I'd say, "Thanks very much, but how did you get in my bathroom?" But although fame still eluded me, I really enjoyed the recognition and felt I had climbed one further rung up the ladder.

In fact the *Showbiz* appearances helped to raise my profile for a couple of years. I still kept working and went back to Germany, this time on the NAAFI tours. A bunch of entertainers would fly out and do a couple of months 'tour of duty' if you like, entertaining British Forces at their bases in places like Dortmund and Osnabruck.

One of the acts I worked with was the comedy show band Scotch Mist, a bunch of mad, musical drunks from Ayr, who were brilliant on stage and relaxed as newts offstage. I made a lot of money on that tour. Not from my fee. From smuggling. No... don't call the police. Let me explain. I had a friend in Swansea called Frank Rossini, who loved a good cigar. He could afford them too, because Frank owned the local Land Rover franchise and before I left for Germany he asked me to bring him back a box of cigars.

Cigars cost a lot less on the continent than in the UK so, knowing that Frank was prepared to recompense me for my outlay, I decided to bring back a load of cigars so I could make a little bit of profit. When the rest of the entertainers on the tour found out it was an easy way of making money, they bought cigars too, because they all knew someone who'd be prepared to buy them. I decided to go for broke and used the money I earned on the tour to purchase fifty boxes of King Edward cigars, twenty to a box, for around £4 each. The big problem of course was getting them through British customs on the way back as tobacco would have to be declared and there was no way I could admit to bringing in fifty boxes. The other entertainers also had a huge stock of cigars between them. We were like a mobile tobacconist shop.

We all travelled together around Germany on an old coach, which had seen better days – and much better entertainers – so to ensure we got our contraband through the customs without being stopped, we tore away all the upholstery, hid dozens and dozens of boxes of cigars in the nooks and crannies, and replaced the upholstery without any sign of it being disturbed. When I got back home I sold Frank Rossini all fifty boxes of King Edwards for *£20 a box*, which made me a profit of £16 per box!

I was offered a few more NAAFI tours but decided against it. The pub was doing well and I had a load of gigs lined up… and besides, Frank Rossini wouldn't need any more cigars for at least ten years. As far as Kath and I were concerned, The Hafod Inn was a great pub, the customers loved the live music nights and we had no intention of leaving it, even if some big cheese from the Brewery came along and offered us somewhere even better. So guess what happened? Some big cheese from the Brewery came along and offered us somewhere even better…

The Starlight Rooms was an 800-seater nightclub in Port Talbot which I knew very well because I'd performed there. I felt ready to take over a big place like The Starlight Rooms, but there were a couple of things that needed sorting out before I agreed. There were some design faults in the building, such as the seats nearest the stage were the furthest away from the toilets, so people were up and down like a bride's nightie all evening. This and the layout of the seats, which were in tiers, made the place unworkable for a performer. I told the Brewery that they would have to bring the seating down to one level as best as they could and, give them their due, they spent a fortune on refurbishing the place.

While the nightclub upstairs was being refurbished we opened the downstairs bar and a small lounge, and we got to know and like all the local people who'd pop in for a drink. Many of them recognised me from the *Showbiz* series and that helped to create a great, friendly atmosphere. It was a really good time for Kath and me.

A memory from that period just came back to me and I'll throw it in for no other reason than to embarrass my daughter Katy, who was two at the time. I remember taking her down to the club one day and I don't know what we'd fed her, but it obviously didn't agree with her because she suddenly pooped all over the dartboard! That wouldn't have been so bad, but one of the darts players standing at the oche was eating a pasty at the time.

By the time we opened the nightclub upstairs in 1983 I'd spent £30,000 on lighting alone and it looked so futuristic, so 'out of this world' we called the nightclub Close Encounters after that famous Steven Spielberg film. You know the one, *Jaws*.

With the vast amount of money spent on the nightclub, it couldn't help but look anything other than fantastic. I wanted the very best for the club and I got it. New carpeting, fittings, decor, PA system, toilets... everything. But there was one vitally important part of the building the Brewery didn't spend money on. The roof.

It was a *flat* roof and anyone who's ever had a flat roof on their conservatory or kitchen extension knows that every few years it'll need attention otherwise tears will start to appear in it. Maybe that's why they called the place The Starlight Rooms, because there were so many holes in the roof when you looked up at night you could see Venus and Mars twinkling away. We would have sorted the roof out once we were up and running but, for the time being, it wouldn't be a problem provided it didn't rain. And on our opening night, it didn't just rain, the Heavens opened! It rained so heavily, even ducks didn't think it was nice weather. It rained so heavily... well you get the picture. And the club was due to open in a couple of hours.

The flat roof could put up little defence against the deluge of heavy rain that started to pour into the building. It had all the makings of a major disaster, for the club, for my thirty thousand pounds worth of lights... and for me! I had to do something fast. I managed to get hold of some black tar, and went up on the roof in the pouring rain, filling in all the holes and sealing the roof as best as I could. What an experience! It was the last thing I wanted to be doing on such a special night, but if I hadn't taken control of the situation before matters got any worse, we would never have been able to open the club.

It really was a case of 'all hands to the pump' as Kath and me and all our staff frantically went around the club mopping up the puddles, ensuring that the electrics were safe and making the place look presentable. Everyone in town knew the club was opening that night so we couldn't let them down. Our efforts paid off because at opening time we had loads of customers pouring through the door and no rain water pouring through the ceiling.

I can only describe the two years that followed our opening night as pure magic. The club was always packed and my comedy career really started to take off. I was so busy as a comedian I had to hire a full-time manager for the club and the person I chose was my old friend Roger Bell who had acted as roadie for me back in the 60s and Roger did a great job. He knew what it took to run a nightclub because he'd managed the Valbonne Club for Bonnie Tyler. We also had a resident DJ named Mike, who eventually took over as manager when Roger became my personal assistant.

I managed to attract some great acts to the club and the very first performers I booked were the Platters, a vocal group who had become famous in the 1950s for million-selling international hits like 'Smoke Gets In Your Eyes', 'Only You' and 'Twilight Time'. Today there are roughly two-dozen acts touring the world who call themselves the Platters (there are a similar number of Drifters around too), most of whom have no connection with the original line-up or management company, which is not surprising as the singers would now have to be in their 80s or dead!

I don't know if the Platters I booked in 1983 included any of the original members, but their name and 30-year reputation meant the club was more jam-packed than a Hartley's factory.

It was a big night for the club (*and* Port Talbot) with this legendary American group on the bill and my agent, Alan Phillips, and his wife came down to enjoy an evening of great entertainment. As I mentioned, the Platters were a vocal group, but they had their own backing musicians who had arrived in plenty of time for a band call.

I went on for twenty minutes and did my best to get everyone in a great mood. I mentioned how honoured we were that the great American group the Platters were going to appear in our club and that the audience were going to love them. I had no idea if they would, but you have to say *something*, don't you?

So now it's nearly nine o'clock and show time. The Platters' backing band walked on, looking very slick in their expensive stage suits, and got a little ripple from the audience who were anticipating the arrival of the American stars. The band did a quick tune-up and I was all ready to introduce the Platters. The only problem was, there weren't any Platters in the building. Not even one. I went around backstage looking for them. I went outside looking for them. But it was obvious that we were totally and utterly Platter-less.

Then came the phone call. "Our car's broken down, but we're getting it fixed and we should be with you by ten o'clock *latest!*" So, on I go and announce that our star attraction had broken down on the M4 but they would be with us in less than an hour. I got a huge laugh. They all thought I was joking! I heard a woman in the audience turn to her husband and say, "He's an awful boy! The Platters broken down on the M4! That's the funniest thing he's said tonight!"

The Platters' backing band walked *off,* looking very slick in their expensive stage suits. They went back to their dressing room and changed into their equally expensive leisure clothes while they waited.

The audience, most of whom by now realised I wasn't joking, were still in a good upbeat mood, drinking and listening to the music Mike the DJ was playing. But I wondered how they and I would feel if the Platters *didn't* turn up at ten o'clock. It didn't take me long to find out. One hour in fact. Because the Platters *didn't* turn up at ten o'clock. I was feeling sick and the audience were feeling no pain.

Then came the next phone call from the Platters. "We're very sorry about this, but are on the way and we'll be in Talbot Port in one hour!"

I said, "It's not Talbot Port. It's *Port Talbot!*"

There was a moment's silence down the line and then... "Make that *two* hours!"

I had a room full of people who had paid to see the Platters; yet all they were getting was disco music, pork scratchings and a selection of jokes, announcements and interruptions from me. Now I had to tell them it could be midnight before the Platters turned up. I explained to them that the Platters had apologised for the delay, but they would definitely be here, that I really appreciated their patience and that I quite understood if anyone wanted their money back. A few of them did, because it was getting very late, but 500 people remained in their seats.

Another half-hour went by and still no sign of the Platters. Then a fellah shouted out good naturedly "I hope they get here before I start work tomorrow. I'm on *two 'til ten*!" This was received by a lot of laughter, which told me the audience were still in a good mood and unbelievably patient.

The Platters eventually turned up at half-past eleven, full of apologies. They said they'd go straight on stage and because it was so late, they'd just do a few of their hits. Because I had been so worried they weren't going to appear at all, I'd had a few drinks – quite a few – to calm my nerves, so I said, "Yes, that's fine!" Frankly, I was so relieved they'd arrived, if they'd said they were only going to sing The Latvian National Anthem in Chinese while juggling two pounds of soot, I would have said, "Yes, that's fine!"

When they walked on stage they had a terrific welcome from the audience, who by now were all well away. It had been such a long night; even the teetotallers had turned to drink. The Platters went down an absolute storm, getting a wild reaction to every song. Instead of just singing a couple of songs they did forty-five minutes and everyone went home with a smile on their face. And yours truly had the biggest smile of all, because the Platters told me that because they had been so late in arriving, they wouldn't be charging me a fee! So apart from all the money we'd made behind the bar, I was also £1,500 to the good. I felt like a fish on the end of a rod. I was landed.

We brought a lot of stars to the Starlight Rooms. Bands, singers, comedians – big names who ensured that the place was packed from floor to ceiling. The late 60s and early 70s had seen the start of the cabaret boom in Britain and it continued, thankfully, for the Starlight Rooms into the 80s before a mixture of soaring prices, the success of the 'Don't Drink and Drive' campaign, the lack of big name attractions and the arrival of 'alternative comedy', killed it off.

But during the heyday of cabaret, huge American stars who would normally play venues like the London Palladium or the Royal Albert Hall, would appear for a week at a time at provincial venues like Batley Variety Club, Blazers at Windsor, the Fiesta at Sheffield and the Lakeside at Camberley. Names like Dionne Warwick, Victor Borge, Louis Armstrong, Jack Jones, Guy Mitchell, The Four Tops (the originals – not a tribute act!), Roy Orbison and Eartha Kitt. And *The Man in Black* himself, Johnny Cash, and his band appeared for a week at the late, lamented Double Diamond Club in Caerphilly.

The Starlight Rooms did well with attractions like the Syd Lawrence Orchestra, Chas n' Dave, Bernard Manning and the Real Thing, but I began to notice that the people of Port Talbot had a strange attitude. They would strongly support a new venture like the Starlight Rooms, but as soon as another venue opened, their loyalties would switch at the drop of a hat. That's not a complaint by the way, that's just an observation on the quirks of human behaviour. But what it meant for me was, after two years of doing great business, the third year was a disaster. I lost a fortune, because I was trying to chase my once-loyal customers back to the Starlight Rooms, and having found other places to spend their hard-earned money, they just wouldn't come back.

Whilst I was running the nightclub I was still gigging on a regular basis and because I was slowly becoming a bit of a 'name', I was occasionally invited to appear on big charity shows around Wales. It's always an honour to be asked onto these shows to help to raise money for a worthwhile cause by standing up and telling a load of daft jokes!

Towards the end of 1986 I appeared on a charity show – and I wish I could remember *exactly* where it was – with that fine singer, song-writer and BBC Radio Wales broadcaster Frank Hennessy, who was (and still is from time to time) lead singer with the folk group the Hennesseys. Little did I know when I agreed to take part in the show that it would turn out to be a stepping-stone to my career in radio, which in turn would make me a household name in Wales. Okay, maybe not in *your* household. But it certainly is in mine!

At that time I didn't listen to BBC Radio Wales very often (I was more of a Radio Three man!) but I knew Frank was 'Cardiff born and Cardiff bred' and had been on Red Dragon Radio before he moved to the BBC. The charity show turned out to be a good night for me and to be honest I was at a stage where I'd had very few *bad* nights. Whether this was down to the fact I was improving as a comedian or because I was becoming more well-known due to my odd appearances on TV, I can't say. But on that charity show with Frank, I went down a storm.

Now, two things could have happened after that show. Frank could have seen the audience reaction and considered me to be a rival entertainer who might end up stepping on his toes at some point, as my career progressed. Or he could have genuinely liked me and my comedy and decided to give me a leg up in the business when the opportunity arose. In the end it's all down to Lady Luck.

In any walk of life, in any business and in any career, an unexpected piece of good luck can make a huge difference. Some people don't believe in luck. Others say you make *your own* luck. Here's a little story that sums up my attitude to whatever 'luck' might be. A famous and very successful theatrical producer, who came from an impoverished background, was once interviewed by a journalist who obviously wasn't a fan of the producer's work. The journalist looked around the producer's opulent Mayfair home and, in an envious and slightly sneery manner, said, "Well, I must say you've been very lucky!" To which the producer, who had known the sort of childhood poverty and deprivation that the middle-class journalist could have no possible concept of, simply replied, "Yes, you're quite right. I am lucky. And the funny thing is, the harder I work, the luckier I get!"

That's what I believe. *The harder you work, the luckier you get.*

This talk of 'luck' brings us back to Frank. After the charity show he made a point of asking me for my telephone number and at the beginning of 1987 he rang me to ask me if I'd like to appear on another charity show, this time for Kidney Research, which was going to be held on level three of St David's Hall, Cardiff. The comedy singer/guitarist Jake Thackeray was going to be on the bill along with Frank and his band, the Hennesseys, and Frank wanted me to open the show with a ten minute spot. I immediately agreed and put the date in my book.

When I got to know Frank, I realised this was a typically kind gesture of Frank. He specifically invited me to appear on the show, because he thought it might do my career a bit of good. There were going to be a load of people in the audience from BBC Wales, including the Editor of Radio Wales, Bob Atkins, and the assistant Editor, David Peet – who is now married to Ruth Jones, the star and co-writer of *Gavin and Stacey*.

I turned up at St David's Hall all ready to do my ten minutes of jokes, which I had lovingly prepared weeks in advance – alright, I put it all together in my head in the car on the way in. When I walked through the doors of the Hall, I was met by a nervous producer who said, "Hello, Owen. Um... we've got a problem. Jake Thackeray's car has broken down on his way here from Monmouth and we have no idea when he'll get here or *if* he'll get here!"

I wanted to ask if Jake used the same driver as the Platters, but I could see from the producer's face that he was on the edge of a nervous breakdown. Some years later, after I'd worked with a variety of producers on my radio and television shows, I came to realise that producers *permanently* look like they're on the edge of a nervous breakdown. It's what keeps them healthy.

Frank Hennessey joined us and calmed the producer down by telling him that if Jake Thackeray didn't make it to the show, the Hennessys could easily extend their set from the handful of songs they were supposed to do and fill the entire second half. But with a packed audience, including those high-level BBC bods, waiting for the show to start, what they desperately needed was someone to fill the entire first half – someone able to entertain an audience for forty-five minutes.

Now I'm no genius but, apart from the Hennesseys, I was the only entertainer in the building, so my super-human sixth sense kicked in and I realised that *I* was that someone they needed to fill the entire first half. The ten minute act I had gone over in my head went straight out of the window. Thankfully, as long as I had a couple of minutes to get my head together, I didn't get flustered or nervous whenever I was asked to do more than my allotted time, even an additional thirty-five minutes, which is a heck of a lot of material. I was delighted to help out and went on, did forty-five minutes and, aware of the presence of the BBC, I kept the material squeaky clean.

The audience reaction was very positive, as was the reaction I got afterwards from Bob Atkins and David Peet, who were very complimentary about my act. I was getting used to audience members telling me they enjoyed my comedy – and the odd one who thought I was rubbish, naturally – but to get such a positive reaction from BBC honchos was something else.

Bob Atkins said, "We thought you were absolutely marvellous. You're exactly what we're looking for!" I was mystified. Why would the Editor of BBC Radio Wales be looking for an ex-pop singer, turned stand-up comic, who also ran a Port Talbot nightclub and grew his own tomatoes in his greenhouse?

He went on, "Wyn Calvin has been presenting a radio show for us on Sunday mornings called *Sounds Unforgettable*, but because he's got so many other commitments, he has to step down from the show. We don't want to cancel the programme and replace it with something else because it's very popular with Radio Wales listeners, so we're looking for someone to take over from Wyn!" I said, "Someone to take over from Wyn? Ooh. That's a tough one. Off-hand I can't think of anyone who could step into Wyn's shoes."

Bob looked at me. Then he looked at David Peet. David Peet looked at Bob. And I looked at Bob. It was like the end of *The Good, the Bad and the Ugly*, with less sweating and only half as many flies. Bob said, "We think *you* could take over from Wyn". Me? Present a radio show? I was thrilled that they'd consider me, but I had no broadcasting experience. I barely knew how to tune-in my car radio, let alone sit in a studio twiddling knobs and playing records to thousands of listeners.

Bob could sense my mixed emotions and clarified what they planned on doing. "We'd like to get you in to make a half-hour pilot radio show for us, a sort of try out, to see if it works. Just be yourself, chat a bit and play a few records. What do you think?" I told him I'd love to have a go and he said he'd be in touch, to fix up a time and date for me to make the pilot. True to his word, a week later he called me to invite me to Broadcasting House in Llandaff, Cardiff, where they would have a radio studio laid on for this 'experiment'!

On the day, not really knowing what I was letting myself in for, I was met at BBC reception by a young lady PA/researcher named Sian Roberts, who took me down to the studio. Well when I walked in, I realised immediately why they called the show a 'pilot'. It was like being inside the cockpit of a jumbo jet. There were red lights and green lights and buttons and knobs and switches and record decks and cassettes and little speakers and big speakers and microphones... I felt sick.

To coin a phrase we've recently nicked from our friends in the US of A, I was *well* outside my comfort zone. Of course they didn't expect me to work any of the equipment; I just had to introduce each record, which a studio assistant would play. Being surrounded by all this equipment in a claustrophobic, soundproof room was very daunting to a man who was used to communicating with a live audience and getting an instant reaction, but I was determined to grab this chance with both hands... which would have made it difficult for me to play records and twiddle a few knobs at the same time.

The red light came on in the studio as if I really was going out live on air and Sian cued me to start speaking... "Good morning! Owen Money here and this is Luther Van Dross with 'Always and Forever'!" It was a bit shaky but not bad for a first attempt. I'd managed to get my name, the singer's name and the title of the song correct. I was a born broadcaster! This was a piece of cake.

The cake was immediately exchanged for a slice of humble pie when I saw the expression on Sian's face and she pulled my opening piece apart in her cut-glass accent. "No, no, Owen! Stop there! You're talking to the floor! You need to be up! Up! Up! Up! Up!" Sian wanting me to be 'up' was already getting me down.

"On the radio we don't say 'Good morning!'"

"Don't we?"

"No! We say... 'Good MOR-ning!'"

"I've never said good MOR-ning in my life. If I went around Merthyr shouting out 'Good MOR-ning' to everyone, they'd call the men in white coats and have me put away!"

"This is BBC Radio Wales and we say 'Good MOR-ning!'"

This didn't feel right to me at all, so I bit my tongue and

swallowed my pride. If I'd done that the wrong way around I'd have been a goner.

"Good MOR-ning!"

"That's better! Now let's try again! And remember… "

"I know. Up! Up! Up! Up!"

"Excellent. Now… cue Owen!"

"Good morning! Owen Money here and this is…!"

"No, no, no, no, no! You're down when you should be up!"

That was it. I said, "I'm sorry, Sian. I can't pretend to talk posh like that. I couldn't keep it up for more than a minute. This is how I speak and this is what Bob Atkins heard when he saw me at St David's Hall. I don't think this is for me. But thank you very much for giving me the chance." And to Sian's astonishment, I walked out, waving 'Ta ta!' to my future in broadcasting, or so I thought.

A day or so later, David Peet, the assistant Editor, called me, wanting to know what had happened. I said "They wanted me to talk posh and I can't. You know how I speak. You heard me at the charity show!"

"Yes, yes. We obviously put you with the wrong person. Look, I'd like to give you another chance. Leave it to me and we'll bring you in again and make another pilot."

A short while after, I was invited back to the BBC to have another bite of the cherry, this time without having to put a plum in my mouth. See what I did there? I created a mildly amusing sentence using two fruit-based metaphors. Be fair! That line all by itself was worth the price of this book!

This time around, a day or so before I went into the studio again, I first had an informal meeting with my producers, Penny Arnold and Eli Williams, who were job-sharing at the time. They took me into one of the small side offices they used to have in the Radio Wales department, where you could have a private conversation. Now it's mostly open-plan, designed to give office workers space, light and the opportunity to eaves-drop on their colleagues at every available opportunity.

Eli (daughter of the famous BBC Wales broadcaster Alun Willams) and Penny knew all about my disastrous first pilot and tried to put me at my ease. They wanted to know about my own personal tastes in music and I explained that I was around in the 60s, playing in bands and listening to other bands and singers and I still loved that music, which at the time wasn't played a lot on the radio.

Having established the music element of the pilot, the girls told me that they wanted me to interview someone during the show. I thought they may have lined up a Radio Wales personality or a sporting hero for me, but instead I was to interview a lovely lady in her 90s, named May Wheway, who was a big fan of Radio Wales. Between Eli, Penny and May the three of them decided on a subject that I was going to talk to May about, which might have been Siamese cats or Welsh love spoons or those great entertainers Steele, Novak and Good for all I know. All these years later I can't remember.

I *can* remember that when I got back in the studio to make the second pilot, the first disc I 'spinned' was Bruce Willis singing 'Under the Boardwalk'. After I played it, I said something like, "Bruce Willis there, with the old Drifters hit from 1964, 'Under the Boardwalk'. Very nice, Bruce, but I gotta be honest, I prefer the original. What's that detective show he's in? Moonshining with Cyril Fletcher?" I knew it was *Moonlighting* with Cybil Shepherd, and Eli and Penny thought it was funny enough to leave in.

Then I played a record by Billy J. Kramer and the Dakotas and mentioned that I'd worked with them in the Grand Pavilion, Porthcawl, many years before and the girls thought this sort of informative-but-informal chat would be interesting to listeners – should the pilot be successful enough to lead to a series.

I introduced May Wheway and she asked me who I was

and I asked her who she was and we were away. We had a little chat and it was all very light-hearted and hopefully funny too. I had to interview someone else on the pilot, but I've done thousands of interviews since, so it's no surprise that I can't recall that one in any detail. I just hope it wasn't anyone who's famous now!

The pilot lasted half-an-hour, unlike the original which lasted half-a-minute and Eli and Penny thought it had gone well and told me that they'd really enjoyed it. The next stage was to let Bob Atkins and David Peet listen to it and whatever the decision was, one of them would let me know how I'd done.

The following week was a nightmare. Every time the phone rang I'd pick it up half-hoping and half-*not*-hoping it would be the BBC, because I knew that if I'd messed things up a second time, there was little chance of me being asked in to make a third pilot. Well, just over a week later, the call came through from Bob Atkins. He didn't tell me whether I had the job, he just asked me to come in to see him and when I walked into his office he put me out of my misery straight away. "Owen, we loved the new pilot show. And we'd like to offer you a Sunday morning programme, from 10.30 until noon!"

Owen Money had his own BBC radio show! How the hell did that happen? As I'm sure some of you have asked over the years. Okay, here's what I think led to this moment. It was all down to pure luck. The BBC happened to be actively looking for someone to replace Wyn Calvin and I had learned my craft and honed my own conversational style of comedy over many years. In other words... *Opportunity Met Experience*. If that's not *the* classic definition of what luck is, then I'm a monkey's uncle. I like my bananas with custard, by the way.

A Sunday morning show was ideal for me. People would be at home getting the dinner ready or relaxing with the papers. Perfect! Bob added, "We don't really have any specialist music shows on Radio Wales, apart from Stan Stennett's country music programme. They tell me you're a fan of 50s and 60s music."

"That's right. I used to be in bands in the 60s and worked with loads of the big stars of the time."

"Well we'd like you to feature a lot of that music on your show. And as you got on so well, I'm going to put Eli and Penny with you. They'll both be producing your show", which was great news for me.

The week before my first show I went into the BBC and Penny, Eli and me worked out a running order, picking out some great 50s and 60s tracks. Once I knew what records I'd be playing, I'd do a little bit of research about the artistes and drop the information in before and after I played the disc. There were also times when I'd throw in my own personal memories of the performer and I stuck to this format for the rest of the series.

We had Julie Stevens, who is now a Senior Producer, as our Broadcast Assistant and she used to record the shows on reel-to-reel tape and, somewhere in my house, I still have the tape of my first radio show. In fact I have the first two years of the show on tape. I'm thinking of selling them on *d*-bay, which is like e-bay, but not quite as expensive. So in May 1987, at the age of 40, Owen Money made his debut on BBC Radio Wales and twenty-three years later I still haven't been found out. Yet...!

CHAPTER ELEVEN

WE THOUGHT OF VARIOUS titles for my new series, using all the well-known sayings and song titles that included the word 'Money' and eventually came up with *Money for Nothing*, which it's still called today. Well, as my old Grannie used to say, "If it ain't fixed, why break it?" She was a lovely lady, but easily confused.

On that first show I was surrounded by a great team, all willing me on to do well. Apart from the engineer, I had Julie Stevens as my Broadcast Assistant, and Penny and Eli as my Producers. As the studio clock ticked the seconds away to ten-thirty, I quickly checked my equipment was all working (I told you once, don't make up your own jokes!), the red light came on and I was broadcasting live to the nation!

My introductory music was, as it is now, 'Money' but in those days I played the Beatles version. I faded the intro music, said "Good morning! My name's Owen Money, live on BBC Radio Wales and this is 'Money, Money, Money' by Abba" and I pressed the button to play the track. But I was so nervous, instead of releasing my finger, I kept it on the button, so nothing happened! Silence ruled the airwaves. I jumped in and said, "It's not working!" released my finger and as the song started, I shouted out over the opening lyrics, "It's working now!"

What a start to my first show. I felt terrible, sure that any Radio Wales listeners who were still bravely tuned-in at that point must be thinking, "Who's this comedian?"

I'm glad it wasn't a half-hour show, because with 90 minutes stretching out ahead of me, I began to settle down a little and took my time over pressing buttons and knobs. Before every record I'd make a reference to the performers, maybe giving out some little-known fact about them, or relate a funny anecdote about the time I worked with them. About half-way through the show, a funny thing happened. After I gave out the show's phone number, people started calling in, asking for dedications and making comments. Comments like, "Who's this comedian?"

They were complimentary on the whole, saying they liked the music and in fact May Wheway, the lady who helped me with my pilot show, came on the line to wish me well. Then, suddenly, it was noon and the show was over. Everyone 'behind the glass' was elated, saying they thought it had all gone well. I was pretty happy too. I'd managed to keep a radio show going for one and a half hours, with only the occasional glitch. I didn't think of myself as a broadcaster, even though I had my own radio show. I was a comedian who was lucky enough to go on the radio once a week as a sort of paid hobby. When I say 'paid', the money the BBC paid me wasn't very much, but I would have paid them to host my own show!

Traditionally (but there are notable exceptions of course), radio doesn't pay anywhere near as well as television. Which is why many radio performers, once they have built up a fan base, move across to TV.

Money aside, one of the great things about being on the radio on a regular basis is the exposure it gives you. It gets your name known quickly and if you happen to be a performer as well as a presenter, it can increase the size of the fees you charge for live appearances in clubs and theatres. And it didn't take me long to discover the power of radio; in fact it only took me the time it takes to drive from the BBC studios in Cardiff to Aberdare.

On the afternoon of the Sunday that I began my radio career, I was booked to play in the Senator Windows golf day at Aberdare Golf Club. I was playing with a friend of mine, who is no longer with us, Dave Jenkins, and as I got out of the car he came over to me and said, "I listened to you on the radio this morning. You were fab'less!" Then someone else came over to me and said they'd heard me. I was knocked out. I had two listeners! Then when I got on the first tee, Colin Price was standing there and with a big smile on his face – well I think it was a smile, it could have been wind – he said, "Here he is, boys! The Welsh Wogan! Why don't you work on the radio full-time and pack in the comedy? That'll stop you pinching all my gags!"

After that first day I had so much to learn about broadcasting. For example, how to play the records.

In 1987, although CDs were on sale alongside cassettes and albums, we were still using vinyl and the BBC sent me on a week's course, learning, amongst other things, the very delicate method of lining up the record and the needle at the right place so that the exact second I stopped my introduction, the song started immediately.

I quickly learned how to mix from one turntable to another and work the desk – meaning that, not only did I find out what all the knobs and buttons and switches were for, I also learned how to use them! I didn't have to rely on the team 'behind the glass' the whole time. I always had a selection of cartridges to play in each show, a mixture of trails for upcoming BBC shows and various 'stings' or 'intros' to the news, travel and weather items that are part of every radio show.

Mentioning items like turntables and cartridges makes it sound like I was broadcasting during the War, but in the late 80s that's what every radio studio in the land used. Today's radio shows have dispensed with vinyl, cassettes and CDs and the music is supplied via a computer. And, no doubt, one day broadcasters like me will also be replaced by machines.

But it wouldn't be the same having a dedication read out by a Dalek, would it? "ATTENTION! WE... WOULD... LIKE... TO WISH... OUR MAM... A SPEEDY RECOVERY... AND WOULD LIKE TO THANK... THE STAFF... OF MORRISTON HOSPITAL... FOR ALL... THEIR... HELP...

ESPECIALLY HER DOCTOR!! (PAUSE) DID YOU SAY... DOCTOR? EXTERMINATE! EXTERMINATE!"

I didn't have a contract with Radio Wales and they didn't tell me how many weeks I'd be on the air. It was all a bit open-ended really, which suited me. Being involved with a large media organisation like the BBC with so many employees was all new to me of course and although I already knew Frank Hennessey (and have never forgotten how he managed to get me seen by the BBC bosses), because I only went in on a Sunday for a long time, I didn't meet or socialise with the established BBC Wales broadcasters like Roy Noble, Vincent Kane, Chris Stuart and Mike Flynn who were on air Monday to Friday.

Julie would phone me on a Wednesday with the running order, so I could familiarise myself with it, and then all day Thursday I'd write my links for between the records and look up interesting facts and information about the songs and performers. Then on Sunday morning, I'd turn up and do the show.

This was the pattern for the next few years, until I was transferred to the BBC's small studio in Swansea – there was no transfer fee payable – which meant that I had no contact with *any* other BBC employee! It didn't cause me any problems, in fact, as I was living in Neath then; it was easier to get to Swansea and I could enjoy an extra five minutes in bed.

I was still running the Starlight Rooms, which was losing money every week. I decided to get out of the nightclub game, managed to sell it and bought a pub in Tonna called the Whittington Arms. It was run by my niece Nicola and her husband Mark, while my wife Kath did a lot of the cooking, but I didn't ever spend much time there. My heart wasn't really in it and by now, with my live gigs and radio work, I was getting better known.

Colin Stevens of HTV called me one day and told me

that they were making a one-hour special with Tom Jones and wondered if I'd be prepared to warm-up the audience, prior to the recording, just a short spot to get them all in a good mood before Tom came out. It was paid work, it was a chance to be seen by television executives and it was also an opportunity to work with the great man from Pontypridd.

When I got to the studios, Colin asked me to do forty minutes which, I found out later, is a long time to warm-up an audience. Most professional warm-up artistes are asked to do fifteen or twenty minutes and then be on stand-by throughout the evening to go out and entertain the audience between set-ups or if, as they invariably do, technical problems bring the show to a halt. But at the time I didn't know this, so happily went out and did forty minutes. When the show started recording, I got out of the way and watched Tom performing. What an easy gig.

Well it *was* until Tom, clad in a leather suit that fitted him so tightly around the crotch area you could almost see what religion he was, made one of his famously energetic moves in the middle of a song and then suddenly stopped his performance and raised his hand in the air to halt the band. He was obviously unhappy about something and the audience didn't know what was happening – until Tom shouted "I've split my bloody pants!" and revealed a great big tear in his trousers, to huge laughs and squeals of delight from the females in the audience. You might remember seeing that clip on Denis Norden's *It'll Be All Right On the Night*.

Tom went off, surrounded by wardrobe girls and producers and goodness knows how many people from his entourage and I got called on to the floor to keep the audience entertained while, what I thought would be, a quick repair job was done to Tom's trousers. I'd already given them forty minutes of gags and tried to remember which ones I'd told. There's nothing worse for a comedian to tell a joke and then hear the cry of, "Heard it!" from some wag in the audience.

Luckily, I had several fall guys I could take the mickey out of in the fine shape of the renowned Treorchy Male Voice Choir who were there to provide backing for Tom on a couple of numbers. I managed to milk humour out of the choir for as long as I could, all the time waiting for someone to interrupt me at some point and tell me that Tom was on his way back to the studio. But there was no sign of him, so I had to back into my act and hope I didn't duplicate any jokes.

After I'd told every gag I could remember, even going back to stuff I'd heard in the playground when I was six, Tom Jones came back, the show restarted and I melted into the studio shadows, hoping Tom wouldn't have any more leather 'wardrobe malfunctions'. The 'short' warm-up spot I had been booked for had ended-up as a comedy marathon. But, as with my extended performance at the Kidney Research charity show, it was worth the effort because a few weeks later, out of the blue I received a call from Peter Elias Jones from HTV Wales, asking me if I'd be interested in making a television pilot.

By now I was as familiar with the ins and outs of pilots as an RAF medical officer. The pilot they had in mind for me was going to be called 'The Tom and Shirl and Owen Money Show', and please bear with me because it's a little bit complicated. The show they wanted me to make would be a *real* show about an *imaginary* show starring Tom Jones and Shirley Bassey and I was playing the warm-up man for the *imaginary* show... in my *real* show. Clear, so far?

The floor manager of 'The Tom and Shirl and Owen Money Show' was played by Welsh actor Michael (sometimes known as Meic) Povey, who had appeared in several episodes of the original series of *Minder* as Detective Constable 'Taff' Jones. The producer was played by the legendary Nicholas Parsons who, apart from hosting the long-running Radio Four series *Just a Minute* without hesitation, repetition or deviation for over forty years, had also been the definitive straight man to two of Britain's greatest television comedians – Benny Hill and Arthur Haynes. So you can see that HTV had pulled out all the stops to give this pilot of mine every possible chance to fly.

The idea behind the show – obviously based on what happened on the night I had to fill in for Tom Jones' absence – was that Tom and Shirley were having problems getting to the studio, so I had to entertain the audience until the stars put in an appearance. I'm not sure if there was a script written for the show and if there was, who wrote it, but it basically consisted of me telling my own jokes to the audience – who were supposedly waiting for the 'Tom and Shirl show' to start – while Michael Povey and Nicholas Parsons came up to me from time to either tell me that Tom and Shirley were delayed, or to assure me they would be out any minute. The show went well, the audience had a great time and the HTV bosses seemed pleased with my performance.

There's an old adage amongst comedians that goes something like, "If you ever get unexpected laughs, check your flies!" I hadn't checked mine before I started the show and it was only after the cameras had been switched off and the audience had left that I discovered my flies had been open throughout the whole of the recording. And nobody had noticed! What a blow to my ego.

If Tom Jones had walked out onto the studio floor with his flies undone, he would have caused a riot. The women in the audience would have been in a wild frenzy of sexual excitement. Owen Money walked out onto the studio floor with his flies undone and not one bugger noticed.

I was thrilled when HTV told me that they liked the pilot show and that they were going to give me a series, which was going to be called *The Owen Money Show*. Apparently they'd thought up that title several years before, but couldn't use it until they found there was a comedian living in Wales called Owen Money. Just think, if my name was Reg Jenkins I would never have been offered *The Owen Money Show*.

Obviously we couldn't make six shows based on the format of the pilot, because that would have been boring and repetitious. So, apart from me telling gags, they wanted me to appear in comedy sketches. Well, they were sketches, but whether they contained any comedy is not for me to say. There were loads of them too, all written by Gareth Williams, including a weekly parody of the Australian soap *Neighbours*, which we called 'Butties', set in south Wales rather than Ramsey Street and I had a small cast of regulars around me including Michael Povey and Menna Trussler. I'm reminded of the joke that was going around at the time: "Do you know why *Neighbours* is shown twice a day? Because you can't bloody believe it the first time!"

HTV gave *The Owen Money Show* a big launch and managed to give it a great early-evening slot, which isn't always easy to achieve for regional television programmes. Most regionally-produced shows have to be content with late-night slots, so they don't upset the majority of viewers who want to see the network shows that everyone else in Britain is watching. Even big audience winners like my two hugely successful BBC Wales series, *Just up your Street* and *Money in the Bank*, which I'll be dealing with in a later chapter, were broadcast after 10.30 at night.

To be honest, I wasn't altogether happy with my first TV series and the reaction from critics and the public was, to put it kindly, 'mixed'. Maybe I wasn't ready for television. Maybe the sketches could have been sharper and funnier. Whatever the case and wherever the blame lay, let's just say the series didn't take the world of comedy by storm. Nobody at HTV said, "Sorry Owen, that's it, you've blown your chances" and I didn't feel I'd let anyone down. But if I was going to do any more television for them, it would have to be an entirely different format, one that I felt more comfortable with. In a way I was lucky that the show was only seen in Wales, because many comedy performers have been given their own network series before they were ready and the critics have crucified them.

I suppose every performer who comes into the business has ambitions to star in their own television series, although these days you stand more chance of getting one if you're a chef or a gardener, but having your own series isn't necessarily the key to a long career in show business. Television has always been notorious for chewing-up personalities and performers and spitting them out. Any aspiring performers, busting to get on the telly-box, should bear this in mind. There is no better example of this than the case of Simon Dee. In 1967 he was the darling of Saturday night BBC television, chatting with pop stars and Hollywood actors on his talk show, watched by eighteen million every week. But his reign at the top only lasted until 1970 – three years, for those of you who are rubbish at sums – when, a few months after he took his show from the BBC to London Weekend Television, he was sacked. Off the air. Out of the door. Gone! Why? Well it depends on who you believe. Either he had the push because he was arrogantly making outrageous demands of his new employers... or, David Frost, who had shows on London Weekend Television on Friday, Saturday and Sunday nights – and had shares in LWT – saw him as a threat.

Simon Dee's fall was spectacular. Literally weeks after being 'the' cool and hip talk-show host, he was signing on at Fulham Labour Exchange. He found a job driving buses for a while, spent 28 days in Pentonville Prison for non-payment of rates and when he passed away in August 2009 at the age of 74, he had been a forgotten name for almost 40 years.

But sometimes performers do get given a second chance. You might be familiar with what one cynical reviewer, unimpressed by Eric and Ernie's first ever venture into TV comedy on BBC Television in 1954 in a series called *Running*

Wild, famously said about them – "Television is the box they buried Morecambe & Wise in". Ouch!

The great comedians were so upset by the vicious reaction to the series by the critics, they begged the head of the BBC to pull the show half-way through its run! Just a few years later they switched to ITV; they were supplied with quality scripts by Sid Green and Dick Hills (remember 'Boom, Ooh, Yatta-Ta-Ta'?) and became household names by the early 60s. When they became established stars and moved to the BBC they became the stuff of television legend. That first series could well have killed their career, because at that time they just weren't ready for television.

Here's another, slightly more recent, example of what television can and can't do for your career. In the 1980s, a young comedy impressionist named Paul Squire, proclaimed as being the next big thing in comedy, arrived on the scene and was given not one, not two, not three, but *four* series (one on BBC One and three on ITV and all in prime-time slots) which were all received with indifference by unimpressed viewers. To be fair to Paul, at that time there were entertainment shows and game shows and talk shows, hosted by big name comics and singers on almost every night of the week (hands up who remembers that 'golden age'?), so however good he was, he suffered by comparison. Almost as quickly as he arrived, he disappeared and now we can barely remember what Paul Squire looked like, proving, I think, that it's not television that can make you a star – it's the public.

Not surprisingly, after my HTV series finished, I didn't get dozens of television producers beating a path to my door, offering me another contract. Working on my first series did give me an invaluable insight into the technical side of making television programmes and I was very grateful to have been given the chance to get my face seen all around Wales. And although there were no more television appearances in the pipeline, I did get offered my first role in a pantomime since the one I did at the Swansea Grand, with Tomfoolery for the 1979/1980 season.

From the 9th of December 1989 to the 20th of January 1990, I played the part of the bo'sun in *Robinson Crusoe* at the New Theatre, Cardiff, along with a fantastic line-up of performers: Hope and Keen; Russell Grant; Ruth Madoc; John Nettles (now known around the world for playing Inspector Barnaby in the long-running *Midsomer Murders* series, but then famous for playing the Jersey policeman *Bergerac*) and comedian / impressionist / singer / magician and all round show-off Andrew O'Connor, who went on to create Objective Television, which makes hit programmes like *Peep Show*, *Star Stories*, *100 Greatest Magic Tricks* and Derren Brown's mind-blowing series and specials.

Andrew and I shared a dressing room for the run of the panto and we became great friends. Apart from being a media mogul, he's now directing films and you may remember his debut feature, the comedy *Magicians* that came out a couple of years ago. I'm told he still has my phone number, although funnily enough, he hasn't offered me a part in any of his films or television shows. Yet...!

Robinson Crusoe was a real star-studded panto with plenty of money spent on the sets, props and costumes by the producers E & B/Paul Elliott. I wouldn't say the part of the bo'sun was small, but they didn't give me a script to learn. They just gave me two sheets of paper. On one sheet it said "Hello!" and on the other, you guessed it, "Goodbye!" Naturally I was very careful not to mix these pages up; otherwise I might have walked on stage and made a fool of myself. And that would never do!

The truth is that once the 'Saucy Sal' had sailed off to look for treasure at the end of act one, with the bo'sun on board, you never saw me again. I couldn't even get out of my costume and go home, because I had to be there for the walk-down at the end. I'd sit in the dressing room for an hour, reading the print off my newspaper, waiting for my call to go back on stage in the show's closing minutes. After a week or two of this, I got so bored, I offered to play the part of the gorilla that Robinson and his chums encounter on the island in the second act. I was glad to have something more to do in the show, but that gorilla suit was years old and smelt so bad; I'm convinced that the last person to wear it was a real gorilla.

By the time the pantomime ended I was pretty much established on BBC Radio Wales, but as I wasn't under any sort of contract with the BBC, I was free to make programmes for 'the other side', namely HTV, provided of course they didn't clash with my radio show.

Ironically, the next series that HTV offered me, entitled *Ready Money*, was based on the fact that on my radio show I was always coming up with bits of interesting information about the performers of the 50s and 60s whose records I played. That was partly because I did a bit of research but mainly because I loved the music and was already a bit of an authority on the songs and stars of those decades.

Ready Money was a nostalgia-based quiz show which made good use of the many hours of black and white film and tape that were stored in the HTV vaults, left over from the days of the previous company that held the ITV franchise in Wales, Television Wales & the West, better known as TWW. We made twenty-four shows and they went out in a great slot for family viewing, five o'clock on Sunday afternoons. Not only that, twelve of them were repeated the following year, so I had a lot of television exposure. The great thing for me was, as it was a game show, I didn't have to crack a load of jokes every week using up material I did in the clubs.

When *Ready Money* finished I didn't know whether I'd be offered any more TV work so I concentrated on my successful BBC Radio Wales show and my club work. I then received a phone call from Menna Richards, who was then second-in-command at HTV Wales – a lady who would continue to be involved with my television career when she eventually became the Controller of BBC Wales.

Menna asked me to pop in to see her at the HTV studios at Culverhouse Cross, Cardiff, and when we met a couple of days later, she told me that *Ready Money* wouldn't be recommissioned and asked me what sort of show I'd like to do. I wanted to make a pilot for a different type of programme because, while I didn't want to appear ungrateful, I knew that my first comedy series hadn't really done me any favours. Menna agreed with me and quickly made a studio and crew available so that I could make the pilot show that I wanted. It was very generous of Menna and I was very grateful that she was giving me what was, in effect, a second chance to establish my character on television. I contacted several performers like Rosser & Davies, Powys & Jones, Wendy Kane and the pilot we made was a sort of hybrid sit-com and a chat show, called *A Night Out with Money*.

While I waited to hear what the verdict was on the television pilot, changes were happening at BBC Radio Wales. Out went the old Editor and in came new Editor Megan Stuart, who made the odd decision to move me from my Sunday morning slot, for which I had built up a large, loyal audience, to a slot on Saturday mornings. To be fair, I was also given an occasional series on Sunday afternoons called *Golden Money*, but that wasn't as open-ended as my Saturday show. It was only on the air for so many weeks before being replaced by other shows. Then I would take over for a few more weeks and so on, which is not the sort of deal that fills an entertainer and broadcaster with confidence.

I honestly think that if Megan Stuart hadn't left the BBC to have a baby, she would have shown me the door when the first opportunity arose. Which of course, as the Editor of BBC Radio Wales, she was perfectly entitled to do. People talk about the insecurity of being in show business and that insecurity is as much a part of broadcasting as it is in film, television and theatre. Very few broadcasters, especially outside network radio, are safeguarded by rock-solid contracts that guarantee them continuous employment for three, five or ten years work.

Saturday mornings had traditionally been pretty bleak, listener-wise, for Radio Wales, perhaps because of the competition from Radios One and Two and the increasing popularity of Saturday morning television shows like *Tiswas*, *Swap Shop*, *Saturday Superstore* and *Going Live*, all of which were enjoyed by adults as well as the children they were aimed at.

But as it turned out, if there *had* been any motivation behind the decision to move me from Sunday to Saturday mornings, it totally back-fired. Because not only did my regular listeners follow me across to my new show, they were joined by a growing number of new fans so, as the weeks went by, my audience figures – and the Radio Wales Saturday morning figures – actually increased.

As it happens, the lady who took over the Editor's role, Gaynor Vaughan-Jones, was a fan of mine and she was well aware how popular my Saturday morning show had become. I've had quite a few editors since then and I still haven't been found out, because at the time of writing this book, I'm still broadcasting on Saturday mornings and Sunday afternoon to a large, loyal and enthusiastic audience, many of whom take the time and trouble to come and see me when I'm performing live, in pantomime, doing a solo stand-up spot or with my band, the Soul Sharks. Having this 'army' of fans is great for me as a performer and it doesn't do BBC Radio Wales any harm either.

I'm not being big-headed (honest!) when I say my Saturday show is probably the most listened-to couple of hours on BBC Radio Wales, thanks to my loyal listeners – Wally and Gladys Jones of 863 Gasworks Terrace, Lower Treharris.

I did eventually progress from **BBC Radio Wales** to **BBC Wales Television**, where apart from making several music documentaries, I also hosted two incredibly successful series – the star-studded entertainment show *Money in the Bank* and the long-running talent show *Just up your Street*. But the irony is, I wouldn't have been offered these shows by the **BBC** if I hadn't already enjoyed some television success with two series of the entertainment show *A Night Out with Money*, which was made by HTV Wales (now ITV One Wales).

A Night Out with Money, like the shows I went on to make for **BBC Wales** a couple of years later, went out just after ten-thirty on Friday evenings and regularly slaughtered the viewing figures for whatever programme **BBC Wales Television** tried to put on against it. I believe there was one Friday evening when my show attracted half the available audience in Wales. So I must have been doing something right.

I'm telling you this purely to illustrate why the **BBC** bosses weren't very happy when callers to my Saturday morning show on **BBC Radio Wales** regularly used to praise the TV programme they'd seen me in the night before... over on 'the other side'. I'll explain the full story of why and how my television career moved from HTV to BBC Wales later in the book.

By the way, if you're reading this in a bookshop and you've got this far into it but still haven't decided to purchase it, here's some advice – it's people like you who cause bookshops to close... *so go and pay for it, you cheapskate!*

My life is studded with coincidences and chance meetings, and all my successful television series since 1998, particularly the talent show *Just up your Street*, have links to the man who helped me to write this book – Alan Wightman. You won't know him, because he prefers to stay in the background. And if you saw the state of him, you'd understand why. I'm not saying he's ugly, but when he went to the pictures to see the 2010 remake of *Nightmare on Elm Street* the audience thought Freddy Krueger was making a personal appearance! And fat! My God, he's so huge he has his own post code. It's alright. Alan is great at taking a joke. It's *writing* the buggers he has trouble with...

I was first introduced to Alan in January 1995 by Joe Pasquale when Joe and I were in our third pantomime together, *Aladdin* at the Grand Theatre, Swansea, which, like the previous two we'd been in, was a superb production by Britain's premier panto producers, Qdos Entertainment, run by Nick Thomas and Jon Conway.

At the time I was looking for a comedy writer – hopefully somebody local – who could supply me with gags for the first series of *A Night Out with Money* which was going to be made by HTV Wales the following spring. Despite the fact that Alan lived in Newport, south Wales, I'd never heard of him, but Joe assured me that Alan was an experienced writer who had penned material for many star comedians including Joe himself and had been the Script Associate on the 1993 Royal Variety Show which had catapulted Joe to stardom.

Joe knew Alan and his work well because, at the time, Joe and Alan shared the same agent/manager (Michael Vine) and Alan went on to be Script Associate on *The Crazy World of Joe Pasquale* special for London Weekend Television at the end of 1996 and was the author of the best-selling *The Big Thick Joe Pasquale Book*, which is *still* available from Amazon for the bargain price of 99 pence – so no wonder it was a best-seller! As Alan lived less than an hour away from Swansea, I thought it was worthwhile Joe setting-up a meeting with him at the Grand. If it turned out he wasn't on my comedy wavelength, if he was a fan of 'alternative' comedy for example, then I'd have to look elsewhere.

Joe phoned Alan, told him about my upcoming television series and invited him to meet me at the Grand Theatre for an informal chat. A couple of days later, Alan jumped on an Inter-

City train (I think he might have even *paid* for his ticket) and came down to Swansea. I can't pretend to remember much about our first conversation, but I do recall discovering that we shared two mutual interests: the music of the sixties (in particular the Beatles) and chips. You may laugh, but I'll have you know that throughout history, many successful working relationships have been built on far shakier foundations. Fifteen years later he's still scribbling the occasional page of jokes for me. And quite a few of them are reasonably funny.

The first time Alan met me in my dressing room was just before a matinee and I was dressed in a rainbow-hued frock and a red wig, sat in front of a mirror, applying bright mauve eye-shadow which clashed with my bright red lipstick. But he didn't bat an eyelid. As he said at the time, "I've seen far worse, Owen. I've worked with Phyllis Diller. And you're *much* prettier."

In retrospect it's funny that he and I should have met during a pantomime run because a few years later when I was setting up the Owen Money Theatre Company, I asked Alan if he would be the company's 'writer-in-residence' and create our pantomime scripts. I knew he was capable of writing a full two hour show because by then he had already written pantomime scripts for Qdos Entertainment, including the 1996/97 production for the Swansea Grand, *Robin Hood*, starring Little and Large and Ruth Madoc. Which is about as contrived a way as I can possibly think of to set up the next chapter, which is all about the greatest family entertainment form of them all – pantomime.

Altogether now... "Oh yes it is!"

CHAPTER TWELVE

PANTOMIME
Three things are required of Christmas time.
Plum pudding, beef and pantomime.
Folks could resist the former two...
Without the latter, none could do!

(From an old pantomime playbill)

LET ME GET DOWN off the fence and say this as loud and as clearly as I possibly can to those of you, whether you're in or out of show business, who have *never* seen a professional pantomime, have no regard for pantomime and think that pantomime is just a load of tired old jokes and routines performed by third-rate performers who couldn't get work at any other time of the year... you're *so* wrong!

And let me also say to those people who might look down their snooty noses at this ancient and enduring art form and think it's distasteful because (as tradition demands), regardless of the title of the pantomime, it will always feature middle-aged men dressed as old women in outrageous clothes and pretty young girls dressed as virile young boys wearing tights and thigh-high boots... you're *so* wrong!

I defy anyone – man, woman or estate agent – to sit amongst a pantomime audience, surrounded by families roaring with laughter at the silly slapstick, witty wordplay, barmy banter and tricky tongue-twisters that are the foundation stones of a successful pantomime, and not emerge from the theatre feeling the world is a slightly better place than it was before the houselights went down, the curtain went up and the band went into their opening number.

A good, solid professional pantomime never pretends to

be anything other than a couple of hours of out-and-out fun for all the family, set in a colourful fairytale land where the cast of loveably eccentric characters, particularly the star comedian, know enough about the *real* world to enable them to make a constant stream of jokes and humorous references about it. If it all works, the grown-ups in the audience will forget about their everyday worries, either because they'll be enjoying hearing their children and grandchildren laughing or because they themselves are helpless with laughter. And let me say to anyone who thinks that we don't need more laughter in this world these days... you're *so* wrong!

Like my old pal, the legendary Stan Stennett – who, at the time of writing, still tours around Wales every Christmas in his own fun-packed pantos featuring his perennially popular characters Billy and Bonzo (that dog must be the oldest in captivity!) which Stan also produces and directs – I'm a committed champion of value-for-money family pantomimes. Yes, only last week I heard someone say, "That Owen Money really ought to be committed".

But do be aware that there are still some cheap and cheerless pantomime companies that tour around the UK in November and December, although I'm not going to name them because my solicitor's hourly rate is far too high for me to take the risk. But what I *will* say is, you should be wary of any panto company that descends on your town to appear at a local theatre for 'one day only' with threadbare scenery and an even more threadbare (and often far too crude) script. The company will cram in a couple of performances of their truly amateurish production before grabbing their share of the takings, piling back into their van and heading for the next unsuspecting town down the motorway. Don't say I didn't warn you.

The best pantomimes are put together with care, written with family audiences in mind and while they don't necessarily have to be huge spectacles with breath taking

3-D sequences and huge television stars in the principal roles, they should always have a bit of money thrown at them so that the scenery sparkles and the colourful costumes and props always look like they're brand new, even at the end of a long run.

Despite my love of pantomime, there's no doubt that it can sometimes be hard work for performers, especially people like me who won't see 29 again, particularly on days when you have to do two or three performances. And because pantomimes are always staged in the coldest, bleakest and most germ-active time of the year, there's also the issue of coughs and colds and flu amongst the company. Inevitably one of the performers will come in one day and start sneezing in a shared dressing room and before you know it, the theatre will be echoing with sneezes and coughs from all the other dressing rooms.

Not that you must ever let a runny nose and a sore throat prevent you from going on stage twice a day to entertain the audience who have paid good money to see you, maybe having bought their tickets five or six months before. A visit to a pantomime could well be the highlight of some children's Christmas, so I have always done my best not to let an audience down. I've gone on stage to clown around as Wishee Washee or Buttons, suffering from a raging temperature, sweating like a good 'un, and desperate to climb under the duvet and sleep for a couple of days. But while I was on stage and heard the audience laughing and shouting, I was able to keep going, even if my singing voice sounded like a strangled frog on helium. Who said "That could only be an improvement?"

While I'm talking about the risk of catching a cold during the run of a panto, that wonderful actor and brilliant raconteur Victor Spinetti doesn't appear in pantomime so much these days, but for years he was one of the greatest Abanazar's in Pantoland – and he rarely suffered from coughs or colds during the run of a show.

When he appeared with Welsh entertainer Mike Doyle in *Aladdin* at the New Theatre, Cardiff, in the early 1990s, after the matinee performance, Mike and the other cast members, including sit-com stalwarts Vicki Michelle and Jeffrey Holland, would go down to the stage door and sign autographs and have a brief chat with their fans. Meanwhile Victor would remain in the dressing room he shared with Mike, eating his tea and relaxing before the evening show. When Mike got to know Victor a little better he plucked up the nerve to ask his far more experienced co-star why he never joined the cast at the stage door.

Victor, who is one of the nicest, funniest and most approachable stars you're ever likely to meet, explained, "You see the thing is, Mike, I usually love meeting the public and will happily sign autographs at any other time of the year. But during a panto run, all it takes is one child to sneeze in my direction and the little bugger will give me a cold that I won't be able to get rid of until Whit bloody Monday!" He then paused for a moment before asking, "Did I ever tell you I knew John Lennon?"

What's so special about pantomime? Well, as someone once put it, many years ago...

George Bernard Shaw can't write it.

Laurence Olivier can't act it.

Benjamin Gigli can't sing it.

Margaret Fonteyn can't dance it.

And there's no other art form like it...

How's that for starters?

Although I love the sound of children screaming, "He's behind you!" at the tops of their voices, it always amuses me that by thirty minutes or so into the show, all the adults have dropped any pretence of only being there 'because the children wanted to see the show' and are joining in just as enthusiastically.

I've produced, directed and performed in dozens of

pantomimes over many years and I still enjoy the rehearsals, the mess-ups, coming out with ad-libs when things go wrong (which they do, regularly) the camaraderie of working with an ensemble cast, the competitive backstage games and meeting the children at the stage door after the show and seeing the excited expressions on their faces – all the time conscious of the fact that whatever the pantomime is, we always have a story to tell, with a beginning, middle and an end. Though not always necessarily in that same order!

As 1990 was rapidly coming to a close, I was gearing up to appear in my third pantomime – my second as a solo performer – this time at the theatre where I'd appeared in my first panto with Tomfoolery, the Grand, Swansea. The show was *Snow White and the Seven Dwarves* and before you ask, no, I didn't play 'Dopey'! In fact I was making my debut as the Dame. Yes, every day I dressed up in outrageous frocks, multi-coloured tights, huge wigs, enormous ear-rings and red and white spotted frilly knickers, with bright orange make-up and ruby lips. Then once I got out of my car and into the theatre, I'd change into my Dame costume!!

I was again surrounded by some big showbiz names, amongst them the beautiful actress and ex-model Linda Lusardi; the roguish star of *Men Behaving Badly* and the voice of Bob the Builder – Neil Morrissey; the comedian Stu 'Ooh, I could crush a grape!' Francis, from *Crackerjack*; Nikki Kelly from *Hi De Hi!* and, playing two of the dwarves, musical double-act the Mini-Tones.

The Mini-Tones were made up of two vertically-challenged performers – Jack Purvis, who sadly died after a car accident in 1997, and the 3' 8" tall Kenny Baker, who was famous for playing the little robot R2D2 in the *Star Wars* films – a role he would go on to reprise in the three prequels. But long before Kenny got into films like *Time Bandits* and *The Elephant Man*, he and Jack Purvis were big, if that's the right word, on the cabaret scene, with their music and comedy act, which lasted thirty years.

I don't mean *their* act lasted thirty years. Plainly that would be ridiculous. Well it would require a *massive* commitment on the part of their audience, who'd have to make all sorts of arrangements (organising baby-sitters, giving up work and sacrificing holidays, cancelling Christmas get-togethers with friends and family etc.) to cover the three decades they spent watching two very short men playing instruments, larking about and falling over. Not to mention the enormous repertoire of tunes the Mini-Tones would have to learn. I meant *they worked as a double act for thirty years*, before, during and after Kenny's involvement with the original Star Wars trilogy – which he managed to get Jack involved in too. So, although the Tones were small in stature, in view of the fact they had appeared in three of the most successful films of all time, they were easily the biggest stars in the panto!

The pantomime ran from the 19th of December 1990 until the 3rd of February 1991, which gave me the opportunity to really establish myself as a pantomime Dame. During the run, the actor Owen Teale came to see the show with his then-girlfriend, Dilys Watling, daughter of British acting stalwart Jack Watling. It seemed to me that Dilys and her sister Deborah – who were both real lookers – were never off the telly in the 70s and 80s, popping up in loads of sit-coms and thrillers.

Swansea-born Owen Teale was already well-established as a stage actor when he came to see the pantomime and has since worked for the Royal Shakespeare Company and appeared in loads of films (he was in the remake of the 1977 horror film *It's Alive!* in 2009), as well as guest-starring in TV series like *Lewis* and *Torchwood*. Anyway, after the show, Owen and Dilys came around to see me and raved about my performance. Mind you it was a bit confusing, with two Owens in the crowded dressing room. Sometimes the conversation sounded like this...

"Will you sign this for me please, Owen?"

"Certainly!"

"No, not you, him!"

"Sorry!"

"Fancy coming for a bite to eat, Owen?"

"Yes, that'd be nice."

"Not you, him!"

"Sorry!"

"Can you lend me a tenner for a taxi, Owen?"

"Which Owen are you talking to now?"

"You! So *can* you lend me a tenner?"

"Sorry!"

So through my involvement with pantomimes in Swansea and Cardiff, I was starting to work and socialise with performers who were well known, not just in Wales but throughout Britain. When I was in panto with John Nettles in Cardiff, we'd go for a drink or a bite to eat in Henry's Café Bar across the road from the New Theatre between performances and have some fascinating conversations.

John, like a lot of straight actors, is a big admirer of comedians. Actors can't understand how comedians can stand on a stage, all alone, armed with just a microphone, a head full of jokes and a rock-solid confidence in their own ability to make people laugh. When actors go on stage they're always in disguise, playing a character. They never reveal their true selves. On the other hand, comedians can't understand how an actor can learn a script for a play and go on stage night after night, reciting the same lines over and over for maybe a year or more.

Being unable to ad-lib or change the lines occasionally in order to get a laugh would drive a comedian insane! It's only in a pantomime that these two worlds, these two disciplines if you like, can complement each other and by the end of the run, the actor and the comedian have learned a few new skills from each other.

John had been in pantomime with one of his comedy heroes, Les Dawson, at the Wimbledon Theatre a couple of years earlier. Les was notorious for having a drink or two, usually double whiskies to 'steady his nerves' before stepping on to the stage and, no matter how many he knocked back, it never affected his performance, which was always superbly funny. He was one of *the great* pantomime dames, along with Terry Scott, Arthur Askey and 'The Welsh Prince of Laughter' – Wyn Calvin. The great dames never played the part as a drag queen. They all played the part as a man in a frock and made this plain to the audience from their first entrance, which is the funniest and truest way.

At the end of one Saturday evening performance, Michael Aspel appeared from the wings, hiding, out of Les Dawson's eye line, behind John Nettles and the rest of the pantomime cast, which included the delectable Rula Lenska and my comedian pal, Jeff Stevenson. As Les was thanking the audience for their kind applause, Michael Aspel walked over to a surprised Les, spoke those immortal words, "Les Dawson, comedian, This Is Your Life!" and handed him the famous big red book. The audience went wild of course, the curtain eventually came down and as soon as Les and the entire company had changed out of their costumes, they were taken in a fleet of cars from Wimbledon to the Thames Television Studios in Teddington.

Les, who could never be described as 'athletic' or anything remotely close to being fit, was playing the Dame in the pantomime, which meant he was on stage for most of the show and that day, as usual, he'd done two long, tiring performances, with lots of energetic comedy routines and costume changes. By the time everyone was assembled in the Thames Television studio and the show's familiar, four-note introduction to the *This Is Your Life* theme tune started, it was already past midnight.

The recording took about an hour and when it was over,

the audience were let out and Les, his family, friends, guests and pantomime colleagues adjourned to the Green Room for some liquid refreshment.

At three o'clock in the morning, after many of the guests had gone home to their beds, including John Nettles and Jeff Stevenson, Les was still refreshing himself with free champagne, courtesy of Thames Television. What a constitution that man must have had – well, up to a point. All of a sudden he collapsed, an ambulance was called and he was rushed into hospital with a suspected heart attack.

Jeff Stevenson was at home asleep in bed at half-past eight the next morning when he got a call from the manager of the Wimbledon Theatre, asking him if he'd ever played Dame before. "No," said Jeff, "I've played Muddles and Buttons, Wishee-Washee and Silly Billy… but never Dame!" "Well, Jeff, you'll be playing the Dame this afternoon and this evening, and maybe for the rest of the run, because Les is in hospital. We have two more sell-out performances today and frankly I can't think of anyone else to call at half-past eight on a Sunday morning! Now you're a foot taller and several stone lighter than Les, so please be here within the hour so Les's costumes can be altered to fit you!" Now *that's* pressure!

As Jeff had been playing the Dame's son, he had no 'Dame' gags to throw into the script, so one of the first things he did – after calming himself down – was to phone several of the professional comedy writers he paid to supply him with new gags, asking each of them to come up with half-a-dozen lines he could use as the Dame. Co-incidentally, one of the writers he phoned to ask for gags was Alan Wightman. That man gets everywhere.

That afternoon, having done his best to memorise his new script in a few short hours and armed with a pile of newly-minted jokes, Jeff made his debut as Dame. He did so under very difficult circumstances – not the least being that the audience were expecting to see Les Dawson in the role and were obviously disappointed – but he performed like the great pro he is, repeating it all over again that evening. John Nettles, Rula Lenska and the rest of the company all rallied around to get him through the two performances.

In the meantime, with still three weeks of the pantomime to run, the management realised they needed a headliner to replace Les and managed to persuade none other than the great Bernard Cribbins to take over as Dame. Jeff was relieved to go back to his normal part and the rest of the run went as smoothly as any pantomime can.

Les never returned to the Wimbledon pantomime, having been ordered to rest by his doctors. But of course he did return to work eventually, making an appearance on the 1991 Royal Variety Performance and starring in several summer seasons in Blackpool. I find it ironic that on the 10th of June 1993, Les passed away from a heart attack in the very hospital he was visiting for a routine heart check-up. Ever since I read about that, I've made a point of avoiding hospital check-ups. They're obviously very unhealthy.

Even when I was booked for a long pantomime run, I would still do my stand-up gigs at social clubs. As soon as the curtain came down after the evening performance in the theatre, I'd quickly get showered and changed, jump into the car and drive off to a club and do a forty-five minute spot. I still do it today when the opportunity arises and you can always tell whether I've got a late night gig after the pantomime. If I *haven't* got a gig, the curtain will go up at seven-thirty and might not come down until ten o'clock. If I have got a gig, the curtain will have come down, the auditorium cleared and the building locked-up, all by nine-thirty. Don't think that means the audience are short-changed. They still get the full performance from the company, with all the dialogue and songs and funny bits still intact. They just have to pay a little bit more attention to what we're singing and what we're talking about, because we're going at it at twenty per cent faster than we normally do. The other tell-tale sign is that I'll have left my car-engine running in the car park.

Neil Morrissey was fascinated by the fact that after I'd finished work (as far as he was concerned) I'd go off somewhere and do another job. Although he was an expert at playing comedy roles – in fact he's adept at both comedy and drama – he's an actor rather than a stand-up comedian. Like John Nettles he liked being around comedians and I think he envied my ability to go from playing a role where I had to, mostly, stick to the script, to standing on a stage in a social club, rattling off a pile of gags. He often used to accompany me to gigs and would stand at the back, fascinated by this 'other world' of the social and working men's clubs.

The following year, I was back in pantomime at the Swansea Grand from the 18th of December 1991 to the 1st of February 1992, playing Dame again, this time in *Cinderella* alongside Linda Nolan and someone who I think is one of the most talented, yet under-rated, all-round performers of the past 20 years – Bobby Davro. Bob and I got on great and we are still pals all these years later. He appeared twice on my BBC Wales entertainment series *Money in the Bank* in 2000 and 2001 and was brilliantly funny and inventive both times.

I started to become a bit of a fixture at the Swansea Grand every Christmas, to such an extent, the posters used to describe me as "Swansea's Own – Owen Money!" even though I was born in Merthyr and lived in Neath. But to be honest I was delighted to be associated with Dylan Thomas's 'ugly, lovely town'. I liked the town, the theatre, the people and the fact that just across the road from the Grand, was the place that served the best chips in Wales – the Highway Café. Don't bother looking for it next time you're in Swansea because it's shut, permanently. You may not be aware of this but I have a first class degree in Chip-ology and Applied Batter-matics, so consider myself more than an expert. I have tasted chipped potatoes all around the world, from the frozen tundra of Aberystwyth, to the rain forests of Porthmadog and all the way down to the scorching deserts of Abergavenny.

And let me tell you, for a chip con-o-sewer like me, seeing a 'Closed Down' sign in the window of the Highway Café was comparable to an art-expert discovering that someone had sneaked into the Louvre and drawn a moustache and glasses on the Mona Lisa! It was devastating. All around the potato farms of the Swansea Valley, flags were lowered to half-mast. But luckily it was still open when I appeared at the Grand again for the *next* Christmas and New Year season from the 17th of December 1992 to the 31st of January 1993. The subject that year was *Robinson Crusoe* and once again I was working with some big names. There was also an unknown young comedian on the bill who went on to much bigger things. But more about the 'squeaky voiced love turkey' in a moment.

Looking at old pantomime posters is fascinating, because they often feature names and faces you remember... names and faces you've forgotten... and more often than not, names and faces that make you scratch your head and think, "Who the hell is *that*?"

Robinson Crusoe at the Swansea Grand that year featured, apart from 'Swansea's Own – Owen Money', Emu, aided and abetted by the late Rod Hull. Not that he was late at the time. Just a little unreliable. Along with Rod and Emu, the principal boy was the delightful ex-Bucks Fizz singer, Cheryl Baker. So far, so good. But here's a name to test your memory. Sharing equal billing with Rod and Cheryl, with his name and face above the pantomime title, was none other than... Mark Greenstreet! How about that! This is the point where you can feel free to scratch your head and think, "Who the hell is *that*?"

Which again proves a point I made a couple of chapters ago. Television doesn't make you a star. The public does.

At the time he appeared in the Swansea pantomime, Mark Greenstreet was a 'hot' actor, having appeared in the popular BBC television series *Trainer* which was set against the world of horse racing. I can't be sure but I think he played an Arab stallion. A year or so after the panto, he disappeared from our screens. Which in box-office terms means that, if his name appeared on a pantomime poster this year, it wouldn't sell one extra seat.

To satisfy my curiosity regarding his current whereabouts – and because I knew you'd want to know too – I did a little bit of research and it seems that when *Trainer* finished he turned to directing films. Apparently, at the time of writing this book, he was set to direct a new film due out in 2010 which is entitled *Househusbands*. Come to think of it, he's *another* one who has my phone number and never thinks to offer me a film role. I wouldn't want any special treatment. I'm very easy-going and willing to share my eighty-foot, air-conditioned Winnebago complete with Jacuzzi, giant plasma screen telly and a fridge full of the finest champagne with any number of beautiful actresses.

So, back to *Robinson Crusoe* 1992/1993. The young comedian with the squeaky voice I mentioned was, of course, Joe Pasquale. That year, his face and name were well below the title of the pantomime on the posters but he has since become one of the biggest stars in the country and all these years later he's still a mate of mine. In fact because we're friends, he agreed to appear on my BBC Wales television series *Money in the Bank* just for peanuts. Admittedly, a lorry-load of dry roasted peanuts delivered to his door did cost the BBC a *lot* of money, but it was worth it.

Joe's debut video, *Live and Squeaky*, was the first-ever comedy video to go platinum, selling over one million pounds worth. I should add here that my comedy video *Made in Wales* did very well too. Don't look so surprised! You've heard of pop stars' albums going double-platinum?

Well, I don't like to brag but my video went *treble-tin*! Not many comedians can claim that! Since then Joe's annual UK tours and summer seasons and pantomimes have done fantastic business and his voice has been heard in at least one Hollywood film. He's *another* one who has my phone number and never thinks to offer me a... hang on! There seems to be a pattern emerging here!

Robinson Crusoe was Joe's first pantomime at the Grand and he was pretty-much unknown at the time. He'd been discovered a few years before by the well-known theatrical agent Michael Vine, who had been told about a bright young comic with a very strange, not to say indescribable, act that he ought to go and see. So he eventually saw Joe perform in a run-down holiday camp on a stretch of the windblown Essex coastline that edged-out so far into the North Sea it appeared to be closer to Holland than to London. It was the end of the season, the place hadn't seen a lick of fresh paint since the Coronation (that's Queen Victoria's Coronation), the carpets were sticky with spilt beer, the camp was half-empty... and the October rain was lashing down like heavy rivets on the corrugated-iron roof of what the management laughably referred to as the theatre.

You'd expect the next part to read, "Yet despite all that, Michael Vine was so impressed with Joe Pasquale's performance he thought he was a comedy genius and signed him up straight away". Sorry to disappoint you. Show business rarely works like that. The truth is, Michael Vine thought Joe's act was terrible. He was undisciplined, lacked any stage craft, was obviously nervous and was far too frenetic. Basically, he was all over the place.

Yet there was *something* about him, some *small, promising glimmer of talent* amongst the chaos, that made Michael sign him up. He made him work hard on his act day after day after day, and before long he started to improve as a performer. In fact, by the time he was booked to appear in *Robinson Crusoe* he had made a couple of television appearances, including *Saturday Live*, but was still unknown to the general public.

Joe's crazy style of comedy, with his magic tricks that rarely worked and his ramshackle props that seemed to fall apart every time he picked them up, proved to be very popular with the audiences at the Swansea Grand, so much so that the management asked him to come back the following year.

Harold Wilson once famously said that a week is a long time in politics. That may or may not be true, but *one year* is definitely a long time in show business. Between appearing in *Robinson Crusoe* and the Grand Theatre's next pantomime *Sleeping Beauty*, Joe toured the UK as the support act for Richard Digance, won the television talent show *New Faces* and was *the* surprise hit of the 1993 Royal Variety Performance at London's Dominion Theatre.

This was a remarkable achievement when you consider the line-up on that year's Royal Variety included Frank Carson, Bradley Walsh, the Muppets, Lesley Garrett, Cilla Black, Brian Conley, Michael Barrymore (who was then still *huge* on TV), Shane Richie and the cast of *Grease*, the Bee Gees and Hollywood superstar Mel Gibson. Joe's frantically funny six-minute spot went down a treat with the Queen and Prince Phillip, the theatre audience and the 12 million viewers at home.

The Royal Variety turned him into that almost mythical creature, the one the newspapers love... the unknown who becomes a star overnight! The fact he'd been learning his craft the hard way, in soul-destroying clubs and run-down holiday camps, week-in and week-out for ten years, was something the papers chose to ignore. But when Joe returned to Swansea for *Sleeping Beauty* (which I wasn't in) the following year, his name and face were still featured *below* the main stars on the posters, because when the billing had been discussed earlier in the year, no-one had any idea that by Christmas 1993 he would be the hottest new name in British comedy. The above-the-title stars were sit-com veterans Windsor Davies and Paul Shane and Australian 'soap' actor Bruce Roberts. Repeat after me... "Who the hell is *that?*" But it was Joe who got the audience rolling in the aisles at every performance.

The following year when he returned to the Swansea Grand for his third pantomime, *Aladdin* (his second with me), which opened on the 15th of December 1994, he was by then a big enough star to share top billing with *Eastenders* actor Adam Woodyatt.

That 1994/5 pantomime season was, as I mentioned in the previous chapter, the first time when I met Alan Wightman, who, some years later, when I decided to set up the Owen Money Theatre Company, would create several successful, family-friendly pantomime scripts. Alan and I also worked together on high-rated TV series for ITV One Wales and BBC Wales that gave television audiences what they were desperate for – entertainment!

I'd been thinking of setting-up a theatre company to produce my own pantomimes for quite a while, but every year, Gary Iles, manager of the Swansea Grand, would call me and make me an offer. The money wasn't bad; the Grand was one of my favourite theatres with a wonderful back-stage crew and it was always interesting (on several levels) performing alongside straight actors who were usually the stars of popular television soaps. The Australians were the weirdest. Well you'd have to be a little bit crazy to travel all the way from the sunshine of Oz to work in Swansea in the middle of the winter, with the snow and the ice and the cold wind blowing-in off the Bristol Channel.

But before I gave up the Swansea pantos to take a gamble and start producing my own, I had three more to do at the Grand. In 1995/96 I was in *Jack and the Beanstalk* with the Chuckle Brothers and Australian soap star Dan Falzon, who had absolutely no comic timing and had a singing voice that wasn't so much trained as strained. Whenever he practised his scales, we all practiced sticking our fingers in our ears. But Qdos Entertainment knew what they were doing by booking him, because his TV role had given him an army of young fans who persuaded their parents to buy tickets for the show and it made a fortune.

I wasn't in the Grand's 1996/97 panto *Robin Hood* – a brand new show for which, co-incidentally, Qdos hired Alan Wightman to write for Ruth Madoc, Little and Large and Sarah Vandenbergh from *Neighbours*. No, I've never heard of her either! But then the odds are, she's never heard of me.

I was back the following year in *Peter Pan*, with Michaela Strachan in the title role and yours truly as Smee, the First Mate and idiot assistant to Captain Hook, played by Norman Bowler, who was then one of the main stars of the long-running soap, playing Frank Tate in *Emmerdale Farm*. This was before ITV decided to drop the 'Farm' and keep the 'Emmerdale' to attract younger viewers, which seemed an odd decision to me. I mean they wouldn't think of dropping the 'Miss' from 'Miss Marple' and re-name it 'Marple' would they? That would be ridiculous!

Norman Bowler and I didn't really hit it off, which may have had something to do with the fact that at the first rehearsal he overheard me say to someone, "Norman's been in *Emmerdale Farm* since it was an allotment!" And what made matters worse was that, during one performance he came on stage in full flow, waving his sword around and bellowing how he was going to kill Peter Pan – and me and the rest of the cast noticed that he wasn't wearing his hook! Captain Hook without a hook! That's like Keith Harris walking on stage without his hand up Orville's... well, you get the picture.

He must have removed his hook to have a quick cuppa or a jimmy riddle and when he heard his cue, he rushed back on stage, leaving the hook in the wings. In a straight stage play, when something unexpected happens, such as a wardrobe malfunction or a prop is mislaid, it can either be ignored or covered-up by dropping in an additional line. This is what an actor like Norman Bowler was used to. But this was a pantomime, I was the comedian in the show... and a comedian will try and get a laugh *wherever he can*.

By the time Norman realised he was hook-less, most of the audience had also noticed that the villain's famous false appendage was missing, so when I addressed him as "Captain Hand", the cast and the audience burst into laughter. It was a genuinely funny moment and if he'd been a comedian or a comedy actor, he would have seen the potential *for both of us* to squeeze as many laughs out of the situation as we could. And if it got *huge* laughs, we would have ensured that he 'forgot' to wear his hook at that point in every performance. But although the theatre echoed with laughter, the only person keeping a straight face – which was now a bright purple mixture of thinly-veiled anger and embarrassment – was Captain Hand... err... Hook. I didn't want to antagonise him more than I already had so instead of milking it to death, we got back to the script and continued the show. After that incident he didn't say more than two words to me off-stage for the rest of the run – and of those two words, the second one was 'off'.

As a footnote to this incident, to prove that Norman couldn't have been all bad – and to give you an example of what can happen to an actor once he leaves a long-running soap – he's now living in southern India, where he and his wife do a lot of charity work. So you've got to hand it to him.

My last pantomime at the Swansea Grand was *Cinderella* with Melinda Messenger in the title role. When I say 'my last' I mean, my last... *so far*. I'm not going to rule out a return to that 'grand' theatre one day. As for Melinda, I liked her a lot. I know you might expect me to come out with some rude, sexist joke about the bubbly, blonde, big-busted ex-topless model at this point, but I'm not going to. I don't want to be associated with that sort of juvenile humour these days. All I *will* say about the delightful Melinda is this – she was two of the nicest people I've ever worked with.

Jonathan Morris, who played Buttons was an entirely different kettle of fish. And if you've ever had the misfortune to work with a kettle of fish, you'll know how hard it was for me to perform alongside one in a pantomime for five weeks. He was a big star at the time, having starred in the sit-com *Bread* for several years. With the main comedy (and pathos) part in the show taken by Jonathan, I was cast as Cinderella's father, Baron Hardup – stepfather of the Ugly Sisters – a part not usually filled by a comedian because it's quite a small role compared to Buttons and the Ugly Sisters.

The Baron is usually played by a straight actor because he has few, if any, funny lines, has no funny 'business' to do – like throwing out sweets to the children or showering the front row with water fired from a giant water pistol – and he's off-stage more than he's on. It was a bit like that first pantomime I did, except there was no gorilla in the show that I could volunteer to play. I took the job because it's always nice to be offered work; it was another glitzy Qdos pantomime with no expense spared on scenery and costumes... and the pay wasn't bad.

Despite my short 'on and off' appearances in the show, every time I stepped out on stage, my comedy instinct would automatically kick-in and I'd try and get laughs wherever I could. I didn't just do this for my own amusement. I felt that the audience expected Owen Money the comedian to be funny. Although it was obvious from their laughter that the audience enjoyed the topical gags and the local references I threw in as often as I could, Mr Morris thought I was upstaging him, meaning I was stealing his thunder. Although I was never a fan of *Bread*, I knew that he was a big TV star, which is why he was hired for the show. I've been in this business long enough to know you never, *ever* try to upstage the star.

But if you can get a few extra funnies in by bouncing lines off each other, why not? Like Norman Bowler, he didn't realise that a pantomime is a couple of hours of fun, during which, provided you stick to the story and the script most of the time, the performers should keep the audience laughing the whole time. Laughter brings the performer and the audience closer together, helping them form a close bond throughout the show. Even the nastiest pantomime villain should make a few self-deprecating jokes and no matter how evil he appears, there should always be an undercurrent of 'I'm not so bad, really!' It's not to be taken too seriously.

This was brought home to the American actor and writer Henry Winkler, best known for his role as the Fonz in the TV series *Happy Days*, when he made his pantomime debut in Wimbledon a couple of years ago. Qdos Entertainment brought him over at great expense to star as Captain Hand... err... Hook, and the part of Smee was played by my old friend Bobby Davro. Apparently, Henry, being an American, only had a vague idea what a pantomime was, so I'd love to know how he was persuaded to cross the Atlantic to spend a couple of months working in a suburb of south London! Anyway, all through rehearsals, Henry played the part of the Captain completely straight and made no reference to *Happy Days* or his famous leather-jacketed role.

The pantomime run was a complete sell-out because, although the youngsters who came along had no idea who Henry was (*Happy Days* was on our television screens from 1974 to 1984), their parents and grandparents... the people who put their hands in their pockets and bought the tickets... did.

The show opened and, at every performance, Henry performed professionally, word-perfect from day one, and

Money in America tour – April 1999; with Frankie Avalon in Las Vegas.

With Martha Reeves and the Vandellas at the Fox Theatre, Detroit.

With a gospel choir at the Gospel Hall, Detroit.

At Antone's in Austin, Texas with Jimmie Vaughan.

With the Crickets at Jerry Naylor's ranch in Nashville, Tennessee.

With the Temptations in Los Angeles.

The Detroit cityscape in the background.

On a Harley Davidson, riding through Texas.

Flying over Buddy Holly's hometown of Lubbock, Texas in a replica of the plane which crashed and killed Holly in 1959.

Driving around Lubbock, Texas…

…and meeting the locals!

At a Willie Nelson concert in Hillsboro, Texas.

On horseback in the Lone Star State.

Freddie Starr was a guest on the TV series *Money in the Bank*.

Leo Sayer was also a guest.

With Jimmy Saville in Leeds. The bus in the background is used in the TV series *Heartbeat*.

Telethon 1988, with Arfon Haines Davies, Ruth Madoc and Aled Jones.

With Shakin' Stevens at the Coal Exchange, Cardiff in 1998.

Tomfoolery
with Ken
Dodd at
the Civic
Theatre,
Darlington
in 1978.

With John Nettles at the BBC studios in 1990.

With Max Boyce at the Max
Golf Day in Glynneath Golf
Club.

At the Grand Hotel,
Swansea in the company of
Tommy David, Wyndham
Rees, Steve Fenwick and
David Howells.

At the revamped Cavern
Club, Liverpool.

With the Searchers at the Grafton Ballroom, Liverpool.

At the Rockfield Studios, near Monmouth where Queen recorded 'Bohemian Rhapsody'.

Relaxing! Gardening at my former home in Neath.

at the end of each show he took his bow to polite applause. Meanwhile Bobby's routines were getting huge laughs and when he took his bow at the end, the audience went wild. He'd done what Bobby always does. Created comedy gold at every opportunity.

One night after the curtain came down, Henry took Bobby to one side and asked him why the audience always cheered Bobby so loudly, but only gave him polite applause. Bobby told him straight. "It's because the grown-ups in the audience expect you to make a reference to the Fonz at some point in the show. If you did that, I'm sure they'd warm to you more and cheer you at the end too." Henry wasn't having any of that. "I understand what you're saying, Bobby. But the audience must understand that this is not *Happy Days* and I'm not the Fonz anymore. I am giving them my interpretation of J M Barrie's famous villain, Captain Hook, and I can't suddenly step out of character. It would be so wrong for me as an actor to do that."

The show continued to play to packed houses and Bobby had the audiences rolling in the aisles with his giant props and non-stop silly gags. Then at the walk-down at the end (known as the 'who's best' because the audience always give the biggest cheer to the one they think was the best in the show) they would, without fail, let Bobby know they thought he was 'the best'.

Then one afternoon, during a matinee, just before he was about to make an exit into the wings, totally unexpectedly, Henry Winkler, dressed in his Captain Hook finery, paused for a moment and looked into a prop mirror that happened to be hanging from the set. With his back to audience, he made the famous 'Fonzie' hands-in-the-air gesture and said, "Heyyyy!!" in approval of what he'd seen in the mirror. The audience immediately went absolutely crazy! Just for a moment, right in front of their eyes and after a 25-year wait, they'd seen the Fonz live on stage and they wanted to show how much they appreciated it. When Henry did the walk-down at the end, the cheers he got almost took the roof off the theatre and after the show he was big enough to tell Bobby, "You were right!" Henry has now done three or four pantos in British theatres – he was in Liverpool for the 2009/10 season – and always drops in a couple of references to the Fonz.

The days when pantomime was considered 'third-rate' by big stars are long gone. British acting stalwarts like Simon Callow, Sir Ian Mckellen and Nigel Havers have all appeared in pantomime (and thoroughly enjoyed the experience) while Hollywood stars like Mickey Rooney, Pamela Anderson, Mr T, George 'Mr Sulu' Takei and Patrick Duffy were persuaded to appear in pantomime in recent years. And as I was writing this book I read that the Birmingham pantomime for the Christmas 2010 season will star none other than the legendary Joan Collins! I assume Joan will be playing the Wicked Queen and I'm sure she'll look sensational in an array of dazzling costumes. The producers are obviously paying her a fortune, but they're doing this knowing full well that the enormous publicity around Joan's first-ever pantomime appearance will ensure that there are no empty seats during the entire run.

By the way Joan, if you don't get any offers for pantomime *the following Christmas*, we might be able to do a deal. I need someone to play Widow Twankey...

CHAPTER THIRTEEN

BY THE EARLY 1990S my weekend radio shows were gaining bigger audiences and I was being looked after by BBC Radio Wales' Assistant Editor, Mark Owen, who later became famous when he joined Take That. Only kidding! He wasn't the one in Take That. This particular Mark Owen was a Rhondda boy and we got on well, which is always important in radio, because if you're constantly arguing with your boss about everything from music content to the style of your delivery, it can affect a broadcaster's confidence.

I've had a few arguments with producers before, after and sometimes *during* a radio broadcast, always off-mike, while a record was playing. Unless you're careful it can affect your performance, because when you're doing 'live' radio, you usually have half-a-dozen things to do at once, in a specific order and you don't need any dark, angry thoughts rattling around inside your head that might distract you. You need to be, as someone once said to me when I auditioned for the BBC... "Up... up... up... up... UP!"

While I'm talking about radio producers, in case there's no room left later in the book, I *must* mention my friend Gary Price who I worked with on many of my weekday shows. He was a walking encyclopaedia of popular music and had the most amazing contacts book. Through Gary I was able to get dozens of great 'live' acts on my Thursday afternoon shows, like the Crickets, Jet Harris and Joe Brown. For my very last show he managed to book the veteran American singer-songwriter Tom Paxton. At the end of the show the whole production team joined Tom in my studio and we all sang along with what is probably his most well-known song, certainly in this country, 'The Last Thing on my Mind'. Like all creative partnerships Gary and I had our ups and downs, but I always respected him as a true professional, a radio man through and through. Sadly, Gary passed away in January 2010 at the age of 64.

I was still broadcasting my weekend shows from the BBC's Swansea studio, which was so small if I ever wanted to interview a guest, one of us had to leave the room. That studio was *so* small I couldn't play albums, only singles. That studio was so small, I could only read out dedications from people with very short surnames. That studio was... well, I don't have to spell it out. I was always well prepared for my shows, having written-out the running order and what I was going to say about each piece of music I played.

April 1992 saw the start of the Garden Festival of Wales, which was held on a mountainside site overlooking Ebbw Vale which was so high up, the car park attendant was Sherpa Tensing. I remember asking someone, "Is that Sherpa *Tensing*?" and told, "Well he isn't very happy!" The Festival site was so high-up, there was a café by the entrance selling teas, coffees and oxygen. So, anyway, in 1992 Mark Owen thought that to freshen things up, it would be a good idea for me to come out of the studio and broadcast my Saturday morning show from the Garden Festival site.

In those days my Saturday show started at ten o'clock and ended at noon, so Mark thought that would be an ideal time-slot to catch all the happy visitors arriving on the site every Saturday morning and I could chat to them and have a bit of a laugh between playing records. It would bring a real touch of spring sunshine to BBC Radio Wales, which I thought was a great idea.

As we all know, whenever we plan any outdoor event in this country, whether it's a wedding, picnic, sporting occasion or a tap-dancing routine whilst juggling ten over-ripe bananas on top of Mount Snowdon (or is that just me?) the one thing we can never rely on is the British weather. I know he won't mind me disagreeing with him, because he's very busy at the moment... pushing up the daisies... but when Al Jolson sang 'April Showers' he was wrong when he warbled 'It isn't raining rain, you know, it's raining violets'. I am here to tell you that when it rains in Ebbw Vale in April it definitely does *not* rain violets. Violently, yes. Violets, no. It came down like stair-rods.

BBC Radio Wales had a permanent stand and broadcast studio on site and BBC Television had a studio next to ours which used to put out a 'live' entertainment show on BBC One every weekday lunchtime throughout the festival's run, hosted by Caron Keating. It had some connection with *Pebble Mill at One* even though it didn't come from Pebble Mill and it started at 12.30p.m. The television show featured loads of big stars that were brought up the mountainside to the Festival site by Sherpa Tensing and half-a-dozen Nepalese guides every day. I have an abiding memory of that eccentrically adorable singer Cyndi Lauper in one of her outlandish costumes – leather jacket, tights and boots, looking like Max Wall as dressed by Gok Wan during a migraine – standing next to a big pond in the Garden Festival site, miming to her new single. I remember thinking at the time, that poor girl has travelled thousands of miles to promote her record and straight after she's finished miming she'll travel thousands of miles to get back home – and I bet she hasn't the faintest idea where she is. I empathised with her because I used to feel exactly the same whenever I worked in Llandudno. If you're from Llandudno, I'm sorry, I meant to say Aberystwyth. And if you're from Aberystwyth, I'm just sorry. It's just a joke! Lighten up!

Back to those April showers. On my first Saturday show from the Garden Festival it absolutely bucketed down from the moment we arrived. We had a raised stage protected by a canvas canopy and behind that was a small studio, inside which I would play my records and broadcast to the nation, while hundreds of curious visitors passing-by would have the opportunity to watch a slick, professional broadcaster in action. And me.

As predicted, hundreds of visitors *did* pass-by. They passed-by the Garden Festival site *completely*, and who could blame them when the weather was so wet and miserable? The sad fact was that on that first day I was broadcasting from the site, there were no visitors. None. Zero. Nada. Zilch. Even the Nepalese guides had gone home in disgust.

As I waited for the red light to come on so I could start my show, I looked out at the rain-sodden site, and the only people I could see were two policemen – who, for all I know, may have been off-duty stripper-grams – and my radio producer, getting into her car and driving to somewhere warm and dry. When the programme started I welcomed my listeners to the Garden Festival and immediately revealed that the weather was so atrocious, I'd just phoned B&Q to order 50,000 planks of wood so I could build an ark. Big mistake! While my first record was playing, I had a phone call from one of the Garden Festival organisers, asking me not to mention the bad weather as it might put visitors off. I was going to say it didn't need *me* to put them off. Anyone who was thinking of visiting the site only had to look out of their window to see how bad the weather was, but as I didn't want to upset the people running the Festival, I did what I was told. In fact I did more than I was told.

When the record finished, I announced to the listeners, "The rain's stopped... the sun's come out and it's boiling here now! I've got my sunglasses on and someone has very kindly bought me an ice-cream. Come on up here, but make sure you slap plenty of Factor 20 on first, or you'll burn!" While I was coming out with all this nonsense, I could hear the rain hammering down on the canopy above me and great waterfalls pouring off it and splashing onto the ground. I then introduced the next record... "Which sums up how I feel at the moment. Roy Orbison and 'Only the Lonely'!"

As the morning slowly crept by there were still no visitors about and the site looked bleak, wet and miserable, which really got me down because Mark Owen had told me that my Saturday show would be coming from the site for the entire run of the Garden Festival... which was to last *six months*! I somehow managed to get through that first show, mostly talking to myself and the listeners, because there were no people wandering around for me to interview.

All through the following week I was dreading doing the second show, praying that it wasn't going to rain again. My prayers were answered because the next Saturday wasn't a bad day weather-wise, cool but dry and I actually had an audience. It wasn't a huge crowd, only fifty or sixty people, but that was fifty or sixty more than the previous week. Seeing all these people arriving made me feel a lot better and I asked someone on the BBC team to run the desk, i.e. play the records, for me while I talked to the visitors using a hand-mike. They were a little shy at first, but as soon as one or two visitors chatted to me and the crowd could see I wasn't going to make them look foolish or embarrass them, they were happy to take part.

My experience as a stand-up comedian enabled me to have a lot of fun with the audience, picking-up on little things like unusual names, taking the mickey out of where they came from and (something I still do to this day) spotting members of the public who might resemble a well-known celebrity. I was able to tell pretty quickly which audience members are good sports and which ones might be tricky customers. Anyway that second show worked so well, with me free to wander around with my mike, not having to worry about whether I featured every record on my play-list, from that day onwards I have never pre-scripted or done any preparation for my Saturday and Sunday radio programmes. And many of you will say, "Yes... and it shows!"

Of course I always check the running-order a couple of times just before each programme, so I have an idea of what's coming up, but once I've checked it and the red light comes on, it's a case of "Right... let me at 'em!" and away I go. When you're broadcasting 'live' the adrenaline keeps you sharp and on the ball, although verbal mistakes can happen when you're jabbering away nineteen to the dozen, reading out requests and dedications and cracking gags. Provided these mistakes don't involve obscene language, blasphemy or rude, unflattering, distasteful and totally uncalled-for comments about Prince Charles's enormous lugholes, you can usually cover yourself by quickly playing a record. Then three minutes later you carry on chatting to your listeners as if nothing had gone wrong.

I know I've mentioned many incidents and performances that have boosted my career, but that Garden Festival of Wales in 1992 was, without a doubt, the biggest turning point of my broadcasting career. Once April had come and gone, the weather in May, June and July was very warm and pleasant, which helped to boost the visitor numbers and, in turn, my popularity on Radio Wales. People who had only heard me on the radio came to see me working and seemed to like my conversational style of broadcasting, peppered with my own brand of home-grown humour. They knew I wasn't your typical BBC broadcaster. I was one of them. A working-class bloke who, through a combination of hard work, a little bit of talent and a shed-load of lucky breaks, managed to make a career for himself in show business.

Like the majority of people in Wales (around 80 per cent at the last count, although if you know any different I'm willing to be corrected – but not now, finish the book first), I'm not a Welsh-speaker. However I'm fiercely proud of my roots and my country and don't feel any less a true Welshman than someone who is fluent in Welsh.

If you ever listen to my radio shows – and if you don't,

why the flippin' 'eck are you reading this book? – whenever someone calls in, no matter what part of Wales they're from, I usually know the town or village they live in or at least have some idea where it is. That's down to all the travelling I've done in the course of my career, going right back to the pop band days of the sixties, my stand-up gigs and all the wonderful places we visited when we made *Just up your Street* between 1998 and 2003 in every corner of the Principality. I know the names of the local clubs, pubs, theatres and hotels and also remember the hundreds of old dance halls, ballrooms and discos of the 1960s and 70s which have been demolished to make way for supermarket car parks or converted into mobile phone shops. This local knowledge enables me to relate to my listeners and more importantly, for them to relate *to me*.

Those six months I spent broadcasting from the Garden Festival also boosted my profile as a stand-up comedian to such an extent that on one particular night I worked a club for which I agreed to be paid out of the takings on the door and the place sold out in half-an-hour. They wanted to see the man they were listening to every Saturday morning.

So, through the 1990s, my diary was always full. I had wall-to-wall stand-up gigs... charity shows... my summer shows at the Grand Pavilion, Porthcawl... pantomimes for Jon Conway and Nick Thomas at the Grand Theatre, Swansea... and my regular programmes on BBC Radio Wales. As for television, there was nothing forthcoming from BBC Wales because they had closed down their entertainment department – luckily for me they later reopened it, not long before *Just up your Street* was created – and were concentrating on news, current affairs and sport. It was a shame really because they had performers like me, Max Boyce and Mike Doyle on their doorstep, who, given the right format, could attract an audience.

So, at the beginning of 1995, I seized the opportunity when HTV Wales offered me a series of six one-hour entertainment shows entitled *A Night Out with Money*, loosely based on the pilot they'd made some time before, to be filmed in nightclubs around Wales. I was to host and co-produce the show with the ever-reliable Phil Lewis, who was also the director and an enthusiast for entertainment television. It was this up-coming series that I discussed with Joe Pasquale during my 1994/95 panto season with him at the Swansea Grand. I urgently needed to find a writer who could supply me with gags to complement the reservoir of material I had, but which I was reluctant to 'give away' on television, which is where Alan Wightman came in.

Apart from being a fan of sixties music and chips, he was also on my wavelength when it came to comedy. He'd worked for Jimmy Tarbuck for five years, written television shows for the likes of Les Dawson, Marti Caine, Andrew O'Connor, Richard Digance and Bob Monkhouse and we both admired the great comedians of the past like Tommy Cooper and Eric and Ernie.

Phil Lewis and I, as joint producers of the series, decided that rather than just hiring Alan to write jokes at home and send them in to our production office at the HTV Studios at Culverhouse Cross, Cardiff, we would make him the Associate Producer, which meant that he could be permanently on hand to scribble gags for me on the road and at the venues. Having a writer around was a bit of a gamble for me because I had never worked closely with one before. As it turned out, hiring Alan for the series was a wise choice because a couple of years later when BBC Wales television were looking for a series format for me, he came up with a winner. I won't say any more at this stage or he'll get even bigger headed than he already is. If that's at all possible! No, he's a great bloke really. And very generous. I once saw him give a tramp twenty quid. She wanted *fifty*, but he only gave her twenty...

For that first series of *A Night Out with Money* we visited three venues – the Maes Manor Hotel in Blackwood, which was then run by George Savva; Ashleigh's Nightclub in

Swansea, which was one of the few clubs in Wales that was *never* run by George Savva and the Springfield Hotel in Pentre Halkin, north Wales. I think it was called the Springfield because it was so dusty. I'm kidding! It was and still is one of the nicest, friendliest hotels I've had the pleasure in. Err... I've had the pleasure of *staying* in.

We recorded two shows at each venue over two nights and the places were always packed. We didn't have any big name stars – we couldn't afford them on the budget – but we did feature rock-solid entertainment from many great singers, bands and comedians from the length and breadth of Wales. A mixture of semi-professionals and professionals like the knock-about comedy duo Powys & Jones and Amanda Normansell, the girl who won the very first series of *Stars in their Eyes* in 1992 as Patsy Cline.

The series started a month or so later on HTV Wales, in what was to become 'my' slot, just after the 10.30 local news on Friday nights and within a couple of weeks the viewing figures grew and grew. What would then happen, which was a bit of a mixed-blessing for me, was that the following morning while I was presenting my Saturday show for BBC Radio Wales, my listeners would call in and tell me how much they enjoyed *A Night Out with Money*. As you can imagine, hearing such praise and enthusiasm for a show that was going out on their rival station didn't go down too well with BBC Wales television bosses at the time.

When the first series of *A Night Out with Money* ended in 1995, I was told by the then Head of HTV Menna Richards that, because of its success, she wanted a second series but not until early 1997, when there would be a little more money in the budget. With that bit of good news delivered, the production team all said their goodbyes and then, as is the case with television series, they all went their separate ways. Alan went off to London to work on *Des O'Connor Tonight*, *Blind Date* and *The Crazy World of Joe Pasquale*; Phil Lewis went back to directing in the HTV News Department; and me... I went shopping in Asda's. Well after all that travelling around Wales without a chance to get my laundry done, I needed twelve new pairs of boxers. That's right, twelve. January... February... March...

I returned to my radio shows and 'live' work, plus the usual five or six week panto run, safe in the knowledge that in 1997 I would be returning to HTV for a bigger and better series. It was around that time that a man who became my greatest ally at the BBC joined the organisation as the Head of English Language Programmes. His name was Dai Smith, a stocky, bearded, highly intelligent man who was the forthright type who, whenever he had something to say, would never beat around the bush. He left that to the BBC gardener. I've always liked people who don't mince their words and I've often wondered if vegetarians can bring themselves to do it.

I remember a producer once telling me that Dai Smith had come to the BBC from the world of 'Academia' and I asked him if it was anywhere near the World of Leather. I could tell from the pained expression on the producer's face that it was a daft thing to ask, because he obviously didn't know the answer.

Dai, was (and still is, of course) from the south Wales valleys and was a big fan of mine. Well *someone* had to be. When he called me into our first meeting he told me straight that as far as he was concerned he wanted me to be on Radio Wales five days a week. As soon as he said this I realised that moving from two days a week to five would involve a substantial increase in money and after nearly an hour of really tough negotiations, Dai eventually agreed that I should pay the BBC an extra three pounds fifty a week.

As soon as Dai could arrange things, true to his word, he cleared the morning schedules and put me on the air from Monday to Friday. Now, it's a funny thing with radio. There are people who listen to it at home, at work, in the car or in the cab of their lorry during the week, and never think to listen at the weekend because they have plenty of other diversions. Which meant that from Monday to Friday, once I was in my stride, as well as broadcasting to fans who were able to follow me across from my weekend shows, I attracted a new army of fans who might not have heard me before. And I'm sure there were one or two who, having heard me once, never wanted to hear me ever again!

So as the size of my fan-base increased and my ratings got higher, the BBC Wales bosses, including Dai Smith, began to regard me as an enormous asset to the station. And as those of you who could do with losing a few pounds will know, when the size of your fan-base increases, it can often result in an enormous asset!

Luckily for me, it wasn't just the big cheeses at BBC Radio Wales who thought I was doing a pretty good job. In 1997 I was amazed to be told that I was going to be nominated for radio's top honour, a Sony Award. The Sonys are the radio industry's equivalent of the Oscars and Baftas, which not only meant that my work was being recognised by my peers in national radio, it was also catapulting me into a higher league.

After ten years toiling at the turntables, even if I didn't win the award, for the industry to nominate me for a Sony meant that I was no longer thought of as just a stand-up comedian 'having a go' at working in radio. Dai Smith was delighted with my nomination as regional Presenter of the Year, as were all the other bosses at BBC Radio Wales.

But things then went from the sublime to the absolutely ridiculous when I realised that apart from being nominated as regional Presenter of the Year, my five-days-a-week show was nominated for the Music Programme of the Year. For a few weeks, Broadcasting House in Llandaff was buzzing. But eventually the Health Department took away the wasps nest and all went quiet again.

Arrangements were made for me, the BBC bosses and my production team to travel to London for the awards ceremony on the 10th of May by coach, but there was no question of us staying overnight. As soon as the event was over, we would have to pile back onto the coach and head back to Cardiff. See how BBC Wales respects licence payers' money?

Amongst the BBC personnel on the coach with me were Nick Evans, the then Editor of Radio Wales, plus a handful of radio producers, production staff and my faithful broadcast assistant (and all-time worst singer in the world), Cynthia Robinson. Those of you who remember Cynth's various, painful attempts at vocalising will know she has Van Gogh's ear for music and that her favourite key is 'N'. So you won't be surprised to learn we all thought it best not to have a sing-song on the way up to London in case it spoiled our jolly mood!

The awards ceremony was due to take place in the Great Room of the Grosvenor House Hotel and was, as you might expect, a black-tie event. Black trousers too and socks! Rather than wear our best bib and tucker for the entire three-hour coach journey and take the risk of being dropped off in Park Lane looking as if our tuxedos and ball gowns hadn't seen an iron for months, we wore informal clothes for most of the journey and when we got to the Heston services we all dashed into the loos, quickly got changed and re-emerged in our glittering finery. Yes, we got a few odd looks when we queued-up in the café for our burgers and chips, but we just ignored them.

There's an unwritten rule that applies to all awards ceremonies, from the Hollywood Oscars to the Llandudno Grocer of the Month Prize – the closer your table is to the stage, the more chance you have of winning the award(s) for which you've been nominated. There's a practical reason for this arrangement. It enables the winners to get to the stage to receive their awards as quickly as possible, so that the bitter and twisted losers in the room don't have to keep up their reluctant applause for too long.

Bearing in mind that unwritten rule, you can imagine how we felt when we got to the Grosvenor House Hotel and walked through the entrance into the Great Room (in case you were wondering, it's not *that* Great by the way) to find that the BBC Wales table was the furthest away from the stage, situated right at the back of the room, next to the kitchens. If we'd been any further back we could have helped with the washing-up. I'm telling you we were *that* far away from the stage; we needed powerful binoculars to see who was hosting the show. Little Cynth reckoned it was Michael Parkinson. Dai reckoned it was Gloria Hunniford. And I thought it was Cannon and Ball.

There were 1,500 people in the room, mostly famous faces from the world of broadcasting. I was the only person there I'd never heard of. I slowly looked around surrapti… surrupti… without drawing attention to myself. Which wasn't easy because I'd borrowed a pair of powerful binoculars from Bill Oddie who was on the next table. I don't know why they didn't give him a chair. Bill had brought the binoculars with him because he was combining a posh night out in Mayfair with a bit of bird-watching. Apparently he'd heard there was a nightingale singing in Berkeley Square.

As I peered at the celebs, I recognised the man who was *the* voice of *Pick of the Pops* in the 1960s and 70s, Alan Freeman. I saw Ken Bruce… Steve Wright… oh, loads of them. Dozens of waiters and waitresses bustled around serving drinks and meals to the guests, but my stomach was in a right knot, worrying about whether I had a chance of winning one of the two awards for which my weekday show had been nominated – regional Presenter of the Year and Music Programme of the Year.

The dinner plates and cutlery were cleared and the awards ceremony got underway. Presenters appeared, names were announced and people went up on stage to collect their awards, but because of the vast distance between us and the stage – I'm sure we were in a different time zone – it wasn't easy to see or hear who had won what. But all our ears pricked-up when the host announced that the next award would be for Music Programme of the Year. The nominees were me... Chris Tarrant and Steve Wright. That's wright... I mean that's *right*. I was up against the *Who Wants to be a Millionaire* host who also happened to have the biggest breakfast radio show in the London area (on Capitol Radio) and the host of Radio Two's popular afternoon show.

Just before the winner's name was announced, I closed my eyes and crossed my fingers. Or I might have crossed my eyes and closed my fingers. It was such a long time ago I can't really remember. Then a few seconds later I was amazed to hear those magical words... "Izzee Wizzee! Let's Get Bizzee!" Yes, Matthew Corbett and Sooty were also on the next table.

But then... I heard six *even more magical words*. "And the winner is... Owen Money!" As soon as realised that I was the only Owen Money in the Great Room (well with 1,500 people in there, you never know) I leapt out of my seat and ran up on to the stage to collect my award from Nigel Kennedy, who was taking a night off from his job playing music in the lifts at Morgan's Hotel, Swansea. And if you don't get that reference, you've obviously skipped through too many pages without reading them properly!

As I walked the two and a half miles back to the table, I happened to pass Steve Wright who, instead of giving me a friendly smile or even a nod in my direction, looked like he wanted to place my Sony Award where the sun doesn't shine. I don't think he was familiar with the expression "be gracious in defeat". I can't listen to his *Sunday Love Songs* show without remembering that sulky scowl on his face as he saw the Sony Award glide past in my hand. He's still one of Radio Two's top broadcasters and I'm sure he's won plenty of

208

awards since, but that night it just happened to be *my* turn. When I got back to the table and was able to relax and enjoy a glass of wine, I reckoned that winning one Sony award was a bloody great achievement and the chance of me winning another one was remote.

The regional Broadcaster Award was presented by Caroline Aherne and the nominees were from Ulster, Scotland and... so glad you're paying attention... Wales! And to my utter amazement... I won *that* award too! *Two* Sony Awards in one night! Steve Wright must have been stabbing himself in the leg with his after-dinner toothpick.

The second time I went up on stage I was a little more composed and managed to do a couple of minutes of comedy, which went down well, especially with Caroline Aherne; someone else who has my phone number and never calls to offer me a job! Anyway I didn't overstay my welcome and left the stage to loud cries of "Well done!" and "Congratulations!" and "Who the hell *is* he?" This time when I got back to the table, with no more awards to worry about, I was able to really relax and got stuck into the vino along with everyone else from Radio Wales. Which perhaps wasn't a great idea, because ten minutes later it was time for the Station of the Year award. And unbelievably Radio Wales won that too!! By now Steve Wright must have been outside in Park Lane, looking for a red bus to throw himself under.

Quite deservedly, the whole of the BBC Radio Wales contingent went up on stage to collect the award and savour the moment of victory. When the ceremony was over we were all whisked to a palatial room upstairs with all the other winners to meet an impressive array of BBC bosses in Armani suits – Heads of various important departments at Broadcasting House in Portland Place – who all wanted to congratulate us on our extraordinary achievement. After we started complaining of severe back pains because of the number of times we'd been slapped, we all got on the coach and headed back to Wales... with enough bottles of champers smuggled aboard to keep the party going all the way to 'Llandaff Towers'. We were in such a great mood we even let Cynthia sing. *One* song. We were in a great mood, but we weren't delirious!

The enormity of what I – and Radio Wales – had managed to do at the Sony Awards only really sank in the following day, after three black coffees and six aspirins. It was a massive achievement by any standards and as Dai Smith and Nick Evans were suitably generous with their praise I thought it was a good idea to ask for a whopping great rise.

So I said to Dai Smith, "If you think so much of me and want me to be a big part of BBC Wales like you keep saying, then I demand that you pay me another £10,000 a year... plus a ten per cent Christmas bonus. I also want my own dressing-room with a jacuzzi and giant flat-screen television and I want a car... preferably a Bentley or a Rolls Royce... to bring me to and from Broadcasting House every day!" I've no idea what he said in reply because I'd already put the phone down.

My career was on a bit of a roll now, because around the same time – April 1997 – I was preparing my second series of *A Night Out with Money* which, instead of being filmed in venues around Wales, was going to be made at the HTV studios in Cardiff.

Once again I was co-producing with Phil Lewis, who was also in the director's chair and Alan Wightman was back on board as Associate Producer and writer. Menna Richards had given us a slightly bigger budget and an extra two shows; so as soon as we opened our production office, we had to start planning on how we were going to fill eight one-hour shows and make them bigger and better than the first series.

First-off we needed a house band, to provide musical intros and out-tros, known as 'stings' as well as providing musical backing for our 'name' guest stars, up-and-coming local talent, our resident vocal quartet Baroque (who had been a huge asset to our first series)... and me! On my weekday radio show I had been working with a great keyboard player and musical director named Nigel Hart and he agreed to put together a small but multi-talented band for the show.

This was quite a task, as apart from composing the show's theme music, he would also have to write out the arrangements for all the solo performers featured on each show, as well as Baroque's song of the week and my opening and closing numbers. I have to tell you that Nigel did such a fantastic job that when I started work on *Just up your Street* for the BBC a year later, he was my one and only choice to be our musical director. After Burt Bacharach refused to return my calls...

As for guest stars on the show, we knew who our core audience were, so there was no point in us booking 'alternative' comedians or young chart bands. This was around the time that television variety shows and 'mainstream' comedians were being dropped from the network TV schedules by incoming new Heads of Comedy who considered the established comics (Tarby, Monkhouse, Ted Rogers etc.) to be old-hat. The fact that they were experienced, quick-witted pros who could be relied upon to host big, popular shows, didn't bother the 'brains' who now ran television. The same 'brains' who then infested the schedules with endless reality shows and lifestyle shows. I've always maintained that if you're hooked on lifestyle shows, *you don't have a lifestyle*. Of course people watched these shows and still do. People also sit in front of their televisions and watch *Big Brother* contestants sleeping for hours, which says much more about people than it does about *Big Brother*.

So although we were aware that we were swimming against the tide, we knew that if we got the formula right, we could attract a big audience to our show every Friday night. You can't always second-guess what every television viewer wants to see in an entertainment show, so you have to try and please as many of them as you can. We wanted to put together a great-looking, fast-paced show which leaned heavily on music, with plenty of comedy from me and various guests thrown in.

From the popularity of the *Solid Silver Sixties* shows that toured British theatres every year (and still do) and usually featured four top acts from the swinging sixties, we knew that there was a huge appetite out there for the music and pop stars from the past. But despite the fact that these tours always sold out, the stars who appeared on them were rarely seen performing on television, if it all.

So for our second series, we decided to feature some of the big names from the pop charts of the 1960s and 70s, acts that the audience would remember with affection. What we didn't know was... would the performers be interested in travelling to Cardiff for our show and if they were, could we afford them?

Between us, we had a lot of contacts in the business and by ringing around and speaking to agents, managers and the performers themselves, gradually our white board, hanging on the wall of our production office, started to fill-up with the names of the guests we had booked for each of the eight shows. But there were some weeks when, on a Wednesday we still had a gap to fill because someone hadn't definitely confirmed they would appear. This was always a bit of a nail-biter, as we recorded the shows 'as live' on Friday evenings. That they were always able to be broadcast at 10.35 the very same night was due to the expertise of the editing team, and Phil Lewis.

Every Friday night for the run of the series, we hired a small function room at the Stakis hotel, next to the studios, so we could watch the show going out. Many of the performers, musicians and production team would rush over there straight after the show had finished recording, to get a good seat in front of the television set.

The bill-toppers on the first show were the Tremeloes and although it was great to have them on the show and they went down well with the studio audience, for some reason the boys insisted on *miming* to their hits. They were the only group on the series who did this. All the others sang and played live. The Trems gave the strange excuse that they couldn't play live because they had to catch an early flight to Germany the next morning, which Phil Lewis and I didn't really buy, but they were a big 'pop' name from the past to have on our first show, and we didn't get one letter complaining that they'd mimed. I wrote one, but decided not to send it in.

The Troggs appeared on a later show and were excellent. They played three songs and went down a treat. Before and after the show, the living legend Reg Presley regaled us with fascinating stories about the UFOs he'd seen flying over his home town of Andover and the Hampshire countryside. Reg is a true believer in UFOs and told us quite straight-faced that aliens from other planets are already living amongst us, disguised as humans. You only have to walk into any town centre at half-past eleven on a Friday or Saturday night to see he's not far wrong. Sorry Reg, I know you take it all very seriously.

He's written a book entitled *Wild things they won't tell you!* which reveals that secret organisations rule the world and that one day soon we're going to be invaded by lizard men from space. If you ever get a little bit of painful constipation, I recommend you read his book. After leafing through one chapter, I guarantee that your constipation will be cured and you'll be rushing to the loo.

Apparently, with the royalties he earned from Wet Wet Wet's version of his song 'Love is all Around' which he'd written 20 years before, Reg bought a helicopter so he could go chasing after flying saucers. I don't think he caught any because (a) we might all have read about it in the papers and (b) the Troggs toured British theatres and concert halls again in 2010 with a brand new *Solid Silver Sixties* show. Long may they continue to tour.

A Night Out with Money also featured other popular hit-makers from the past like Lindisfarne, Marmalade, the Searchers and the Bachelors. A real nostalgia-fest for fans of 60s and 70s pop music. Where else would you see a line-up like that on your tellys? The thing is, what we were doing wasn't a state secret. We were giving the public just what they wanted – great music and hilarious comedy from performers like Bob Carolgees & Spit the Dog... Aiden J Harvey... and John Sparkes, who did a disgusting but very funny routine about 'bob a job' week and cleaning a toilet which I will leave to your imaginations.

It wasn't just the viewers who valued what we were doing with the show. When Bob Carolgees first walked into the studio during the afternoon rehearsals and looked around, he said, "Oh my God! You're making a variety show!" as if we'd re-invented the wheel!

I won't pretend it was plain sailing all the way. Once or twice I felt like the captain of the *Titanic*. There was one particular group, who I totally refuse to name – unless you send me a crisp fifty-pound note care of the publishers – who were, to put it mildly, past it. To put it *not-so-mildy*, they were absolute crap. The lead singer, who had been a bit of a heart-throb in his youth and once possessed a pair of golden tonsils, simply couldn't sing anymore. The gold had long ago turned to rust and the other singers in the group weren't much better.

They were booked on the basis of their forty-year career in the music business and the fact that they were still touring and appearing in summer seasons. Maybe we should have asked them to send us one of their new CDs before we booked them. It was only when they started rehearsing in the afternoon that Phil Lewis, me and the rest of the production team realised we might be in trouble. I'm not lying when I tell you that the lead singer actually *squawked* the lyrics of their first song. It sounded so bad we thought for a minute that he was winding us up, pretending to have a terrible voice. But he continued squawking through the song... the next song... and the medley of some of their hits which they were going to end the show with. End the *show*? It might have ended my *television career*!

There was nothing we could do about it. Contracts had been signed and it would have been impossible – and unaffordable – to find a replacement act at such short notice. So that night they appeared on the show and, I have to say, they gave us the biggest surprise of our lives! Yes, they were even crappier than they'd been at rehearsals! But the weird thing is our viewing figures for that show were just as high as all the others, so maybe viewers were happy to sit through the bad bits so they wouldn't miss the good bits!

Then there was the occasion when we lost our 'top of the bill' just a couple of days before we were due to record the show because she refused to sing any of the songs that had made her famous! Yes, I know. It made just about as much sense to us too. She was a very well-known female singer who'd had several hits in the 1960s, since when she'd made a successful career for herself in jazz and gospel music. I'm not going to name her here, but do keep those crisp fifty-pound notes coming please.

Her agent was also her husband and he seemed to be a decent enough bloke when we started negotiating a fee for his wife's appearance on the show. We explained what *A Night Out with Money* was all about, that we had a superb house-band to provide musical accompaniment for her and that the target audience were the sort of people who would have bought his wife's records when they were teenagers and who still loved the music of that era. So having said all that, you would have thought he completely understood that we wanted his client/wife to perform some of the songs that had made her famous in the 60s.

When we asked which of her hits she'd like to sing on the show, he turned around and said, "Oh no! She doesn't want to sing any of her hits. She wants to sing some jazz and gospel songs!" Which might have kept *her* happy, but I knew it would have bored the pants off our studio and television audience and would have disappointed them too. This was a major hurdle to get over and we diplomatically discussed the problem with him for some time, while trying to avoid blurting out the hard fact that his client/wife was only famous because of songs she'd recorded 40 odd years ago.

In the middle of our conversation he got so angry he just slammed the phone down, but not before telling us where we could stick our programme. And our telephone. So there we were. It was late on a Wednesday afternoon and we'd lost our star name for the forthcoming Friday. Who the hell could we get to replace her at the last minute? We already had my friend Gerard Kenny, the American singer/songwriter on the bill, and we knew what he'd be singing. Nigel Hart had received his arrangements and was busy rewriting them for his band. What we needed was a well-known band or group from the 60s or 70s who were self-contained and could just turn up, plug in and play!

With two days to go we all looked through our contact books and started ringing around but, as you might expect, the groups that we hadn't already booked for the series were already working on the Friday night... or were on holiday or wanted too much money. Then I had a brainwave and phoned up Ray Ennis of the Swinging Blue Jeans who, along with the other boys in the group, still lived in Liverpool.

It turned out to be the best thing I could have done because, not only did Ray and the boys know the show "We watch it every week, Owen! We love it!", they also had a rare night off on the Friday and agreed to come down to Cardiff for a reasonable fee.

What a show that was! One of my favourites. The Blue Jeans did two great numbers, including 'The Hippy Hippy Shake'... comedian John Sparkes was very rude, but very funny... and Gerard Kenny closed the show in a rousing fashion, sat at the piano singing 'I could be so good for you' backed by Nigel Hart and the band and surrounded by all the performers on the show, including the Blue Jeans. And me!

People continued to phone in to my Saturday morning radio show, as they'd done when the first series of *A Night Out with Money* was broadcast on Friday nights, telling me how much they'd liked my TV show. So it was inevitable that when the HTV series ended, the BBC bosses would have something to say to me. I thought I might have been called up to Dai Smith's office for a formal meeting but, instead, he told me was going to take me out to lunch with Geraint Evans, the Head of the new Entertainment Department.

I had to wait over a week before the lunch date (I was starving by then!) and during those seven days, all sorts of thoughts went through my mind. Because when you're taken out to lunch by BBC bosses, one of two things happens. You're either offered a contract that will provide you with some interesting television projects... or you're on your way out of the door!

Come the day, as arranged, Dai and Geraint took me to lunch and I remember being so impressed when Dai read out our orders to the waiter in fluent Chinese. Amazing! As it turned out it didn't do him any good, because it was a French restaurant. Dai came straight to the point, "We'll give you a three-year contract to make television shows, but it has to be exclusive. You can't make any more shows for HTV during the period of your contract."

I was thrilled to bits to be given such an offer and for them to have such faith in me that I could deliver good ratings for the channel. No disrespect to HTV or ITV One Wales as it's called at the time of writing, but if you're in television, for me, the BBC is *the* place to be. Leaving aside all its problems and flaws and the Ross/Brand saga, the BBC is still the most respected broadcaster in the world. When there's any major event, whether it's a national celebration or a tragedy, the majority of people still turn to the BBC for news and updates.

Knowing a good thing when I see one, I accepted the BBC's generous offer. What they didn't know at the time was that I'd already had a meeting with Menna Richards, who was thrilled at the success of *A Night Out with Money* and wanted a third series. However, as regional television has never been awash with dosh, HTV wouldn't be able to afford to make it for at least *eighteen month*s. Financial restraints were starting to be felt in regional television and the repercussions are still being felt.

Although I understood Menna's problem of having to balance her programme-making budgets, as a performer who enjoyed appearing on television and as someone who had brought ratings success to HTV Wales, I found the prospect of an eighteen-month gap before the next series a huge disappointment. It was possible that if we came back – and there was no rock solid guarantee that we would – our audience, who had been very loyal to the show, might have found other things to watch in the interim. I also knew that if a *network* show on ITV achieved the sort of high ratings my series had, the money to make more shows would *definitely* have been found and in those eighteen months they would have made three more series, two Christmas specials and a spin-off show on ITV2.

A Night Out with Money was, for a regional ITV show, expensive to put on, because if you want to use the best musicians and performers and production staff, capable of bringing a professional showbiz gloss to a project, you have to pay them the going rate. But whatever the total cost of the series was, we're talking very small beer compared to the budgets for network shows like *The X Factor* and *Britain's Got Talent*.

The ITV network has struggled recently because of the drop in advertising revenue, but things are now improving in 2010 and they still have several big 'bankers' throughout the year that they know will bring in at least ten million viewers – the two I've mentioned above are perfect examples – so they are prepared to invest in big budget entertainment if they know they're proven to be popular.

Having signed my exclusive television contract with BBC Wales, I was eager to find out what exciting projects they had in mind for Owen Money, but although they were kicking several ideas around, they asked me if I could come up with any suitable formats.

As I always do, whenever I need to come up with new ideas, I sat down in a quiet room with a paper and pencil and went over and over things in my head. Several hours and ten cups of tea later I came up with the perfect solution, "I'll ring Alan Wightman and ask *him* if he's got any ideas!"

So I phoned Alan – reversing the charges as usual – and asked him if he had any television entertainment formats that he thought might suit me. At first he said he didn't think he did, apart from something he'd thought up called 'Nude Pro-Celebrity Window Cleaning on Ice' which, amazingly, had been turned-down by *every* broadcaster in the country. And two or three in the town.

But when I mentioned that I definitely wanted him on board as the writer and he might get paid a few quid, he suddenly remembered a format that he'd worked on for Michael Hurll Television a few years before. It was going to be a mega-budget, sixty-minute Saturday night show for all the family – and anyone who didn't have a family called – 'Street Party', which would be filmed all over the UK. Several well-known presenters were in the frame to host the series, in which they would look around Great Britain for talented unknown performers as well as interesting and eccentric people in each neighbourhood.

The production team would arrive in each town in a fleet of vans and lorries and would de-camp in that town or city for a week. The unknowns would be coached by celebrities and on the Friday night, a variety show would be staged at a local theatre or some other venue, featuring the locals and a big name top-of-the-bill. A shortened version of the stage show would be included in the last twenty minutes of the programme, which on paper sounded like a winner. But Alan told me that it didn't even get to the pilot stage because it was considered far too expensive to make.

I think it's worth pointing out here that as you read about the intended contents of the show-that-never-happened, you probably felt that some of it sounded very familiar. Well it's only my opinion, but I reckon that over the past ten years at least *three* different network series have been broadcast which were loosely or not-so-loosely based on that original format, without any acknowledgement of its source, after being re-jigged and re-titled.

As Alan told me about 'Street Party', I could see straightaway that the show could be an ideal vehicle for me. Because of my enthusiastic response to his description of the show, he said he'd contact Michael Hurll that day to check whether the format was still available. He wasn't even sure if Michael's company still owned the television rights, because production companies and broadcasters often only 'buy' them for a specific length of time before they revert back to the company or individual who created it, which then allows the company or individual who created it to try and sell it elsewhere. Which is fair enough, because if you create a format that a broadcaster thinks might appeal to the television viewing public and will give them good ratings, then it's only right that your creativity and hard work should be rewarded.

If the format *was* available, Alan said he'd spend a couple of days rewriting it to come up with a revised format, which Michael Hurll would still have to approve of before he allowed BBC Wales to make their own version. This revised format would have to exclude a lot of the more ambitious (i.e. far too expensive) segments of the show to bring it in line to suit a BBC Wales budget. He also promised to come up with a brand new title for the show.

It turned out that the format *was* still available and Michael Hurll had no objection to Alan rewriting it, as long as he was provided with a copy of the revised format. If he approved of it, he would allow us to try and 'pitch' the series to BBC Wales television. Alan then came up with the revised format and the title for the series that would eventually become a big part of my life for several years – *Just up your Street*.

We were about to present BBC Wales with a fantastic new format that would give them the opportunity to go out on the road and make contact with the people of Wales – not just those living along the M4 corridor and the north, but way up in the Valleys and across to the far west of the country.

But we had to convince BBC Wales that *Just up your Street* would not only be the perfect show for me to host, but would also be good enough to attract several thousand BBC Wales viewers away from whatever they watched on network television while our show was going out. We'd have to 'pitch' the idea to Geraint Evans, Head of Television Entertainment at BBC Wales, to see if he thought it was a suitable project for the Corporation to invest a hefty sum of money in.

I've never been over-confident about anything to do with my career, but I had faith in *Just up your Street* and I was sure that if it was made with care, by the right production team, it could be a big success for both me and my employers!

CHAPTER FOURTEEN

MOST OF THIS CHAPTER and part of the next one deals with the years I worked on *Just up your Street* and I make no apology for devoting so many pages to this series, which ran, in various forms, from 1999 to 2004. For a BBC Wales entertainment series, that's quite a run. It was a big part of my life for a long time and gave me fantastic exposure on the 'box'.

It proved to be very popular with our viewers, who enjoyed the mixture of pre-recorded items which showed me and the crew interacting with some wonderful people on the streets of Wales, interspersed with half-a-dozen live performances from mostly young Welsh entertainers. In each of the first three series we took the show on the road to theatres and leisure centres, recording two shows at each venue. This was a winning formula which didn't attempt to reinvent the wheel. For half an hour every Friday night, we were giving the audience a bit of a breather from lifestyle and reality shows, with a little slice of entertainment.

But I'm getting ahead of myself! When you pitch (i.e. try to 'sell') a brand new programme idea to somebody in the film or television business, you have to do it in a clear, concise, articulate manner. You have to be enthusiastic about the project without appearing desperate. You have to be absolutely certain that the idea you've created is not only going to appeal to the person or persons you're pitching to, but also to millions of television viewers – make that hundreds of thousands in Wales!

Pitching is a tough business and not for the faint-hearted because you could be in mid-pitch and someone will suddenly stop you and say, "Thank you! We've heard enough and it's not for us!" or "Dear oh dear! It sounds like a right load of old pony to me!" or the ultimate confidence-killer... "Um, sorry. Have you started yet?"

Of course there is another way to get a television executive to buy a format from you and that's to ply him with just enough drink during the lunch to put him in a good, receptive mood. Sometimes this can go badly wrong if the executive drinks far too much, gets rolling drunk and agrees to buy a format that he wouldn't consider in a month of Sundays if he was stone cold sober. Off the record, I think this must happen quite regularly. How else can you explain why there are so many terrible, unwatchable programmes filling the television schedules?

We decided to pitch *Just up your Street* to Geraint Evans one lunchtime at Le Monde Restaurant in the heart (okay, just above the right kidney) of down-town Cardiff. It was the perfect place because we knew that while their food was always sensational, their lunch prices were reasonable enough not to break the bank. In basic terms, if the pitch didn't work out, Alan and I wouldn't be too much out of pocket.

Despite his high office at the BBC (I think it was on the 23rd floor), Geraint Evans was a very approachable man with a sense of humour dryer than the Sahara desert at high noon. There was no chance of us getting him merry with red wine as the restaurant closed at two o'clock, and he had to be back at the BBC for a two-thirty meeting.

So between us, Alan and I did our best to explain the basic idea behind *Just up your Street* and how we felt that it could be exactly the sort of medium-budget, high-quality entertainment show that BBC Wales should be making for their audience – basically the same people who had tuned in to watch me every Friday night on *A Night Out with Money*. We also pointed out that it would be a great public relations exercise for a BBC Wales television series to go out on the road and get involved with local communities.

I think we talked all the way through the starter and the main course, while Geraint nodded politely from time to time. Eventually, Alan and I had said about all we could about the show and waited for Geraint's verdict. He sipped his glass of water and paused for a minute before asking, "Do you have any other ideas?"

Oh bugger! He obviously didn't like the sound of *Just up your Street*! We were sunk. And *he* wasn't going to be treated to a dessert. As it happened we *did* have another idea we thought he might like. In fact it was more than an idea. It was a three-inch thick, 190-page film script entitled 'Another bad day at Black Rock' that Alan and I had written a couple of months earlier. It was a comedy set in a small south Wales town and, with the aid of an experienced script editor, who could cut away half its 190 pages without destroying the storyline and make it more manageable, it could easily be made as a low-budget film for television. So, still a bit shaken by Geraint's reaction to *Just up your Street*, we pitched him 'Another bad day at Black Rock'.

It was based on a true story I'd been told about a group of Welsh rugby fans who set out for Murrayfield three days before a Scotland v Wales game, but only got as far as Abergavenny. As he listened, Geraint seemed to enjoy our pitch, smiling at our vivid description of the many colourful and eccentric characters who inhabit the small Valleys town and the various comic sub-plots and story strands that all tie-up together in the last fifteen minutes of the film... with 'hilarious consequences'. Yes I know I would say that but, hand on heart, the script was, and still is, bloody funny! When we'd finished, Geraint said, "Okay. We'll have the two of them!"

I wasn't sure what he meant by that, until he continued. "We can get *Just up your Street* into production first and then I can get our drama department to sort you both out some development money for 'Another bad day at Black Rock'."

After we got over the shock of having *two* ideas accepted we were suitably appreciative of Geraint's faith in us and decided that we *should* buy him a dessert. While he was waiting for it, he asked Alan, who was now feeling a little more confident than he'd been when we walked into Le Monde, what he thought his involvement might be on *Just up your Street* other than writing my jokes, links and voice-overs. Straight away, Alan replied "As I brought the idea to BBC Wales, I'd like to be hands-on right from day one. So unless you have any objections, I'd like to be the Associate Producer." Geraint, aware that Alan had been Associate Producer on my successful HTV shows, agreed.

When he'd finished his dessert, Geraint got up to leave, told Alan that he'd be in touch in the next couple of weeks and went off in search of a taxi. As the restaurant was just about to close for the afternoon, we paid the bill and went off in search of a bar that *wasn't* about to close for the afternoon. Thanks to Geraint's instinct for a successful television format and his confidence that I could do a great job of hosting the show, we had cause to celebrate and intended to do so.

If you know anything about my career, you'll be aware of the runaway success of *Just up your Street*, but you may be wondering why you missed seeing 'Another bad day at Black Rock' on your tellys. Well as they say, you don't miss what you've never had, because the film wasn't made. Just months after we delivered the script to the BBC Wales Drama Department, the Head of the Department left and his replacement decided not to commission any project that had been on his predecessor's desk. That, as the man said, is showbiz! Nevertheless, we did get paid a few bob, so no complaints there, and the script is still available if anybody's interested. It might take you a fortnight to read it, but it's still bloody funny.

It was in the September of 1998 that our *Just up your Street* production office opened in Tŷ Oldfield, a building just across the road from Broadcasting House in Cardiff. I say 'our' production office, because we had to share the Entertainment department office with several other BBC Wales productions. From memory I think they included the team who were working on a Frank Hennessey music documentary series to be made in America and another team preparing a series for Peter 'The Phantom of the Opera' Karrie to be made at Broadcasting House. The people who were putting together that year's *Children in Need* show were also in one corner.

As this wasn't network television and money was tight, every production had to share the same small group of researchers and runners, so with music playing from various tellys and hi-fis, phones constantly ringing, several conversations going on at the same time and odd people who didn't quite grasp the concept of what an audition was turning up out of the blue wanting to be instant pop stars, it was often chaotic!

Before I relate some of the things that happened to me during the six years I worked on *Just up your Street*, I should point out the irony of BBC Wales agreeing to let me host a talent show. I've already mentioned my shows at HTV Wales and the fact they couldn't afford to make any more of my *Night Out with Money* shows for a couple of years – which was one of the reasons I moved across to BBC Wales. But when I signed my contract with HTV, they kept saying to me, "We've got to do a talent show with you!" but no-one could come up with the right format, so we made that first series of *A Night Out with Money* around the clubs instead. As things turned out, it did okay and paved the way for the greater success of the studio-based version of the same show with bigger names, which in turn got the BBC to sign me up for television. If we had made a talent show at HTV, who knows, it might have flopped and I might well have had the shortest television career in history. So no regrets there!

We've been inundated with talent shows on television in recent years, from shows like *Pop Idol*, *Britain's Got Talent* and *The X Factor* to the Saturday night series on BBC television which aim to find new West End stars. But it's worth remembering that in September 1998, when we started pre-production on *Just up your Street*, every broadcaster considered television talent shows to be yesterday's news and that they would never make a comeback.

The evening schedules were awash with reality shows, lifestyle shows, cookery shows, DIY shows, junk-in-the-attic shows, *How Dirty is my House* shows – most of which by 2010 have been relegated to daytime television. In 1998 if I had taken the format for *Just up your Street* to, say, Granada or London Weekend Television, they would have turned it down without a doubt. Which would have been a short sighted – and as it turned out, totally wrong – attitude for them to take, because the expression 'what goes around, comes around' applies to the television business more than any other.

Talent shows had been the mainstay of both the BBC and ITV schedules since the late 1940s/early 1950s, starting with the *Caroll Levis' Discovery Show* and Bryan Michie's shows on TWW. There was one particular television presenter who was associated with the television talent show from the 1950s to the late 70s.

I am of course referring to the host of ITV's *Opportunity Knocks*, the legend that was Mr Hughie Green. Since his death in 1997, I've read some of the newspaper stories about him being a bit of a Tartar, on and off the studio floor, but I thought he was terrific – and I mean that most sincerely, folks. Anyone who didn't have the chance to see Hughie in full flow missed a real treat. At the end of every show, he'd run through the list of performers who'd 'entertained' us and encourage us to write in and vote for our favourite act.

It's the norm on today's TV talent shows to vote for your

favourite performer by telephone, which helps prevent cheating. When I appeared with Tomfoolery on the popular ITV talent show *Rising Stars* in the late 70s, we were able to win for several weeks on the trot, purely because we sent in postcards and voted for ourselves. I'm sure we weren't the only act that tried this! Unlike today, with telephone voting, there was no way of checking on cheating!

What always made me laugh was the moment when old Hughie would talk to the viewers as if they were all children or morons who thought an IQ was a line of people outside an opticians. He'd say thing like, "That was the delightful amateur opera singer from Oldham in Lancashire, Senorita Lucretia Ramonita Manolita Bonnaventura. And if you can't spell her name, just write down, 'The tone-deaf fat lady with the big ears'."

Opportunity Knocks was revived by the BBC in 1987 as *Bob Says Opportunity Knocks* with Bob Monkhouse. Welsh entertainers did well on the show, with Mike Doyle the runner-up on one series and Rosser and Davies managing to win their series. Coincidentally, both Mike Doyle and Lloyd Davies are now regular performers in my pantomimes.

Les Dawson took over 'Op Knocks' from Bob in 1989 until the last series in 1990. ITV were also busy making talent shows in the 80s, including the long-running *New Faces*, originally with Derek Hobson and then the wonderful Marti Caine.

Apart from London Weekend Television's *Big, Big Talent Show* which had short runs in 1996 and 1997, to all intents and purposes the television talent show was gone forever. We didn't know it at the time but, although only made for viewers in Wales, my series *Just up your Street* was to be the first of the new breed of talent shows.

One of the reasons I wanted to do the show was that I knew there was so much talent in Wales that never had the exposure that it deserved. The clubs were bursting with singers and comedians, who would give anything for the chance to get on the telly. As previous talent series had shown, a performer can work in the clubs for all his or her life and never get that big break. But one three-minute spot on television can change their life completely.

Stars like Little and Large, Victoria Wood, Lenny Henry, Roy Walker, Les Dawson, Jim Davidson, Su Pollard, Joe Pasquale, Gary Wilmot, Mary Hopkin and even Marti Caine who went on to host *New Faces*, all made their television debut on talent shows – some with better results than others. Famously, Su Pollard was beaten into second place by a singing dog. I think he sang 'Anyone who had a Bark'. Or it could have been 'Leaning against a Lampost'.

Apart from club entertainers, the hundreds of amateur dramatic societies in Wales contained many potential West End performers, as did the Saturday morning stage schools that were springing up around the country. I knew that once we advertised the new show and asked for people to apply for an audition, we wouldn't be short of applicants. And I was proved 100 per cent correct!

We advertised in local newspapers all over Wales and asked those who'd like to audition to send in audio tapes, video tapes (this was just before DVDs took over) and CDs – and we got hundreds and hundreds of 'em! We listened to every tape and CD and watched every video.

Some of the performances were so bad, so painfully flat and completely out of tune, it made us wonder what the people who'd sent them in were hearing when they sang. There was always the possibility that they were wearing earplugs when they made the recordings and this was the reason they had no idea how bad they were. To be honest, if we'd had the money in the budget, the entire production team would have loved to have been kitted-out with ear plugs at times.

Was it possible that the hopeless 'hopefuls' who sent in their tuneless tapes and chronic compact discs were so deluded that they actually thought that they could stand up on stage, in front of the cameras and the audience and the viewers, and belt out a song, backed by professional musicians? Or were they so desperate to get on television, that even though they knew they had no talent they applied anyway?

We also wondered why their families and friends didn't sit them down and have a quiet word with them before they slipped the tape or CD into the envelope and posted it to the *Just up your Street* office. If it was your child or grandchild and you knew the general consensus was they just couldn't sing, you'd *have* to stop them, wouldn't you? Yes, you might upset them, but better to tell them the truth now, than see them be rejected time after time.

And here's something else we found fascinating, if not a little depressing. A proportion of the tapes we received from applicants arrived in tatty old brown envelopes, with the production office's address barely legible on the front. Not only that, very often there would be no accompanying letter inside, so we had no idea who'd sent it in, which wasn't helped by the fact that that there was also no label on the audio tape with a name and contact phone number.

It's not as if we didn't have a huge reservoir of talent to pick from. Hundreds of applicants had the sense to send in reams of details about themselves with their photos, videos, audio tapes, CVs etc, and they were the ones who had more chance of being asked to audition.

With the office up and running and our desks choc-a-block with application forms, we arranged for the first auditions to take place in the rehearsal room at Tŷ Oldfield, which was used by the cast of *Pobol y Cwm* several days of the week. Yes, I thought that would surprise you. They *do* rehearse! We had the room for three days, Friday, Saturday and Sunday. And they were long days. I mean loooong!

I was there to see all the acts, along with Geraint Evans, who was going to produce the series; Clive Harpwood, the director; and Alan Wightman, Associate Producer. Between us we had years of experience in the world of television and theatre entertainment, having worked with the biggest and the best... and one or two of the worst. Not only that, we were the finest judges of up and coming talent you could find in our price range.

We also had a cameraman videoing each performance, several production assistants and runners and a couple of heavy security men to stop the hundreds of nubile young ladies, who had never seen Owen Money before in person, from throwing themselves at me. I was worried that they might try to have their way with me, in the hope that it would help them pass the audition. I didn't want accusations in the press about jiggery-pokery. Actually I wasn't so much worried about the jiggery as I was the pokery.

The show's musical director, Nigel Hart, was there with his rusty, err, trusty keyboard, ready to play for anyone who had brought along sheet music, although I knew from when he worked on my Thursday radio programmes that he was capable of remembering thousands of songs and could busk them brilliantly. We also had a superb sound system set up by our ever-reliable sound man 'Buzz', which could provide mini-disk, CD or tape backing – whatever format the auditonees had brought along with them.

Unlike the cruel format of *The X Factor* we wanted to give everyone who walked through the door a chance to shine and if that meant they should have musical backing, they got it. They didn't have to stand there, singing unaccompanied. Obviously they were all nervous, but we didn't want them to have the added worry about being humiliated or made fun of, no matter how awful they were. And believe me, some of them were *way beyond* awful.

We couldn't believe the massive reaction we got to the ads we placed in the papers. This was the first television talent show in Great Britain for several years and the first in Wales for goodness knows how long (probably since the late 50s and

Bryan Michie's show for TWW). We had been warned before we started advertising for applicants, that the vast majority of people who'd be responding would be female singers.

So, it was no surprise to us when we received loads of tapes and CDs from the fairer sex. Many of them sounded good enough to audition, so we invited them to Cardiff and hoped they could perform in front of us as well as they could on tape or CD. What we were totally unprepared for was the fact that more than 50 per cent of the girls were going to sing *exactly the same song*. What? No, I'll tell you the title of the song in a minute.

Now, we all have our favourite songs and we love listening to them from time to time, but you wouldn't want to hear the same song over and over again, forty, fifty times a day... for three days. Well *you* might, but most normal people wouldn't. If I tell you the song in question was sung by Celine Dion... that it won the Oscar for Best Original Song in 1997... was a titanic world-wide hit... and is best heard underwater... you'll know the song I'm talking about. That deeply moving ballad, with the soaring music and brilliant lyrics. Yes it's the classic love song 'I keep her picture hanging upside down 'cos I can't stand the sight of her face!'

In actual fact it was 'My Heart will go On' from *Titanic*. What a film that was! Talk about realistic. When that huge ocean liner started to sink, I asked the usherette if I could move seats. She said, "Well, where do you want to sit?" and I said, "By the lifeboats!"

When the first girl singer walked into the audition room, we had a friendly chat to calm her nerves and when I asked her what she was going to sing she said 'My Heart will go On'. Which was fine with all of us and I quite liked the song at the time – which was just after 9.30 in the morning... She sang the song (which is almost four and a half minutes long) and we politely applauded and sent her on her way. She wasn't a bad little singer, so I put a small tick next to her name on the list of auditioners we all had in front of us. We marked them all out of 20 and anyone who scored 10 and above, were going to be added to the short list.

Following the first girl singer we watched a couple of boy singers who were okay, and then another pretty girl singer walked in.

"What are you going to sing, love?" I asked.

"'My Heart will go On'," she replied.

"Great! In your own time," I said.

It was still early in the day and it was a pleasant enough song. She performed it quite well, slightly better than the first girl, she left and we ticked our forms, waiting for the next singer. In walked another pretty girl.

"What are you going to sing, love?" I asked.

"'My Heart will go On'," she replied.

"Great! In your own time," I said.

She sang the song... four and a half minutes went by... and off she went.

In walked another girl. We chatted for a minute, and then came the question which you will already know the answer to. "What are you going to sing, love?"

"'My Heart will go On'."

"Great! In your own time."

And so her heart went on... and on... and on. And as it did, our hearts began to sink because it became apparent that, because of the enormous popularity of the film and the song, every girl singer in the country wanted to have a go at it. That Friday we were serenaded by it around forty, maybe fifty times. And this was only the first of three days of auditions in Cardiff.

We also had further auditions set up at the Dylan Thomas Theatre in Swansea and the Springfield Hotel, Pentre Halkin, north Wales.

As I mentioned, we all had a list of the performers in front of us, with room at the side of their name for us to mark them out of twenty. By the end of the day, Geraint Evans had stopped marking them on his paper and instead drew a miniature 'Titanic' next to each girl singer's name. He wasn't being detrimental to any of the performers, because he was very much aware how nerve-wracking it must have been for the youngsters to stand there in front of us and sing their hearts out. But by mid-afternoon, after listening to the same song over and over, sometimes performed well, but often performed badly, if he thought the singer was any good, the 'Titanic' stayed afloat. If she was so-so, he drew an iceberg hitting the ship. And if she was terrible, he drew a little cartoon of the 'Titanic' sinking.

By the way, *that* song will be coming back to haunt you all over again in 2011. James Cameron, who directed *Titanic*, has been tinkering with his 1997 multi-Oscar winner, using the latest technology he used on *Avatar* and will be re-releasing it in 3-D! Can you imagine watching *Titanic* in 3-D? They won't have usherettes in the cinema, they'll have lifeguards. All the non-swimmers will have to sit way up at the back for Health and Safety reasons. And I can dust off all my old *Titanic* gags and, with any luck, get another 12 months' use out of them!

Apart from Celine Dion's international hit, we noticed that most of the girl singers had a very limited repertoire of songs. This might have been because their audition choices were the 'knock out' numbers that went down well for them in the clubs, where a lot of the girls made a living. But it did show a lack of imagination on their part when it came to showcasing their voices. I'd say, at a guess, there was a pool of around a dozen songs that more than 60 per cent of the girls dipped into. We must have heard 'Black Velvet', 'The Wind beneath my Wings', 'I Will Always Love You', and 'River Deep, Mountain High' ten times a day at least. Hearing the same song performed by a succession of female club singers who, for the most part, all had similar voices and a limited vocal range, didn't really help us in our search for *really* talented performers who could stand out from the crowd.

Obviously the ones who didn't make it through the auditions were disappointed and if they could bring themselves to watch the series they'd auditioned for when it eventually went out on BBC Wales, they probably wondered, "Flipping heck! Why did they choose *her*? I can sing better than that!"

There are plenty of girls out there (and men too) who can sing in tune, but the reality is not *everyone* has the whole package – voice, looks, style, determination, personality, confidence, and a great big helping of luck! It's also important they have the strength of character to understand that every time they get turned down for a job or fail an audition, it doesn't mean they're not talented. It just means they weren't right for that particular job.

In the world of the professional theatre, when a performer walks out onto a bare stage and does his or her audition piece, only to be told then and there by the producer sitting in the stalls, "Thank you, my darling! You were very good but we don't think you're right for this particular part," the professional doesn't burst into tears. They might be feeling disappointed, but their experience and professionalism kicks-in and they smile bravely, thank the producer for seeing them and walk off with their head held erect. Later, in the privacy of their own home, if they desperately wanted the part they'd auditioned for, they might well be upset. But they don't let the world see it.

That's the difference between pros and amateurs. You've all seen the wannabe stars on *The X Factor*, sobbing their hearts out, the tears streaming down their crumpled little faces when they're told they're 'not going through' with ten million people watching. They think it's the end of the world. And for some of them it's probably better that they don't pursue a career in show business, because they're just not good enough. But some of them will lick their wounds and keep on trying. They might not necessarily succeed, but this first rejection will help them when they get their next rejection and the next. Everyone in show business from Frank Sinatra to Robbie Williams and the Beatles were told, "You're not good enough" at some point in their career. I get told it every couple of weeks!

If you ever watched *Just up your Street* you'll know that we found some fantastic girl singers and plenty of great male singers, quite a few bands, trios and duos too. But very few comedians, which was a bit disappointing for me because I would have loved to have mentored a couple of up and coming comics.

We did have talented Welsh funny men Phil Evans and Rod Woodward on the series, but they had already started to establish themselves as after-dinner speakers and corporate functions and have since both gone on to make audiences laugh all over the world. Someone else who we discovered a decade before he made his sensational appearance on *Britain's Got Talent* in 2010 was the brilliantly funny impressionist Paul Burling who, although not born in Wales, lived in Cardiff for many years.

If any raw, inexperienced young comedians had wanted to come on the show and have a go at making people laugh, I would have done my best to knock off the rough edges and help them make a start.

Whatever younger comics think of my material and my style of comedy, they can't deny my years of experience and that I know the mechanics of comedy. How to judge an audience as soon as you walk out on stage. How to work a room if it's a social club environment. How to deal with hecklers and drunks. How to time a joke. When to hit them with a series of quick gags one after another and when to slow down and tell them a story-joke with a big finish. Many young comics, who do a few open-mike spots and get on the comedy club circuit, don't even know how to walk on and off stage properly. You may think that's not important these days and, to be honest, you're probably right. Times have changed.

I'm lucky enough to remember the confident-to-the-point-of-arrogant way that Jack Benny and Bob Hope used to walk out on stage and look at the audience. They were in charge from the second they appeared. Jimmy Tarbuck used to watch the two American greats on TV when he was growing up and learned from them. He always walks on with a confident swagger and it's not through big-headedness. It just lets the audience know that *he's the man*!

The very first episode of *Just up your Street* came from the Coal Exchange in Cardiff, an historic building where, many years before, rich merchants in black frock coats and mutton-chop whiskers would exchange lumps of coal with each other. What fun that must have been. Well there was no telly in those days. Even if there *had* been, no-one could have watched it. There was no electricity.

As I was saying, the first venue was the Coal Exchange; we had five acts on the show and in between some of the acts we ran five, two-minute film clips of me and the crew looking for talented people around Cardiff and persuading them to perform on camera, which established the format of the show for the first three series.

One of the performers on that show was Caroline Cooper, an experienced club singer with a very distinctive voice. She also happened to have a very famous niece – a then very young Charlotte Church – who was sat in the auditorium with her mother. We managed to persuade Charlotte to introduce her relative from the audience and she did, by saying "Singing 'As if we never said goodbye' from *Sunset Boulevard*, here's *my Auntie Caroline*!"

We also had a three-sister act from Ely called Soul Attraction who sang the Diana Ross version of 'Why do Fools Fall in Love'; a singing bus driver from Barry who performed 'I Drove All Night' and a rock band called Peel, who we thought would go on to greater things. So as you can see, we tried to appeal to as many musical tastes as we could, which is why the show very quickly became so popular with viewers.

Meeting so many talented young (and not so young) performers on the series enabled me to give several of them the opportunity to work for me in my touring pantomimes, for my Owen Money Theatre Company.

One girl singer who auditioned, Terina Newman from Caldicot in Monmouthshire, was a real stunner. She had a mass of blonde hair and the face of a fashion model which made her ideal for the part of Cinderella in the Owen Money Theatre Company's second pantomime. She wasn't the world's greatest singer but she looked sensational and had a lovely personality. The perfect Cinders.

You might find this odd, but in the autumn of 2000, when she was an 'unknown' trying to break into the business any way that she could, Kym Marsh, the dark-haired actress who plays Michelle Connor in *Coronation Street* auditioned for our second series in Llandudno. She was part of a double-act with the pretty blonde violinist Claire Gobin and their audition was quite something. While Kym sang 'live' and danced to a backing track, Claire accompanied her on electric violin. I can't remember what the song was but it struck me that their act was visually strong and musically very exciting.

When we phoned Claire a couple of weeks later to give her the good news that we wanted them to appear on the series that we would be recording early in 2001, Claire told us that while she would love to appear, Kym had successfully auditioned without Claire for another television talent show, to be made by ITV, which she wasn't allowed to tell us the title of. Not only that, Kym had been asked to sign a contract that forbade her from appearing on any other television show while she was still part of this 'mysterious' new show.

The ITV show turned out to be *Pop Stars*, which created the short-lived band Hear' Say, of which she was a member until

2002. She then had a solo singing career for a while, before becoming an actress. As for Claire Gobin, she did appear on the series with her electric violin and she looked and sounded fantastic. I heard recently that she is now making a good living as an entertainer on luxury cruise ships. I just hope she doesn't include 'My Heart will go On' in her repertoire. Cruise ships? The theme from *Titanic*? Oh, please yourselves!

Another singer I employed in a couple of my pantomimes was Newport singer and actor Anthony Moulton. I'll never forget his audition, which I think was for the second series. Auditions were held, as before, in Tŷ Oldfield and it must have been a Sunday, because Anthony was in the chorus of *Miss Saigon* at the Theatre Royal, Drury Lane.

We'd already auditioned on the Saturday and had found several potential singers for series two, but the Sunday had been a bit of a disappointment. No-one had knocked our socks off and it seemed we'd seen the best of the bunch on the day before. Then right at the end of the day, as we were about to clear up and clear off, this tall, bald young man walked in and apologised for being late. He explained that he worked in the West End six days a week; he'd spent the Sunday with his family in Newport and he was rushing off back to London immediately after the audition. He seemed a bit flustered, which is not the ideal state to be in for an audition, but he handed Nigel Hart his sheet music and took a moment to focus. His audition piece was going to be Stevie Wonder's 'Lately', which is not an easy song to interpret, with its quiet, reflective opening, building to an emotional, soulful ending. I thought to myself, "Good luck with this one, sunshine!"

Well as soon as he started singing, he blew us all away. He was fantastic. And I would also like to add that Nigel Hart's sympathetic keyboard accompaniment was also, as it always was, just superb. When Anthony had finished we said, "Thanks very much" and off he went back to London. At the auditions we didn't tell anyone whether they would be on the show or not. Before a decision could be made between us all, we had to look back at the video footage and make our decision. There were signs all over the walls of the holding area outside the audition room, making it quite plain that, "We will only be writing to those of you who have passed the auditions. If you have not heard from us within four weeks, you have not passed the auditions."

Even though I wasn't really allowed to do so, I wanted to tell Anthony straight away that he was definitely going to be on the series. All the other performers had gone by then, so no-one could have overheard, But I restrained myself and I'm glad I didn't spill the beans, because some months later the *Just up your Street* film crew and I surprised him in his dressing room at the Theatre Royal, Drury Lane, and told him on camera that he'd passed the audition.

Another talented performer who appeared on *Just up your Street* was the young singer, songwriter and pianist Richard Harris who was, and still is at the time of writing, the resident pianist at the Celtic Manor Hotel, Newport. He was another one who arrived very late in the afternoon and I remember he had to set up his own keyboard before he could perform. He could have chosen any one of the hundreds of songs in his repertoire, from Rat Pack standards to West End and Broadway show stoppers or one of his own fine compositions. If you like good music, you should check-out his CD, *Café Days*.

The audition song he settled on was one that I wasn't familiar with, 'How do you keep the music playing?' and I learned later that the haunting music was written by Michael Legrand and the wonderful lyrics by Alan and Marilyn Bergman. Sometimes you can hear a song for the first time and the combination of the words and melody touch you. That's how I and the rest of the judging panel immediately felt about that song. Richard performed it brilliantly, bringing out every little nuance of the emotion in the lyrics. When he'd finished we thanked him for coming and after he'd gone, the rest of the judges and I were unanimous. Not only was he going to be on the show, he was also going to sing that song!

A few weeks later the crew and I did a surprise 'hit' on Richard as he was playing the grand piano at the Celtic Manor Hotel to tell him he was on the show. Some years later, Radio Two's Chris Evans was staying at the Celtic Manor, saw Richard perform and booked him to appear on his chat show which used to be on ITV on Sunday nights. But I was the one who gave him his first chance on the telly!

These surprise 'hits' on people who'd auditioned for us were a very popular part of the show, but they took some planning and a lot of patience. We were so lucky to have as our Production Manager a man called Rhys Bevan. Without Rhys on the team, I don't think we could have done half the things we managed to achieve with the series. He could juggle half-a-dozen logistical problems at once while appearing to be totally unflappable. He is also the only man I have ever met who carried four mobile phones around – and at least two of them were constantly ringing at the same time. I'm sure he once phoned himself by accident.

You have to remember that when we set out to make that first series we really were in uncharted waters, not knowing whether it would work and Captain Rhys Bevan helped to guide us safely through one or two pretty stormy seas at times. Could I tell you some stories! I could... but the BBC legal department won't let me.

These 'hits' also involved a lot of hanging around for me and the crew inside the *Just up your Street* vehicles in various car parks and side streets all over Wales at various times of the day and night, waiting to catch our 'victim' in their home, or in a restaurant, a hairdresser's shop, a school classroom, a cinema queue, the Celtic Manor Hotel, a betting shop and, in one case, in the middle of painting and decorating someone else's house.

Going back to Anthony Moulton, his performance on *Just up your Street* was one of the highlights of series two and a couple of years later, when BBC Wales decided to turn the series from its established format as a showcase for Welsh performers into a 'Pop Idol' style competition, he re-applied to come on.

In the semi-final he sang 'Mr Bojangles' and once again he delivered a great performance. If he'd stuck with that song for the final he would definitely have won the series, but he decided to change the song to something else that I can't remember, and as a result he lost out to a female singer from west Wales. However, Anthony continues to entertain audiences, both as a singer and club DJ.

One of our biggest finds on the series was that very talented young lady from Haverfordwest, Connie Fisher; several years before Sir Andrew Lloyd Webber discovered her on the BBC network series *How do you Solve a Problem like Maria?* Connie had auditioned for us in Cardiff and her distinctive voice, bubbly personality and obvious unbridled enthusiasm for musical theatre won us over.

Rather than write to her to tell her she'd passed the audition, we decided to set up a surprise 'hit' on her and, with the help of her mother, who was sworn to secrecy, we managed to 'ambush' young Connie – who was only 16 at the time and still at school – at her mother's place of work, Greens of Haverfordwest, a motor dealership which specialised in 4x4s. Her mother made up an excuse for Connie to call in to see her after school and I arrived with the crew about an hour before, so we could find somewhere suitable to hide. And we did, in a store cupboard about five foot by three foot.

Not many of you would have had the experience of standing in a cupboard for half an hour with a cameraman, sound man, and electrician, together with all their equipment. Be grateful that you haven't. It's the sort of occasion when you find out which one of you had baked beans at lunchtime. I don't think I need to elaborate.

When I jumped out of the cupboard, microphone in hand and told her she was on the show, Connie was delighted and when she appeared on the show a couple of months later she didn't let us down. She looked every inch a budding West End star, which of course she went on to be some years further down the line when she won the role of Maria in *The Sound of Music* at the London Palladium for a year, before going on a national tour with the show.

She has also appeared in the television drama *Caught in a Trap*, in which she played an obsessive Elvis fan, and *They're Playing Our Song* at the Menier Chocolate Factory. I know that Connie, who is actually from Lisburn in County Antrim, will go on to have a long career in the business, because she's worked hard to get where she is and will keep on giving one hundred and ten per cent.

But she had a bit of a tough time when she came back to appear on the 'competitive' version of *Just up your Street* a couple of years after her successful first appearance. She was eligible to audition again because after we'd made three series of *Just up your Street*, BBC Wales decided to turn the show from a talent showcase to a talent competition and the change of format meant that the auditions were open to anyone, even those who had already appeared.

I should mention here that when we started pre-production on this new 'competitive' series, there'd been a lot of changes at BBC Wales. Geraint Evans had left, the Entertainment Department had closed down and we'd moved across the road from Tŷ Oldfield to Broadcasting House and set up shop in the newly-formed Music Department.

Connie Fisher had by then appeared on Jane McDonald's *Star for a Night* series and performed in various amateur and semi-professional stage shows, gaining experience all the time. She applied to be a contestant on the revised *Just up your Street* and easily passed her audition. But when she appeared on the new series, she fared less well than she had first time around, through no fault of her own. She was also on the receiving end of some unjustified harsh comments by the judges. Stuart Cable, the ex-Stereophonics drummer, whose sudden death at the age of 40 while I was writing this book came as a terrible shock to everyone, was also a judge on some of the shows and being an out-and-out rocker, he wasn't really qualified to give his opinion on someone like Connie, who sang songs from Broadway and West End shows. When Connie finished her song, Stuart's comments, in which he honestly explained that musical theatre wasn't his scene, and the even harsher ones made by another judge whose name I can't recall, really got to her. I can still see her walking off the set, after hearing the judges' comments, with tears in her eyes, saying, "They hated me!" That wasn't true, but she was upset and feeling vulnerable after delivering what I and the audience thought was a terrific performance. Obviously Stuart didn't hate her. He was a rock drummer (and one of the best in the business) and was simply unable to judge someone whose ambition was to go into musical theatre. I think it's worth pointing out that at the end of 2009 Stuart and Connie appeared together on a Radio Wales show and they both laughed about their experience on *Just up your Street*, proving that there was no lasting ill-feeling on Connie's part.

While we're still talking about Connie, here's something you might find interesting. One of the regular judges was singer and vocal coach Annie Skates, who has been involved with many West End productions over the years. While she was travelling back and fore to Cardiff for our series, she was also employed by Sir Andrew Lloyd Webber's Really Useful Company to look for likely performers for his revival of *The Sound of Music*, which was in the *very* early planning stages then, probably four or five years before it was eventually staged. When Annie saw Connie on our show, she didn't go overboard with her praise. Neither was she particularly negative. But I wonder if, as the years went by, she remembered the girl from

Haverfordwest who looked and sounded like a young Julie Andrews?

There had been huge budget cuts on the fourth series, but we still had just enough to pay for a 'live' band. However, without the film clips of me interacting with the people of Wales and with the addition of three judges each week, it just looked and felt like a micro-budget version of shows like *Pop Idol* and *X Factor*.

I've wanted to say this for a long while. I have no proof to back this up, but to this day I am sure that someone in network television saw an episode or two of *Just up your Street* and decided it was time for talent shows to return to prime-time Saturday night television – obviously with a vast budget, big name judges and hosts... and an enormous set and space-age lighting that BBC Wales could only dream of. The budget just for the set of *The X Factor* was probably more than five series of *Just up your Street*.

When it came to series five, for some reason the BBC decided not to make it themselves, in-house as it were. Instead they asked all the independent production companies in Wales to put in bids to make it. More on that in a moment.

The other popular show that I worked on at BBC Wales, under the then still active Entertainment Department, with Alan Wightman back on board again as Associate Producer and writer, was *Money in the Bank* which was set in a fictitious nightclub – actually a spectacularly designed studio set – called 'The Bank'. Money... in... the... Bank... geddit? This was a straightforward, dare I say the 'V' word...? Variety show. We made two series of that show and in each one we managed to book some great names, like Joe Pasquale, Status Quo, Jimmy Nail, David Essex, Tim Vine, Johnny Casson, Cannon and Ball, Tony Hadley, Roy Wood, Gerard Kenny, Toyah Wilcox, Bobby Davro, Jimmy Cricket... and Freddie Starr!

Freddie appeared on our Christmas show, along with Alvin

Stardust and Leo Sayer *and* Jerry Lee Lewis's piano-playing sister, Linda Gail Lewis. Not a bad line-up for a regional show. Well, when people heard that Freddie was going to be on, the demand for tickets was unbelievable. We could never have fitted everyone who wanted to see the show into the studio. Health and Safety wouldn't have allowed it, although they did let Freddie in!

Viewing figures for that show were touching 300,000. Phenomenal! He hadn't been on television for a couple of years and people wanted to see what Freddie would get up to. But there was a terrible moment – about two hours before we started recording the show – when we thought Freddie wasn't going to take part.

He arrived several hours later than expected, accompanied by his wife, Donna. Because he was so late, we had rehearsed with all the other stars and the band and were desperate to get him in front of the camera so we would have some idea what he was going to do. Geraint Evans was still Head of Entertainment at the time and was also the Producer. So he, I and Alan waited and waited for Freddie to turn up.

He eventually walked into the studio, all smiles, and introduced himself. In fact I must say he was very friendly and outgoing with me. Then he said, "Owen, I've got this great idea. It's called 'Inder Cella' and it's the story of Cinderalla but I keep getting my words mixed up. And there's this really funny bit where I call one of the Ugly Sisters *Betty Swallox!*"

Well I was mortified. I knew this routine. It was first done years before by another Liverpool comedian, Mickey Finn. And it was filthy. Okay in the clubs, if you like that sort of thing. But definitely not for BBC Wales audiences expecting a bit of pre-Christmas fun. I knew Freddie had a reputation for being difficult in certain situations and I thought that telling him he couldn't do a certain routine just a few hours before the show would definitely qualify as a 'certain situation'. More than likely he would walk out and we would have lost our star attraction.

Geraint Evans said "Could I have a word?" and took him into the Green Room. Not to confuse you but the Green Room was actually painted in terracotta with light blue furniture and a red door. The curtains were purple and the carpet was a matching lilac. I have an idea the place was originally designed by Stevie Wonder.

Alan and I followed, not knowing what to expect. Geraint sat down with Freddie and Donna and gave them cups of tea, and while Freddie lit a cigarette, Geraint explained, very diplomatically, that although the show would go out at half-past-ten at night, because it was a Christmas special, it was going to be repeated at a seven-thirty slot the following week. So, could he understand why that routine, however funny, wasn't really suitable?

Freddie pondered this for a few minutes, exchanging glances with Donna and taking drags from his cigarette. I knew that Donna had already retrieved Freddie's musical backing disk from our studio sound department, so she was obviously ready to get up and go the moment Freddie lost it. And from the distant look on his face, I could see it was very likely that he was about to.

Freddie stubbed out his ciggie in an ashtray and stood up, as did Donna. With a face like thunder Freddie said, "Donna! It's time for a taxi!" Geraint didn't seem fazed by this and said, "Freddie, we've been trailing this show and the fact you're on it for weeks. We have never had as many requests for tickets as we have for your appearance. The studio is going to be packed with your fans tonight. And there's one more thing." Freddie lit another cigarette as Geraint continued. "This is a BBC show for which you have signed a contract to appear. If you fail to appear on the show, you will have broken your contract."

Freddie was now taking another cigarette out and lighting it. You can imagine there was a lot of smoke in the room by now. There was so much you'd think they were electing a new Pope. Geraint continued, "If you break your contract, my Entertainment Department will have no alternative but to hand the matter to our Legal Department... and you know what that will lead to?" Freddie still held firm. But the anger in his eyes wasn't shining so brightly as before.

Geraint went on. "But we don't want all that nastiness, do we Fred? And you don't want to disappoint all your fans who've travelled here to see you, or all the viewers who'll be tuning in when the show goes out?"

Freddie smiled. He was savvy enough to know that he was being sweet-talked and having his ego rubbed, but he also knew it wouldn't be the first time the BBC had sued a star for breaking their contract. He sat back down, as did Donna and from that moment he was as nice as pie. Like all big stars, from time he needs to establish that *he is still* a star and his threat to walk out was a bluff on his part to see just how much we wanted him for the show. I also knew that a comic with his many years' experience would have hours of routines to choose bits of comedy business from and as long as he had a couple of hours to get his head together, he would easily find ten minutes of acceptable material. Not only that, if all else failed he also had several songs to fall back on.

He went on that night, sang an old Elvis song ('cos there aren't any new ones), got a girl 'volunteer' up from the audience and indulged in some outrageous physical comedy and then did an interview with me. It wasn't vintage Freddie, but he got a great reaction from the audience and when the show went out just before Christmas that year, the high viewing figures justified the mini-trauma he caused us.

The other guests on the show all delivered too, especially Leo Sayer who drove down to Broadcasting House in Llandaff from his house outside London and got there so early he had a look around Llandaff Cathedral and even had a word with the Bishop! He sang a couple of songs on the show, including his Number One hit from 1977, 'When I need You', backed by our resident band led by John Quirk. Now the sax player with the band was a man named Ceri Rees who, these days, plays in my band the Soul Sharks. If you remember, 'When I need You' has a sax solo in the middle of the song and on our show Ceri played a blistering version. Simply stunning. It would have raised the hairs on the back of Telly Savalas's head. And after the show, Leo went up to him and said, "I've sung that song on TV shows all over the world and that was the best that *anyone's* ever played it!" Quite a compliment.

CHAPTER FIFTEEN

DESPITE ATTRACTING HEALTHY AUDIENCES – and a few people with a nasty cough and cold – after two series *Money in the Bank* was no more. But I was still committed to the next series of *Just up your Street* which was going to be made by an independent company based in Cardiff called Alfresco.

From day one there was a totally different feel about the show. For example, there was a much shorter pre-production period, so they couldn't go through the process of asking people to send in application forms, CDs, DVDs etc, because they didn't have the time or the resources – as we had at the BBC – to vet every applicant. This was the first sign that things were going to be different. So they set up a series of open auditions. In other words, "Turn up and we'll see you!" They had no idea what they'd unleashed.

The first auditions took place in the Newport City Live Arena, which sounds very grand, but was in fact the old, long-since closed Odeon cinema in Clarence Place, Newport. Calling it an 'arena' was a bit ambitious considering it was nowhere near as big as the Cardiff International Arena, but the new owners had spent quite a bit of money transforming it from a disused cinema to a modern venue for live performances.

It eventually went out of business and was taken over temporarily by a church group, who only used it on Sundays and since they left, this fine example of 1930s Art Deco design has remained empty, which is a shame. I think it's a listed building so the council can't knock it down. Anyone out there want to go fifty-fifty with me and buy it? Imagine... *The Owen Money Theatre*, featuring regular shows packed with up-and-coming performers and the occasional big name and every

Christmas a three-week pantomime season with yours truly. Now, just calm down and form an orderly queue before you get knocked down in the rush.

Talking of queues, on the first day at the NCLA, we were due to start the auditions at two o'clock in the afternoon and we thought we'd get a couple of hundred people turning up. The idea was we'd give them just *twenty seconds each* to impress us, without any sort of musical accompaniment, and that we'd all be away by six o'clock, or seven o'clock at the latest. So this was already a very different set-up from the previous three series, where we always started our auditions first thing in the morning and gave everyone a chance to sing a complete song.

Despite the limited time, the hopefuls knew they'd have to impress us. Long before the two o'clock start, the queue stretched from the building's front doors, all the way along Clarence Place to the Newport town bridge – around three hundred yards. There were so many people waiting, I went outside with a small camera crew, to talk to them to keep them cheered up as they stood around in the cold. One of the hopefuls was an eccentric female singer with missing front teeth named Kerry Rees, who later appeared very briefly, a couple of times, on *The X Factor* audition shows.

Kerry was such a lively character, although I had no idea how bad or good a singer she was. I thought she would at the very least add some comedy value to the show, but she was so far back in the queue there was a real danger that, if we did stop the auditions at six o'clock in order for the production team to be away by seven, she wouldn't be seen.

The afternoon flew by and around five o'clock, because new people were joining the end of the queue all the time, it didn't seem to go down. So we had to rush them through even faster than we had before, by bringing in fifteen of them at a time, letting them each strut their stuff for twenty seconds and then they were replaced by another fifteen and so on.

Even with this rapid turn-around it was obvious that there was no chance of us closing the doors on the hopefuls for several MORE hours.

So we did get to see Kerry Rees perform. But at the exact moment she opened her mouth to sing... "Bang!"... a bulb in one of the lights over her head exploded! Not her doing, of course, but *it looked like it was* and the moment was so funny – we were all on our knees, helpless with laughter – we used it in one of the segments where we showed all the auditionees who weren't quite good enough, the bad singers and... the no-hopers, an idea later picked up by *The X Factor*. I know I keep mentioning that show, but it really is true that they 'borrowed' so many ideas from *Just up your Street*.

The six o'clock finish that Alfresco had anticipated went by the board and the auditions went on past ten o'clock... and they were still queuing outside. It was amazing. Because the NCLA's entertainment licence had an eleven p.m. cut-off, we approached the landlord of the Ivy Bush pub next door to see if, after eleven o'clock, we could keep the auditions going in their function room but, sensibly, he refused. So we had to continue the auditions at the NCLA and eventually finished them at one o'clock in the morning.

From there the auditions moved down to the Grand Theatre, Swansea, where exactly the same thing happened. The queue went all along the length of the building and all the way down Nelson Street. The auditions were held in a large room upstairs in the new studio wing and the place was jam-packed.

Amongst the hopefuls waiting to be seen was a character who called himself Kerry Digion who kept everybody entertained, singing songs and generally keeping people's spirits up while they waited hours and hours to be seen.

After what had happened in Newport we more organised by now and we weren't going to be caught on the hop and, instead of starting the auditions at two in the afternoon, we started at eleven in the morning. We should have started a few hours earlier really, because it was still a very long day and we didn't get to see the final auditionee until ten o'clock that night. It can be very draining watching a 'conveyor belt' of performers filing past, all of them singing for twenty seconds before they shuffle off into the wings. When the show was made in-house by BBC Wales the auditions usually lasted from nine in the morning to around six in the evening and even then, by around three in the afternoon, having sat through thirty girl singers either singing, wailing, screaming or gargling 'I Will Always Love You', it was tough to show any enthusiasm.

Because the auditions went down so well in Newport, we decided to make the shows at the Newport City Live Arena. With all the singers selected, it was, like the previous series, staged as a competition. We did five shows as semi-finals and the sixth was the final, which went out 'live' between 7.30 p.m. and 8.00 p.m., after which the phone-lines for voting opened. During the period when people could phone in, we had a one-hour spin-off show over on BBC2 Wales which included some of the more 'eccentric' performers who, and I'm being very kind here, 'just weren't good enough' to take part in the show as contestants. Like, for example, 'John the Song' from Porthcawl, so-named because he tends to burst into song no matter where he is. The fact that he hasn't got the first idea about keeping in tempo or pausing between the lyrics and doesn't have an ear for a melody doesn't deter him from his musical mission in life.

On the BBC 2 Wales show he was going to sing 'Doo Wah Diddy Diddy' unaccompanied (not that any self-respecting musician would have wanted to accompany him). We rehearsed him in the afternoon and he was fine, in his own way, and when he'd finished his very short spot (thirty seconds) we reminded him that when the show went out that night, it was 'live' and we would be very tight for time so he couldn't over-run his time.

So, that night, as the BBC2 show was going out live, I introduced 'John the Song', and he walked on singing 'Doo Wah Diddy Diddy' for thirty seconds, getting an enthusiastic response from the audience, which was packed to the rafters. But when he finished singing, instead of going off stage, he started singing it all over again. And he did an even longer version which lasted a minute and a half, to the delight of the crowd and the dismay of the production team who were outside in the scanner, beaming the show back to the BBC from where it was immediately transmitted out to the tellys of Wales!

We managed to get the show back on track and as ten o'clock approached, I told the viewers that the phone lines would close soon and that they should turn over to BBC One Wales after the national news at ten o'clock, when they would find out who had won that year's series. We had some great singers in the final, including Richard Harris, who was happy to reapply for the show even though it was now a competition. The winner of the series was Swansea's Karl Morgan, another multi-talented singer who went on to work with Steve Balsamo and who now tours and records with his band, The Click.

Connie Fisher. Paul Burling. Kym Marsh. Karl Evans. Can I find talent, or can I find talent?

The viewing figures for the series were, once again, excellent. BBC Wales ordered another series from Alfresco, but by now the financial constraints we'd been up against got even tougher and the budget Alfresco was given was much reduced. Once again they had to make sure they made a profit out of the series, so they had less money available to spend on the actual production.

More cost-cutting ensued, which was the main reason why, after five previous series in which we'd staged the show in theatres and leisure centres, the BBC studios in Cardiff and the Newport Arena, that the final series was made in a converted factory. Like the previous series that Alfresco produced, the 'live' band were dispensed with and the performers sang along to a pre-recorded keyboard backing.

The venue was a place called The Pop Factory in Porth in the Rhondda Valley, and it was a former soft drinks factory which had been reopened as a music and media venue. In fact it was officially opened by Sir Tom Jones, who smashed a bottle of dandelion and burdock pop against the wall of the building as part of the official ceremony. Or it could have been because he wasn't keen on dandelion and burdock. Well it's not unusual!

I was given a co-host for this series, the young actress and presenter Josie D'arby, who was delightful and did a very professional job. Once again the series went out on Friday nights and the viewing figures were consistently good.

However, I had hosted *six* series by now. The first three were a joy to make and involved me travelling around Wales with my production crew, meeting people on the street and being directed by inventive and creative film makers like Richard Pawelko and Deiniol Morris. The fourth series, the 'competitive' one, dispensed with the film sequences but kept the 'live' band. And the final two series had no film clips or band and were made for ten bob and a bag of toffees. Nevertheless the shows were still a big hit with the viewers.

But all good things must come to an end and when, at the beginning of the following year, 2006, I was asked to attend a meeting with BBC Wales' 'Head of Talent', it was no surprise to me when she explained that *Just up your Street* wasn't coming back. But she went on to explain that they were going to create a brand new entertainment series, starring a couple of fantastic new Welsh comics that they'd discovered in London. Aha! So the old *was* having to make way for the new.

As it happened the new series with 'a couple of fantastic new Welsh comics' never happened. Don't look at me! It wasn't my fault! I've no proof of this but the two comics may well have been Rhod Gilbert and Chris Corcoran, who I like and find very funny. Rhod and Chris, together and in their solo careers, have gone from strength to strength and built up a huge fan base. Rhod has done what I never have, toured theatres all around Great Britain and appeared on network comedy shows and chat shows. He creates his own material, works hard at his comedy and his success is well deserved.

In telling you what happens in television in terms of certain personalities falling in and out of favour, I'm hardly giving away a state secret. You've probably noticed yourself how some people seem to be on the telly all the time for a few years – then vanish. Take Cilla Black. After her pop-singing career faded a little, she was off the scene for many years, and then came back to host *Blind Date* and *Surprise, Surprise* attracting huge ratings for both shows. She was 'Miss Saturday Night TV' from 1985 to 2003 and even found time to host the 1993 *Royal Variety Performance*. That's quite a career. Then in May 2003 she walked away from *Blind Date*, since when she has only been seen on our screens occasionally.

How does this happen? Search me!

CHAPTER SIXTEEN

WHEN I HAD MY stroke in 2006 and was off work for several months, Julie Barton, who was my Editor at BBC Radio Wales, came to see me at my house. I knew that she'd announced that she was leaving her job but Julie assured me that as soon as I was well enough, I could return to work whenever I wanted. Julie was always a strong supporter of mine and one of my most vivid memories of her is when she was standing on the other side of the glass while I was presenting one of my weekday radio shows. On Monday, the 11th of September 2001.

I was in the two p.m. to four p.m. slot and you may remember that the news and 'live' footage of the Twin Towers started coming through from New York soon after two o'clock our time. I had to keep everything together for those couple of hours, while snippets of information about the scale of the devastation filtered through our news department and onto the air, courtesy of our news team.

In between the reports I had to keep playing the list of records that had been pre-arranged days before, being alert to the possibility that one of the songs might, quite innocently, contain a reference to what was going on across the Atlantic. I found it a very traumatic experience but, thanks to the years of 'live' radio I had under my belt, I got through it, with the help of my production team and Julie, who continually encouraged me to keep going. Those were the longest couple of hours I have ever experienced in over 20 years of broadcasting.

I was very lucky that the stroke didn't affect my speech very badly, but nevertheless it *was* affected and there was no way I could return to radio until it improved. I think I was off the air for around three months, but it seemed an eternity to me.

I was determined to get back to work as quickly as possible and I thought it would be a good idea to have some speech therapy. Unfortunately that didn't really work because all my speech therapist wanted to do was talk about my radio show and ask me questions about *Just up your Street* and when it was coming back. Anyway, after a few months, day by day, slowly my speech got betterer and betterer.

My speech might have improved but my spelling's still atroshuss.

So, I eventually went back to my four days a week on the radio. I felt like things were getting better for me, even though, after six or seven years of being on the box, I didn't have a television series lined-up. But my radio shows were still popular with the listeners and I was happy to stay in radio for as long as 'the powers that be' at BBC Wales wanted me to.

Then, out of the blue, I was told that my friend, the venerable (and veteran!) broadcaster Roy Noble, was going to take over my week day afternoon shows. I can't pretend I wasn't disappointed, but life goes on and I had to count my blessings. I'd got over my stroke and still had my popular Saturday and Sunday shows. I did the old professional entertainer thing of telling myself that I would be moving onwards and upwards, believing that better things lay ahead. Those positive feelings lasted about a fortnight. Or it could have been two weeks. I forget. And then the gloom descended...

I went from feeling I was on the top of the tree, to the stage where I felt low every day. Weeks went by and I couldn't shake it off. Comedians have always been prone to feeling down in the dumps – remember the story about the great Grimaldi – and I'd had days in the past where everything got on top of me, just like anyone else. But I hadn't experienced such a prolonged and seemingly endless black mood. It wasn't just my broadcasting career that was causing the depression. My marriage was falling apart and it was totally my fault, and nothing to do with my beautiful wife Kath, who I have never stopped loving with all my heart, despite all the 'diversions' I've taken through the years we've been together.

After all the pain I've caused her and our children, it may sound trite to say that I'm sorry for what I did. But I am truly sorry. Hindsight provides us with a crystal-clear window into the past, enabling us to look back at things we've done, choices we've made and decisions we've taken and think, "Why the hell did I do *that*? What a bloody fool I've been!" And I freely admit that in the past I have been very foolish, very selfish and taken a very cavalier attitude to my marriage.

Confession might be good for the soul, but it's really difficult for me to admit to my failings and weaknesses to my fans and loyal listeners. However I do need to get this off my chest. Unbeknown to Kath, I had a secret affair with a young lady that lasted fifteen years. I'm sure some of you reading the last sentence either think I was exaggerating or "How could he keep an affair from his wife all that time?" All I can tell you is, the affair did last all that time and my wife didn't have a clue.

Of course I knew the affair was wrong and that if Kath found out it would break her heart, as well as alienating me from my two children. God knows I tried to end the relationship on many, many occasions. The young lady in question – who is now happily married – also wanted to finish with me several times because she could see I was never going to divorce Kath and move in with her or even marry her. The affair was doomed, but we just couldn't end it. The feeling between us was too intense. Fifteen years is a long time to have an illicit relationship with someone. Many *marriages* don't last that long. I'm not trying to justify what I got myself involved in; I'm just explaining why it was so difficult to end it.

As things turned out, neither of us ended the affair, because fate stepped in. A friend of my daughter Katie saw me and the lady in question out together one night and 'kindly' told Katie that her father had a girlfriend. Katie told Kath and holy hell broke out. It was a terrible, terrible time for my family and it was all brought about by me.

Some wives, understandably, wouldn't hesitate to throw out a husband who'd had an affair behind her back, whether it was for fifteen years or fifteen days. So it says a lot about the sort of generous person my Kath is, that she eventually forgave me. After I had my stroke in 2006, she was the first person I turned to for help and she got me through it. After I came out of hospital she took me back to the house and nursed me and was instrumental in getting my life back to normal. She's a much stronger person than me in many ways and I'm so happy that she was prepared to give me another chance.

That all happened a few years back; since then I have done everything I can to put my marriage on track. These things take time and Kath has to really believe that this is what *I* want and that I won't go philandering again. Our ultimate aim is to renew our marriage vows and get back together on a full-time basis. The fact that we still love each other is undeniable, but a good marriage has to be based on more than just love. Trust is important. As is patience and tolerance. And mutual respect.

But there's something much more important, that has to be discussed in depth, right at the start of a marriage, if it has any chance of surviving. And it's this. You *have to* decide which one of you is going to be in charge of the TV remote control.

I was a bloody fool to have had that long-term affair because it could easily have caused a huge wedge between me and my two children, Matthew and Katie, and my two beautiful grandchildren. I'm so lucky to still have my loving family and loads of friends, colleagues and acquaintances. I've got fans all over Wales and many more beyond Offa's Dyke too. Yet, at the time I'm writing this, I live alone while Kath and I decide how to move forward with our relationship.

The truth is I'm not one of those people who enjoy their

own company for more than an hour or so. Which means that I get lonely at times. I might be surrounded by hundreds of people in a club or at a function and I'm all smiles, just like any comedy entertainer worth his salt *should* be with his public. But when the show's over, I go home to an empty house. Well, when I say 'empty', obviously there's furniture in there. Carpets and curtains. Tea bags. Half-a-packet of Rich Tea biscuits (best before date – June 1997). A digital radio permanently tuned to BBC Radio Wales. And a flat screen television set. Well it wasn't *originally* a flat screen telly but it has been ever since it fell face down on the floor.

Here's an interesting fact that I read in my doctor's waiting room, whilst I was growing a beard. Of all the electrical items in an average house, the television set is *the most watched*.

Did you see what I did then? I switched from bearing my soul to making a funny. I can't help it. It's in the blood. Because whatever's going on his private life, a comedian's job is to make other people happy. Without getting too heavy about it, comedians are there to make the world a slightly cheerier place to live in – and that's quite a privileged position to be in.

There are always one or two miserable buggers who simply refuse to laugh when I'm performing and remain stony-faced even when I tell my best jokes. They're not fans of Owen Money and that's fair enough. There are plenty of comedians who leave me cold. But the so and sos who sit there with their arms folded, determined not to break into a smile, while everyone else around them are doubled up with laughter, would be much better off, as Doddy always maintains, "Exercising their chuckle muscles!" What's that old saying? "It takes two hundred muscles to frown, but only one hundred and ninety nine to smile?" No, that can't be right. Surely?

I think in many respects, certainly when it came to my family, I let my life go by me. From the 1970s right through until the late 1990s I put my career first and took many more things for granted. Even before I became Owen Money, when I was with Tomfoolery, I was always away working in Blackpool, north-east England, Scotland and Italy. Then when I became a solo comedian, after a few false starts, I eventually got on a roll career-wise, riding on the crest of a giant wave. Everything seemed to get better. On the back of my television and radio shows, the club work flooded in and I took full advantage of it, working until late several nights a week, driving miles and miles and getting home in the early hours.

Then there were the long pantomime seasons and the summer shows and BBC Radio Wales outside broadcasts that took me all around the country. All of this was great for my bank balance and consequently my family wanted for nothing... except having me around. When I wasn't tearing around Wales, entertaining audiences, I was having a good time, socialising, meeting people... especially female people. The glitz and the glamour of the world I inhabited attracted equally glitzy and glamorous women. And one or two who made Shrek look effeminate.

I'll be honest with you. I know I'm no George Clooney. I'm more a George Formby. If I was a foreman at Hoover's or an insurance clerk, women wouldn't look twice at me. But because I was well-known, quite well off and possessed a full head of hair (I use L'Oreal, because I'm worth it), a lot of women found me attractive.

No, I never understood it either. But it's called 'the power of celebrity', it's very seductive and it can turn the head of anyone who happens to be in the public eye. You have to have an iron will to resist. Mine was made of bendy plastic that had been left next to a radiator for days on end.

You've probably heard the theory that a man with a sharp sense of humour can 'laugh a woman into bed'. Believe it or not, I never had the chance to test this theory, for which I'm very grateful. I'd be worried that once she was in bed and saw me in my y-fronts, she'd keep on laughing.

In my defence, ninety-nine per cent of the time it was the women who did the running, usually standing at the bar, giving me the eye and making it plain what they wanted a gin & 'It'. Mostly they didn't want the gin. You'd be surprised how many women were up for a bit of fun with a married comedian who wouldn't see twenty-nine... cough... *thirty-nine* again.

They were my only vice. If you believe the papers and the scandal magazines, show business today, especially the comedy scene, is awash with drugs – cocaine, marijuana and a hundred different types of pills to give you a high. But I always thought taking drugs was a mug's game. I've never felt the need to indulge in them, even when I was younger back in the 1960s when so many of the kids in the discotheques and dance halls were regularly taking Purple Hearts and uppers and downers and all sorts. No, not *Bertie Bassett's* type of allsorts! Now you're just being silly.

It made no sense to me to snort a load of unknown chemicals up my nose or throw them down my throat... for fun! That's what drug users like to do and it baffles me. I don't even like taking headache tablets if I can help it. Who knows what's inside those things?

I've never been a massive drinker either. Maybe that's due to the fact I spent my childhood in and around my parents' various pubs and witnessing what too much booze can do to people. Don't misunderstand me. I'm not about to join the Temperance Society. I enjoy a drink or two after a show or on the odd night when I'm not working, but drink isn't a huge part of my life and never was.

Nevertheless, even though drugs don't interest me and drink isn't of any great importance to me, I do enjoy having a good time. And when you're a comedian who's been on the telly and you've got a few quid in your wallet and there are loads of attractive, available ladies around who think you're "Fab'less!"... it's very easy to have a good time. But you then forget the really important things in life. I took Kath for granted, which in retrospect is unforgiveable. She is without doubt the greatest woman, no, the greatest *person* I have ever met in my entire life. An absolute diamond. The mere fact that she's put up with me through good times, bad times and some bloody awful times is ample proof of that.

While I was busy amusing audiences around the country, Kath was at home bringing our children up and running the household. For years Katie and Matthew were like strangers to me because I was hardly ever at home. Also, not long after my grand-daughter Alex was born, her father Matthew split up with his girlfriend, who went back to live with her mother, taking Alex with her. So I didn't get to know her as well as I would have liked.

But now, I have a great opportunity to make up for all those wasted years. I'm a lot closer to my Alex, who comes to visit more often and, thanks to Katie, I also have a new grandson named Gabriel. And yes he *is* a little angel. I know I'm in the autumn of my life but I'm determined to hang around as long as possible to see Gabriel grow up.

I want to do all the things and take him to all the places that I was too busy to do with my own children when they were growing up. Gabriel and I are going to have a lot of fun in the next decade or so.

Katie is well aware of how hard it can be to forge a successful career in show business, but she is now making a name for herself on the club scene as a singer. Apart from the fact she has a great vocal range – which enables her to impersonate everyone from Dusty Springfield to Tina Turner – she has a quirky sense of humour and an unspoiled naturalness about her that endears her to audiences. I hope she does well and, naturally, as she is my daughter, I'll give her all the help and advice I can. And naturally, as she is my daughter, in exchange for all this help and advice I'll only take ten per cent of her earnings!

I think it's worth mentioning at this point, that I haven't been *completely* self-centred since I became a 'name'. I've done little bits here and there to give people a helping hand. Show business is a bit like an iceberg – here we go again, I can't seem to get away from *Titanic*! What I mean is, the public only see what's visible above the waterline. The ten per cent they see on stage or on screen, the so-called glamour of the business.

But ninety per cent of show business is made up of sheer hard work; dedication; dogged determination; disappointment; rejection; enormous highs and rock-bottom lows... and an unlimited supply of naked envy, green-eyed jealousy and teeth-baring bitchiness. It can be a cruel, heartless business with little sympathy to spare for the ones who never made it to the top and even less sympathy for those performers who did manage to make a name for themselves for a while and then fell out of fashion. Just think of all those popular, laugh-out-loud sitcoms you enjoyed watching ten or twenty or years ago. Massive audience-winners like *Bread*, *Hi De Hi!*, *Drop the Dead Donkey*, *The Brittas Empire*, *Red Dwarf*, *Keeping Up Appearances*, *Waiting for God*, *'Allo, 'Allo!*, *Three Up, Two Down* and many, many more.

Sadly, some of the older stars of these shows have passed over, but of those who are still around, very few are regularly seen on television today, if at all. Producers now seem to ignore the talent – and considerable reputation – of great, reliable comedy actors like Paul Shane, Jeffrey Holland, Su Poilard, Robert Duncan, Vicki Michelle, David Janson, Sam Kelly, Barry Howard and Trevor Bannister, who now make a living in the theatre, touring the country in farces and murder mysteries. They attract audiences of a certain age who remember them affectionately from their days on the box – which didn't seem to last very long.

Noel Coward was right on the money when he wrote and sang 'Don't put your daughter on the stage, Mrs Worthington'. The same applies to Mrs Jones, Mrs Jenkins, Mrs Llewellyn-Price and all the other Welsh mothers who want to push their offspring into the glare of the spotlight. Please think before you set your offspring on a road that appears to be paved with gold and diamonds, but more often, not.

I know just how tough it can be to break into the business – and believe me breaking in is a breeze compared to *staying in* the business and making a career of it. So, apart from the young performers I've given a leg-up-to in the business, either through *Just up your Street* or by giving them a part in one of my pantomimes, whenever I've had the opportunity to help someone out, to 'do them a good turn' as they say, I've always done my best to try and do so. I can also honestly claim that I have never deliberately tried to do anyone in or out of the business a 'bad turn', even though I have been on the receiving end of a few.

I've also had many good turns done to me and been given many fantastic opportunities, even at this late stage in my career. Just a couple of years ago, my good friend the multi-talented actor and comedian Rob Brydon called me up and asked me to play his (fictional) father in a couple of episodes of his BBC3 sitcom *Annually Retentive*. He said, "Owen, the part's perfect for you. You play an ageing Welsh comedian who goes around cracking terrible gags all day and just won't shut up!" How could I resist? It could have been worse. He might have asked me to play his *grand*-father!

So, once a contract was sorted out – and a wad of cash left for me under a brick outside the Welsh Assembly Building at midnight – a few weeks later I found myself in a Soho bar playing a scene with the one and only Rhys Ifans, who turned out to be great company. What a day that was!

Since then, I've worked with Rob Brydon a number of times and I have to say he's one of the most genuine and generous people I've met in this business. His performances as the hapless Keith Barrett first brought him to the attention of the great British public, since then he's gone from strength to strength in his career. I never get tired of seeing him play Uncle Bryn in *Gavin & Stacey*. Despite his film and television acting success, he still keeps his hand in with stand-up comedy, so if you like to laugh out loud, next time you see that he's appearing at your local theatre, go and see him.

He won't mind me telling you that many, many years ago, when he was then called Rob Jones, he was employed for a while by BBC Wales in various presenting jobs on radio and television. But because the executives in charge at the time, now all long gone, weren't able to recognise what a talented performer he was, they had no idea what to do with him and they let him go.

I've already mentioned that I've got ideas for new television shows and I've also got a few ideas for radio too. Like a one-hour radio show, once a week, say on a Friday evening around seven, in which I chat with a singer or band from the 50s to the 80s, while playing some of their hits as well as their favourite songs.

Another idea would be for me to play a round of golf with a celebrity. Yes it *would* work on the radio! I'd chat to the celeb and talk about their favourite songs which would be played through the show. It could be called something like 'Bunker Banter'. Don't try and pinch this idea; I've copyrighted it!

Ideas, ideas and more ideas. Here's another one. I've always wanted to take a coach-load of my regular listeners up to Liverpool and show them around the Beatles museum, the recreation of the Cavern Club and all the other parts of the city associated with the Beatles and the Mersey Sound of the early to mid-60s, a time which changed the face of pop music. And I know enough Liverpool musicians, like members of the Merseybeats, the Searchers and the Swinging Blue Jeans, to include some interviews. What a great Bank Holiday or Christmas special that would be!

My listeners know I'm genuinely interested in pop music from the earlier eras, and that if I'm interviewing Gerry Marsden or Joe Brown or Bobby Elliott from the Hollies or the one and only Cliff Richard (and Hank B Marvin at the same time!), I know what I'm talking about. I've heard interviews on local and national radio where it's obvious the interviewer hasn't had a clue about the person he's interviewing and is reading from his researcher's notes, regarding the interview as a short break between playing music.

But as soon as the person I'm interviewing realises that I know so much about their career, and I'm not like the last five radio hosts they've talked to that day, who only had them on the show so they can plug their new tour/book/CD, they settle down and the interview flows much more easily.

I'm genuinely grateful to my many loyal listeners for listening, writing, phoning and e-mailing me at the BBC and I'd like to thank each and every one of them all individually. It'll take me a while, but if I start in Merthyr first and keep travelling west, I should be in Tregaron in about eight months or so. I'll see you good people in Rhyl in 2015. It'll be a Thursday. Make sure you're in.

Thank you for sticking with me whilst I've been bounced around the schedules, from those early beginnings when I started to dip my toe in the deep end of Radio Wales programming, through the years I was on four times a week, right up to today.

None of us knows what lies ahead in the future. Well, apart from the readers of the *Radio Times* who can see what's on the telly this time next week. But I would like to think that as long as my listeners keep tuning-in in their thousands, I can carry on working for BBC Radio Wales for many more years.

As for my stand-up comedy work and acting like a Silly-Billy (or a Buttons, or a Muddles) in pantomime, I'll keep on going until I'm called to that Great Beanstalk in the sky. Look at performers like the ageless Bruce Forsyth or the tireless Stan Stennett – both great pros who are still working well beyond the normal retirement age.

Well, I've just about reached the end of this book. I'd write another couple of chapters, but my arms are aching and my pen's running out of ink. This has been my life spelt out in around 100,000 words. One... hundred... thousand... words! That's amazing, especially when you consider there's only 26 letters in the alphabet.

Believe it or not, I've still got many more stories to tell you. I've not told you about my involvement with Merthyr Town FC and I only briefly mentioned the Owen Money Theatre Company, which now produces plays as well as pantomimes.

Then there was the Merthyr Village Project that aimed to regenerate Merthyr Tydfil. My experience in the 60s, working with record producer Joe 'Telstar' Meek in his famous studio above a leather goods shop in London's Holloway Road. My golfing adventures around the world and the stars I've played with in pro-am competitions.

The thing is, when you're in your anec-dotage like me, so much has happened in your life, it's hard to remember everything. But, as I was finishing off this book, dotting the 't's and crossing the 'i's (I did tell you that my spelling was atroshuss), lots of other, long-forgotten memories and incidents and names and faces started to filter through.

Maybe one day I'll get the chance to get these untold stories down in print in a sequel that I could call 'Money's *Still* Talking'. Who said, "Oh, no!" Until then, thank you for taking the time to read this book and I hope you enjoyed it.

I'll leave you to ponder over this little thought:

The most effective form of propulsion is a gentle pat on the back.

Tarra!

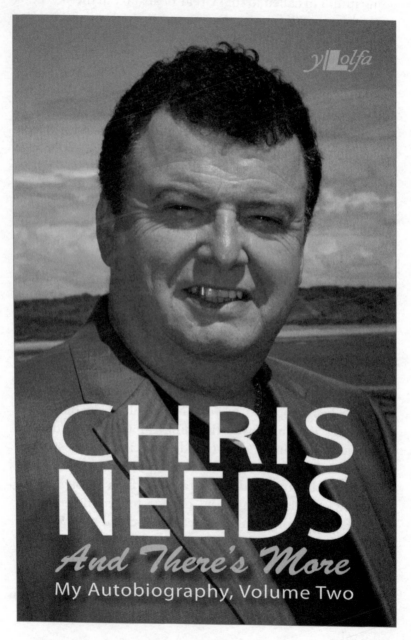

CHRIS
NEEDS

And There's More

My Autobiography, Volume Two

£9.95

y Lolfa

Mal Pope

Old Enough to Know Better

My Autobiography

£9.95

* Published November 2010

Money Talks is just one of a whole range of
publications from Y Lolfa. For a full list of
books currently in print, send now for your
free copy of our new full-colour catalogue.
Or simply surf into our website

www.ylolfa.com

for secure on-line ordering.

y **Lolfa**

TALYBONT CEREDIGION CYMRU SY24 5HE
e-mail ylolfa@ylolfa.com
website www.ylolfa.com
phone (01970) 832 304
fax 832 782